THE GOLDEN KEY

MODERN WOMEN ARTISTS AND GENDER NEGOTIATIONS IN REPUBLICAN CHINA (1911–1949)

MODERN ASIAN ART AND VISUAL CULTURE

Volume 7

Edited by
Kuiyi Shen (Managing Editor)
Patrick Flores
Sonal Khullar

The Golden Key

Modern Women Artists and Gender Negotiations in Republican China (1911–1949)

By

AMANDA WANGWRIGHT

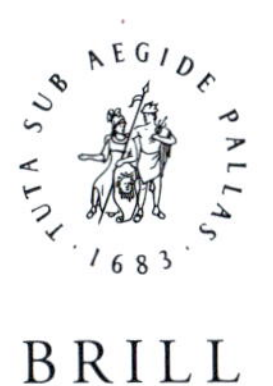

BRILL

Leiden – Boston
2021

Published by
BRILL
Plantijnstraat 2
2321 JC Leiden
The Netherlands
brill.com/maav

Design
Peter Yeoh, New York

Production
High Trade BV, Zwolle, The Netherlands
Printed in Slovakia

ISBN 978-90-04-44190-3 (hardback)
ISBN 978-90-04-44394-5 (e-book)

Library of Congress Cataloging-in-Publication Data
Detailed Library of Congress Cataloging-in-Publication data are available on the internet at http://catalog.loc.gov

Subvention for this publication was generously supplied by the Chiang Ching-kuo Foundation for International Scholarly Exchange; the Metropolitan Center for Far Eastern Art Studies; and the University of South Carolina College of Arts and Sciences.

Cover image:
Detail of Liang Baibo, *Untitled [Wuti]*. Published in *Shanghai manhua [Shanghai Sketch]*, no. 3 (1936): 15.

To women artists the world over: Keep fighting for your due.

Contents

Illustrations

3.3 Pan Yuliang, *Flourish* (*Rong*). *Wenhua* 3 (October 1929). Courtesy of The Li Ching Cultural and Educational Foundation.

3.4 Pan Yuliang, *Meow (Mimi), Xinren zhoukan* 1.6 (October 22, 1934). Also published in *Modern Miscellany* 6, no. 12 (10 October 1934). Photographed by the author, 2010.

3.5 "*Guying*–Pan Yuliang nüshi hui [*Reflection*, by Pan Yuliang]," *The Ladies' Journal* 15, no. 007 (July 1929): 17. Online edition: "Chinese Women's Magazines in the Late Qing and Early Republican Period," at http://womag.uni-hd.de. https://kjc-sv034.kjc.uni-heidelberg.de/frauenzeitschriften/public/magazine/page_large.php?magazin_id=4&year=1929&issue_id=441&issue_number=007&img_issue_page=017(accessed 2018-06-30).

3.6 Photographs of Shanghai's socialites. *Xinren zhoukan* 1, no. 27 (March 18, 1935). Photographed by the author, 2010.

3.7 Zhang Hongfei, "Nühuajia de bianli [The Convenience of Female Painters]," *Arts & Life* 5 (August 1934). Photographed by the author, 2010.

3.8 Article on Pan Yuliang that is illustrated with three of her paintings and a portrait of the artist painted by one of her professors, Umberto Coromaldi. *Shanghai manhua* 33 (December 1928): 6. Courtesy of The Li Ching Cultural and Educational Foundation.

3.9 Liang Baibo, cartoon of a little girl and her artist father. The caption reads, "Daddy, this is art." *Rensheng huabao* [*Life Pictorial*] 2, no. 1 (1935): 17. Source: CNBKSY.

3.10 Yu Feng, cartoon of emaciated model and disapproving artist. *Shidai manhua* 24 (December 20, 1935). Caption reads: "Artist: 'Oh, what a pity there really are no fleshy curves! What I mean to say is, to be a model you should be a bit fatter!' Model: 'Sir! You'll find that only if you go look among the ladies living in mansions!'" Courtesy of the artist's son Huang Dagang.

Chapter 4

Frontispiece: Liang Baibo with the Cartoonists Association for National Salvation (detail of fig. 4.7).

4.1 Fang Junbi, *Portrait of Zeng Zhongming*, 1930. Oil on canvas, 28½ in. × 46½ in. Published as *Studying* (*Dushu*). Courtesy of the artist's son Wen-ti Tsen.

4.2 Fang Junbi's entries in the Salon de la Société des Artistes Français in 1924: *The Flute Player* and *Portrait of Mlle. H.* Published in *The Ladies' Journal* (*Funü zazhi*) 10, no. 9 (1924): 2. Source: CNBKSY.

4.3 Fang Junbi, self-portrait published in *Funü shijie* (*Women's World*) 3, no. 6 (1942): 3. Source: CNBKSY.

4.4 Yu Feng, self-portrait published in *The Young Companion*. Courtesy of the artist's son Huang Dagang.

4.5 Liang Baibo's surrealist illustrations for Lin Huiyin's short story, "Hongcai moyan [Inflammation of the Iris]," published in *Shidai huabao* 8, no. 12 (1935). Source: CNBKSY.

4.6 Yu Feng, *Under the Power of the Times*, exhibited in the Second National Art Exhibition and published in the exhibition catalogue, *A Special Collection of the Second National Exhibition of Chinese Art under the Auspices of the Ministry of Education, Part Three: Modern Chinese Occidental-Painting, Design, and Sculpture*. Shanghai: Commercial Press, 1937. Photographed by the author, 2019.

4.7 "Miss Liang Bai-Poh ready exhibit before school students" from "Cartoonists Take War Area Travel—Nanking First Stop," *Kangri huabao [Anti-Japanese Pictorial]*, 6 (1937): 17. Source: CNBKSY.

4.8 Liang Baibo, "Zeren junyun de jieshi [An Explanation of Even Responsibility]," published in *War of Resistance Masterpieces* (Guangzhou, 1938). Photographed by the author, 2019.

4.9 Liang Baibo, "You qian wan ren zai dengdai zhe ni pi shang zhe tiao guangrong de toujin [There are ten million people waiting for you to put on this honorable headscarf]," published in *War of Resistance Masterpieces* (Guangzhou, 1938). Photographed by the author, 2019.

4.10 Yu Feng, "Aihu shangbing shi laobaixing de zeren! [Taking good care of wounded soldiers is the responsibility of the people!]," published in *War of Resistance Masterpieces* (Guangzhou, 1938). Photographed by the author, 2019.

4.11 Yu Feng, "Rang minzu jiefang de paohuo cuihui le zhe liaokao ba! [Let the gunfire of national liberation destroy these shackles!]," published in *War of Resistance Masterpieces* (Guangzhou, 1938). Photographed by the author, 2019.

4.12 Liang Baibo, "You Take Care of My Children and I'll Take Care of the Soldiers," published in Jack Chen, "Towards a Modern Conception of Art," *T'ien Hsia Monthly* (November 1938). Photographed by the author, 2019.

Conclusion

Frontispiece: Yu Feng, *Under the Power of the Times* (detail of fig. 4.6).

5.1 Liang Xihong's 1948 review of the Chinese modernist art movement. The article reproduces Qiu Ti's painting of sunflowers in a vase *(second image from the right)*, which has been generically titled *Hua* [Flowers]. Liang Xihong, "Zhongguo de yanghua yundong [China's Western Painting Movement]," *Da guang bao* (June 26, 1948). Photographed by the author, 2010.

Acknowledgments

As an expansion of research well beyond my dissertation, this book was made possible through the generous assistance and support of many. The earliest stages of my research were funded by the American Oriental Society's Louise Wallace Hackney Fellowship for the Study of Chinese Art, the Metropolitan Center for Far Eastern Art Studies' Doctoral Grant, Harvard University's Harvard-Yenching Library Travel Grant, and research grants from the University of Kansas' Office of Research and Graduate Studies and the Kress Foundation Department of Art History.

Funding for the expansion of my research for this book was provided by the Fox Center for Humanistic Inquiry Postdoctoral Fellowship at Emory University, which I thank for offering the institutional and financial support that is crucial—but often in short supply—for junior faculty in the humanities. While at Emory, I benefited from the camaraderie and insights of a weekly writing group, its members including Julia Bullock, Maria Franca Sibau, Sun-Chul Kim, and Li Yu. Duke Library and its research travel grant facilitated my collecting of many primary source materials through the CNBKSY database. I especially thank Luo Zhou for her kind and knowledgeable assistance.

I also would like to extend my gratitude to the families of the artists, specifically the families of Qiu Ti, Fang Junbi, and Yu Feng. Qiu Ti's children Professor Pang Tao and Pang Jiun and her grandchild Lin Yan have been exceptionally generous and encouraging from the moment I began my research.

Over the past few years, I have presented portions of the research for this book at various symposia and conferences and I greatly appreciated the support and feedback I received at those times from a number of outstanding scholars, including Kuiyi Shen, Julia F. Andrews, Dorothy Ko, and Aida Yuen Wong. I also am indebted to the anonymous readers of the manuscript.

Two course releases purchased with a University of South Carolina Provost Humanities Grant allowed sufficient time to complete the manuscript. A College of Arts and Sciences Book Manuscript Finalization Support Grant, a Metropolitan Center for Far Eastern Art Studies Institutional Grant, and a Chiang Ching-kuo Foundation Publication Subsidy Grant supplied the funding essential for its production. For helping me realize this published book, I am grateful to editors Inge Klompmakers and Wendy Logeman and the production team at Brill, as well as my tenacious copyeditor Kathryn Kraynik.

My first forays into this area of research began in the Kress Foundation Department of Art History at the University of Kansas. I thank all of the faculty there for providing invaluable guidance and support, particularly Marsha Haufler, Amy McNair, Maki Kaneko, and Sherry Fowler. In the years following graduation, my fellow alumni from the program have become stellar colleagues and stalwart friends who make me proud to be among their ranks.

I thank as well my University of South Carolina colleagues in the School of Visual Art and Design and in Chinese studies, especially Krista Van Fleit, Guo Jie, and Yulian Wu (now at Michigan State University). I owe much gratitude to Kunio Hara and Greg Patterson, who have read countless drafts of this and other manuscripts. I also thank Thomas Cooper Librarian Karen Brown, in addition to the InterLibrary Loan system that supplied so many loan requests, even the ones that I had thought impossible.

Finally, I thank my friends and family who saw me through this lengthy process, especially my husband Di, who always encouraged my professional ambitions (no negotiation required), and my son Ajax, whose arrival encouraged the timely completion of this book as practical necessity and whose presence brings me unimagined joy every day.

With the support of so many, any errors in this book can only be my own.

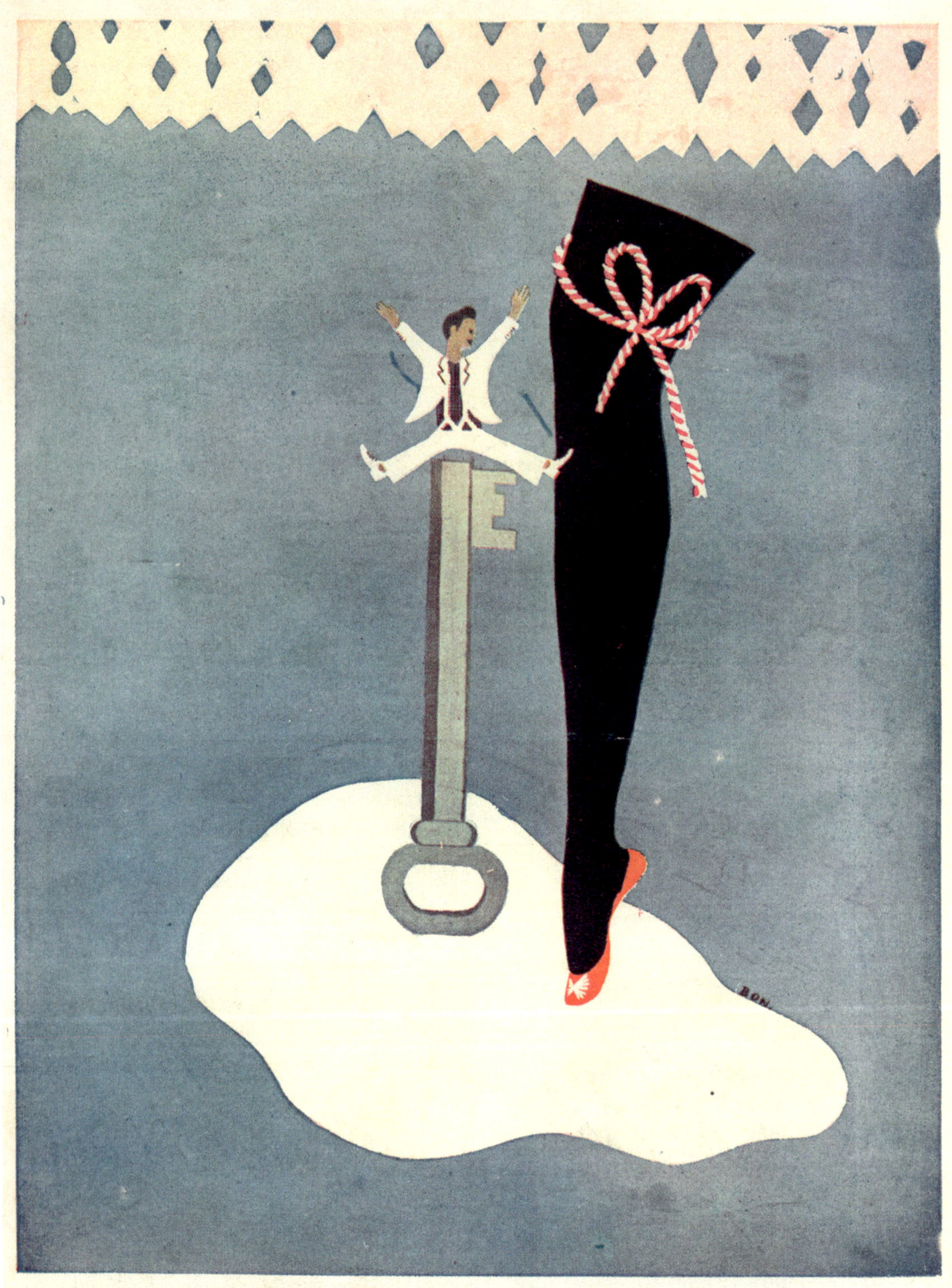

無題

梁白波作

Introduction

The Golden Key of Art

"Day by day female artists increase in number. Indeed, we cannot but consider this is an encouraging thing for our society."[1]

SO CONCLUDES AN ARTICLE in the December 21, 1929, edition of *Shenbao* 申報 (transcribed at the time as *Shun Pao*), one of modern China's foremost commercial newspapers. The article heralded a special issue of *The Ladies' Journal* (*Funü zazhi* 婦女雜誌) that was dedicated to the First National Art Exhibition of that year and, by extension, celebrated the exhibition's numerous female participants. The *Shenbao* article lists and briefly overviews the names and careers of more than a dozen women, conveying a sense of excitement and pride over the growing importance of Chinese women artists. From this article, which was published in Shanghai's most influential newspaper and in turn touted an upcoming issue of a popular women's periodical, one might conclude that women artists maintained an active presence in early twentieth-century China's art world and that their contributions were well received.

Liang Baibo's surrealistic image of a tiny man balanced on top of a giant upright key, his arms and legs thrown wide in his excitement over a massive disembodied leg of a woman. Liang Baibo, *Untitled [Wuti]*. Published in Shanghai *manhua [Shanghai Sketch]*, no. 3 (1936): 15.

Yet, browse any recent survey of early twentieth-century Chinese art and you will find few names of female artists, if any at all. At a time when modern Asian art, previously maligned or simply ignored in art historical scholarship, is finally beginning to receive its due, women modern artists remain forgotten.[2] They are not alone; women artists the world over rarely make it into the art historical canon. A recent authoritative anthology on non-Western modern art accounts for the near total absence of women within the volume by dismally stating, "No matter how closely we peer into the sea of time where our dead sisters' thoughts, feelings, and artistic genius vanished, we can see little.... No amount of art historical research, however, can retrieve a never-created masterpiece."[3]

In fact, women *did* create masterpieces. The women of modern China are responsible for some of the most innovative artworks of their day. Over the intervening years these paintings and sculptures have become undervalued or simply lost to the ravages of war and political upheavals, but our relative ignorance of the artworks produced by China's female modern artists does not diminish their importance. At the time of these artworks' creation, mass-circulated publications celebrated many of them as cutting-edge contributions to modern art. The women who made these lauded artworks were graduates of the top art schools, members of leading art organizations, and professors at major universities. In short, Republican-period female artists pursued and earned the same markers of success as their male peers.

This book uncovers and reclaims the central roles that women as artists played in China's art world, thereby reappraising the accepted understanding of the development of modern Chinese art. Women embraced the agency they acquired through their professions as artists and one female artist even identified art as a golden key that would open the door to a Women's Art Movement. In its examination of the status of professional women painters in China's rapidly changing society between the late 1920s and the mid-1940s, this book also explores the role of art in the newly formed nation and the impact of modernist theory on the avant-garde community. Looking at Chinese painting of the first half of the twentieth century through the lens of popular culture and gender, this book charts the worldwide trends and local events that led to the rise and fall of this profession as an occupational choice for Chinese women of the time. I argue that women artists played a critical role in the emergence and florescence of Chinese modernist art.[4]

WOMEN ARTISTS IN CHINESE HISTORY

In many ways, Chinese female artists of the early twentieth century followed well-established historical precedents. Women of the past made important contributions to the cultural sphere, although they did so in the capacity of refined ladies at leisure. In the late imperial era, when the elite painted as a cultured pastime and an expression of amateur artistic virtuosity, women in more progressive families were allowed to take up the brush as a personal pastime within their homes.[5] Typically, they gained access to the arts only if they were wives, concubines, or daughters of royal or elite families or were courtesans of men of the scholar-official class. And only those encouraged by male family members to take up painting succeeded in developing this skill. Among these accomplished ladies of the brush, Guan Daosheng 管道昇 (1262–1319) stands apart for her development of the distinctive painting genre of bamboo in mist, but also for her role as wife and soul mate of the even more famous Yuan-dynasty painter Zhao Mengfu 趙孟頫 (1254–1322). For a concubine or courtesan, skill in painting was often ranked among her desirable traits: a scholar-official choosing a romantic partner, as opposed to an official wife, might find skill in painting a desirable quality to be counted, along with beauty, poise, or talents in poetry and music, among the attractions of the object of his affection. Sometimes, but less commonly, economic hardship forced talented women of the scholar-official class to sell their paintings to support their families. Painting professionally, however, was disparaged for elite women, just as for gentlemen, and only pursued out of financial necessity.

Considering women's traditional roles within Confucian society, it is not surprising that female artists were seldom recorded in premodern canonical texts of Chinese painting history.[6] A talented female painter rarely had the opportunity to share her paintings with individuals outside of her restricted social sphere. In the few cases that paintings by a woman were appreciated on a wider scale, it was usually because one or more of the men in her family promoted her work to his social and professional network.[7] Such was the experience of the Qing-dynasty female painter Chen Shu 陳書 (1660–1736), whose filial son served as a high-ranking official during the Qianlong period and thereby earned his mother a spot in the imperial collection. But even Chen Shu was better recognized for her successful upbringing of an accomplished son than for her mastery of painting.

Larger compendia of biographies of Chinese painters include biographies of female artists, but these entries are usually relegated to the back of the collection. Moreover, the information provided is not nearly as detailed or significant as that given for men. In her exhibition catalogue, *Views from Jade Terrace: Chinese Women Artists, 1300–1912,* Marsha Weidner relates that a biographical entry for a female painter typically comprises names of her male family members and recycled "stereotypes and clichés" about her feminine qualities but little sense of the artist as an individual.[8] Many of the details included in these biographies are gender specific: occasionally complimenting a woman painter as the female version of a more celebrated male artist or praising her style with terms traditionally associated with feminine characteristics.[9] If, as was believed, the painted image revealed the essential character of its maker, it is understandable that the paintings of the women of the elite class were described in terms that reflected their creators' feminine virtues.

For Chinese women as artists of the twentieth century, husbands and other male family members remained influential on their artistic opportunities and critical reception. Likewise, formulaic descriptions continued in the biographies of women painters that were now published in the new format of popular magazines.[10] But for female artists of the modern era, an unprecedented opportunity to pursue professional careers in the arts sprung from two concurrent societal developments: the New Woman Movement, which radically redefined women's social roles and opened the newly formed occupation of professional artist to female participants; and the New Art Movement, which revolutionized artistic practices and professionalized the occupation.

THE "WOMAN QUESTION" AND CHINA'S NEW WOMEN

The women artists profiled in this book and their peers gained access to the profession though the efforts of the social reformers of the early twentieth century, who championed the elevation of women's rights and the expansion of their vocational opportunities. Women's issues, frequently identified as the "woman question" (*funü wenti* 婦女問題) in newspapers and popular magazines, were both embraced and manipulated by divergent factions.[11] The Communist Party, as early as the mid-1920s, promoted equality between men and women (*nannü pingdeng* 男女平等) as a component of the socialist state to be realized through revolution.[12] And by the mid-1930s, the Nationalist government was promoting women's education as a patriotic means to train the next generation of "Good Wives and Wise Mothers" (*xianqi liangmu* 賢妻良母).[13] Even before either of these calculated political stances on women's roles in the modern body politic, the May Fourth Movement—a student-initiated widespread push to modernize and revitalize the Chinese nation initiated in 1919—had advocated the abandonment of traditional values and culture. Encouraged by the successes of the suffragette movement in the West, May Fourth reformers sought to redefine the role women played in the development of their own country. These reform-minded activists and feminists, many of whom were men, rejected old Confucian social standards and argued for women's rights (*nüquan zhuyi* 女權主義) as part of their effort to overturn the feudalistic remnants of the Qing dynasty.[14] Erudite treatises by male intellectuals and editors—and later essays submitted by female journalists—appeared frequently in Shanghai magazines of the 1920s–30s, popularizing discourse on women's rights.[15] Many of these authors reasoned that in order to develop moral character (*ren'ge* 人格) and be of value to a new society, women needed education, a meaningful occupation, and the independence afforded through personal financial resources.[16] These informed women of the modern era who broke with the restrictive social codes of the past were termed "New Women" (*xin nüxing* 新女性).

The words of the anti-Qing revolutionary Qiu Jin 秋瑾 (1875–1907) capture the fervor of China's early twentieth-century feminist movement and its demands of New Women. Speaking in Tokyo in 1904 to an audience of Chinese study-abroad students, Qiu began with an overview of the oppression of Chinese women at their most transformative stages of life: birth, marriage, and widowhood. She then warned that China was on the brink of collapse and called on her countrywomen to save the nation by asserting themselves.

> Dear listeners, you have to realize that in this world it does not do to be dependent on others, you must rely on yourselves! . . .
>
> Men are afraid that if we acquire understanding and knowledge, we will climb over their heads, and so they do not allow us to study. Why is it that we obey them and do not oppose them? It is all because we women have ourselves abdicated our responsibilities. Whatever it was, as soon as we saw that the men were there to take care of it, we ourselves were content to be lazy and take it easy. . . .
>
> Dear listeners, do you realize that our nation is about to perish? Men cannot be sure of their own survival, so how can we continue to rely on them? If we do not lift ourselves up now, it will truly be too late once the nation has perished. Dear listeners, do not let me down![17]

Qiu Jin admonished her countrywomen to stand up and take charge of their own destiny a full fifteen years before the May Fourth movement. Her words underscore two important facts. Feminist thought did not simply emerge overnight in China, but fermented in the public sphere for years. And women activists participated from the very beginning.

MODERN GIRLS AND FLOWER VASES

Qiu Jin's passionate oratory makes it sound as if Chinese women's rights were but an issue of personal resolve, but her compatriots encountered more obstacles than opportunities. Though the New Women Movement won Chinese women the freedom to pursue vocations outside the home in principle, actual career options remained limited. Modern China historian Bryna Goodman observes that while early twentieth-century discourse on women's issues promoted the advancement of women's equality, social commentary critical of women's motives in the workplace (often circulated in the very same publications) undermined their occupational success.[18] In the early 1920s a hotly contested public debate about the morals and virtues of women working outside of the home erupted, and women professionals encountered ambivalent attitudes toward their role in modern society. On the one hand, women were expected to seek vocations in order to be contributing members of society; on the other, they became targets of lingering cultural biases and disparaging presumptions. By offering their professional skills for pay outside of the home, career women opened themselves to comparison with prostitutes and implications about their wanton sexual habits and greedy dispositions.[19] By the 1930s women with professional careers had become slightly more commonplace, but attitudes toward their roles in the workplace remained ambiguous. Certain occupations deemed appropriate for women, such as nursing and teaching, could be defended as noble service for the good of the nation.[20] In contrast, sales clerks and office workers frequently received criticism for exhibiting salacious behavior.[21] In the 1930s the pejorative term *modeng gou'er* 摩登狗兒, a transliteration of "Modern Girl," came to represent attractive young women who paid close attention to the latest fashion and trends but had little interest in contributing to society or bettering the nation.[22] The prevalence of women office workers employed solely on the basis of their beauty led to the coining of another derogatory term, "Flower Vase" (*huaping* 花瓶). As Chinese women's studies historian Wang Zheng explains, many employers hired Flower Vases to serve as decorations, "to present a modern image or to attract male clients," and when they married, the Flower Vases often found their office careers over.[23]

The women of the Republican period recognized the precariousness of their new social identities, and some wrote to the press about how women should address the issue of their own persona and public perceptions of them. In these essays, the writers appeal to other women, instructing them on how to behave outside the home and chastising them for the use of sexuality to advance in the workplace.[24] A 1934 article by a Ms. Li Ying in *Lin Loon Ladies' Magazine* (*Linglong tuhua zazhi* 玲瓏圖畫雜誌) is representative.[25] Presumably concerned about the reputations of her peers, the author explains that the notion of a modern woman (*xiandai nüzi* 現代女子) is typically associated with the Modern Girl, which in turn is often conflated with the negative images of Flower Vases and "Playthings" (*wanwu* 玩物).[26] She prefers the designations "Girl of This Age" or "Girl of Today" and prescribes five preconditions for such a woman's success.[27] To prosper, she must be strong of body and mind; possess a determined and visionary spirit; have the benefit of an education; maintain financial independence; and renounce jealous feelings. The author places the burden on women and expects them to perfect themselves in order to improve their reputations.

Similar sentiment is expressed in the rousing writings of Lu Yin 廬隱 (1898–1934), who graduated from Beiping Women's Normal College in 1922, found employment as a high school teacher, and wrote prolifically. In an article about Lu Yin's use of feminist rhetoric, Bo Wang, a specialist on the topic, argues that Lu Yin was cognizant of the domination of the women's movement in China by men.[28] Pointing out that the issue of women's equality was naturally more pressing for women themselves, Lu Yin questioned the motives of the men involved in the movement and called on women to take active roles rather than depending on men or copying their actions.[29] In her essay, "The Age of Flower Vases," published in a newspaper supplement in 1933, Lu Yin begins with the sarcastic rationalization that the life of a Flower Vase, being a vast improvement in status for women, may not be an unsatisfactory condition.[30] Nevertheless, she ends the piece with an excited appeal for women to destroy the objectifying net in which they were ensnared:

> And so, the fate of this Flower Vase is actually too tragic. If we want to save ourselves, then we need to have the determination to smash this Age of Flower Vases, and through arduous endeavor be reborn and acquire our own identities. Moreover, this kind of arduous task entirely relies on self-awakening. No longer should you hope to beg for food and favors from men. If men were really as broadminded and selfless as you have imagined, then all of the daydreams of the world would have come true! Furthermore, men's pretense to generosity is exactly what can cause your demise. Don't be coy and flirt with men just so that you may think yourself exceptional. The Age of Flower Vases exposes the populace's shame and stupidity![31]

Lu Yin's cutting diatribe is aimed at women who might be content with an ineffectual existence as a decorative object in the workplace.[32] She implores women to take their lives into their own hands in order to be seen as the equals of men. Like Qiu Jin's speech of nearly thirty years prior, Lu Yin's article expects women to wake to their situation, take stock of their own behaviors, and rise up to their full potential.

Lu Yin's peers seem to have taken her advice, and leading periodicals regularly featured photographs of college-educated young women along with female artists and athletes. The abundant images show women asserting themselves in professional arenas and educated circles. Nevertheless, even active career women remained subject to the tastes of the media and its readership. The editors of Republican-period magazines and newspapers, no doubt conscious of circulation figures, consistently placed greater emphasis on the women's physical attributes and marital status than on their professional abilities and careers.[33] Usually identifying the subjects by name, the captions for these images frequently mention their educational status or professional occupations, as well as their hometowns. The photographs emphasize the beauty of their subjects: female athletes are posed to accentuate their naked limbs and socialites appear in lyrical settings staged to emphasize their fashionable appearances. While publicizing women's accomplishments, such coverage evidences the permeation of the Flower Vase stereotype.[34]

Female artists exemplify the tension between historic and modern notions of womanhood. Not as straightforward as social reformers wished to portray, modern social roles required women of the early twentieth century to "juggl[e] multiple identities."[35] Depictions of women in print media indicate how modern perceptions of womanhood—which included appellations such as the Talented Woman, the New Woman, the Modern Girl, and the Flower Vase—evolved in tandem with the rapidly changing social status of Chinese women. In many cases, social discourse promoted these women in seemingly contradictory terms and the women discussed in this book are not exceptions. For example, Qiu Ti (discussed in chapter 2) won the popular label of Talented Woman (*cainü* 才女)—a designation that increasingly was dismissed as an antiquated notion of ladylike behavior—while receiving recognition for acting out the rebellious prerogatives of the New Woman.[36] The popular press promoted Guan Zilan (chapter 1) as the quintessential Modern Girl, but her public image at times slipped into the easily dismissible role of Flower Vase. Fang Junbi (chapter 4), who embodied the New Woman in her overseas training and prolific career, settled into the public role of Good Wife as a means of maintaining her professional aspirations. Despite these varying labels, these women and their female colleagues in the visual arts uniformly identified as *nühuajia* 女畫家 (women artists), a distinctly modernized social category that, having emerged with the professionalization of the Republican art world, became glorified throughout wider popular culture.[37]

NEW ARTISTIC PRACTICES: EXHIBITIONS, MANIFESTOS, AND THE PURPOSE OF ART

At the very moment that female artists entered the workforce and began defining their roles within the professional field, the art community became embroiled in nationwide debates on the meaning of art and its importance to the revitalization of a struggling nation. The rise of discourse on the role of art in modern China, conducted at a fever pitch and with the same sense of urgency that motivated Qiu Jin, coincided with the ascendancy of *nühuajia*. As such, the future of female artists intertwined with the legitimacy and viability of modernist art in China.

A new spirit of determination swept over the Chinese art community in the 1920s and 1930s and tied into a rousing trend of art activism. In her seminal study "China's Response to the West in Art, 1898–1937," Mayching Margaret Kao detects a growing trend of factionalism among the artists trained in Western styles following the First National Art Exhibition.[38] Whereas Chinese artists had previously adopted Western painting styles and theories more or less indiscriminately, by the 1930s a more critical and nationalistic response had emerged that expected art to contribute toward the betterment of the struggling nation. Artists generally embraced the same nationalistic goal of transforming China through art but split into opposing factions in formulating specific responses "to the demands of a society in transition and a nation in danger."[39] The Movement for the Renaissance of Chinese Art (*Zhongguo yishu fuxing yundong* 中國藝術復興運動), which supported the development of a new national painting (*xin guohua* 新國畫) through the fusion of Chinese and Western art, encompassed a diverse range of work, including examples by Xu Beihong, Fang Junbi, and Liu Haisu.[40] In stark contrast, artists such as Lin Fengmian and the members of the Storm Society made a strong commitment to the styles of the modern European painting schools and explored conceptual issues and the expression of inner emotion. Meanwhile, proponents of academic realism—most famously Xu Beihong, who demonstrated that artists could simultaneously promote more than one theoretical approach to art—advocated the conservative use of traditional Western painting styles.[41] In these heady times, young art students returned from their studies abroad, flocked to Shanghai, staged countless group and solo exhibitions, and debated the proper form and purposes of art—all with the idealistic intent of advancing the discipline and strengthening the national character.

The art community in which all of this turbulent activity occurred provided overlapping venues for professional exposure and public interaction. In her analysis of the Shanghai art scene, modern Chinese art historian Julia Andrews posits "four distinct but intersecting realms in the 1930s": institutions of higher education, art societies, the art market, and periodicals.[42] The Storm Society (Juelanshe 決瀾

社) exemplifies the interplay between these realms. A privately operated art society, it effectively exerted its influence in publications and at the art schools where many of its members taught. And for the Storm Society, like other art groups, the exhibition and the group manifesto were expedient means of distinguishing and disseminating their ideas on how to raise the art of the nation to greater heights.

Chinese interest in public exhibitions originated during the last two decades of the nineteenth century when travelers returned from abroad with knowledge of the exhibition cultures in Europe and Japan and the public spectacle of the World's Fairs.[43] By the beginning of the twentieth century, China was staging its own exhibitions.[44] Initially appreciated as venues for the promotion of the nation, early exhibitions placed emphasis on displays of scientific and commercial worth.[45] As the first generation of Chinese artists studying abroad began to return home in the 1920s, the public art exhibition quickly became a part of the social fabric of the art community. Following the European model, exhibitions for oil painters revolved around a seasonal calendar; autumn became known as the "Season of the Arts," and a number of group and solo exhibitions occurred in and around October.[46]

By the 1930s, the public exhibition was an accepted practice on both the national and local levels. With government sponsorship, the First National Art Exhibition held in Shanghai in 1929 successfully staged a comprehensive and large-scale public display of art. Well before then and on a more local level, major cosmopolitan centers saw the proliferation of exhibitions held in public venues by artist associations and independent artists. As an outgrowth of the New Culture Movement, exhibitions allowed artists to make tangible contributions to the emergent public sphere, and along with their exhibitions modernist artists often published declarations of desires to modernize and improve Chinese society.[47] Exhibitions, therefore, served as vehicles that could express either the perspective of a single artist or a unified group vision to a larger audience. Reviews featured in contemporary pictorial magazines indicate a catholic embrace of Western styles. They also record women artists' participation in group events as well as solo exhibitions.

Like exhibitions, manifestos offered Republican artist societies an outlet for sharing their vision with the outside world. Manifestos were easily disseminated to large audiences via popular journals, and many from the early twentieth century speak of revolutionizing art and nation. All types of art and literature organizations, from traditional *guohua* 國畫 (Chinese-style painting) societies to modernists, drafted and published manifestos.[48] At times quite verbose, these manifestos reveal deep anxieties felt by art society members. Many promote art as a means to alleviate social problems and rebuild China's broken social and political system. The manifesto of the National Art Movement Society (Guoli Yishu Yundong She 國立藝術運動社), printed in *Apollo* (*Yaboluo* 亞波羅) in 1929, epitomizes the zeitgeist of the art community.[49] It boldly declares that the group's "ultimate vision" is "to unite a majority of creative powers in the art community to expedite the realization of a new artistic age, as a lasting spiritual contribution to society."[50] While the group concedes that, "Speaking about Art Movements in this devastated China without addressing the needs of the time seems ridiculous," they also argue that, "the more unstable a society is for its inhabitants, the greater their need for art to serve as an emotional and spiritual refuge."[51] Therefore, the group explains: "We have come to understand the true meaning of art. Although these are times of ceaseless war and displacement, yet without a moment's hesitation [we] raise up the art movement's banner in the midst of screams and groans, spreading the gospel of art! This is our bounden duty!"[52]

WOMEN AS MODERNIST ARTISTS

Female modernist artists stood at the intersection of new womanhood and new art, the import of their space within early twentieth-century Chinese society being that they, more than most of their peers, embodied the anxieties and the dreams of Chinese modernism. Women artists, particularly those working in *xiyanghua* 西洋畫 (or *xihua*, media newly imported from the West), realized the progress of the reforms in the most visual and literal ways possible. Unlike female *guohua* artists, whose choice of medium encouraged comparisons with China's long tradition of talented painters of the inner quarters, the media and styles used by female modernist artists reinforced the perception that their actions were unprecedented.[53] The first generation to benefit from the opening of education and occupations to women, as they filtered into the workplace they performed the role of New Woman while carrying the promise of national rehabilitation. Pushing the boundaries of convention, these women contributed directly to the New Art Movement as students, professional artists, members of art societies, and college teachers. In news features about their education, careers, and social habits as modern women, they publicly performed the emancipative progress of the advancing nation.

Those women most intimately involved in the advancement of both modern art and women's status well perceived the tangled connection between modern women, visual art, and national reform. Jin Qijing 金啓靜 (1902–82), an art educator, high-school arts director, and artist, asserted women's value to the art community with the revolutionary zeal appropriate to the era. Jin believed that a women's art movement would contribute to the florescence of Chinese society and in an article for the National Art Exhibition special issue of *The Ladies' Journal* she speaks directly to her female peers. In "Women and Art" (*Nüxing yu meishu* 女性與美術), she argues that women and art have a special relationship, although she also writes that most women of her time had little appreciation for or understanding of art.[54] Calling woman the "darling of Venus" (*meishen de chonger* 美神的寵兒), the author credits her gender with an intuition for art and maintains that women's fluid nature, intense emotions, and sincere love gave them a profound connection to the creative works of the world. Predicting women will have a brilliant future in the development of the arts, Jin concludes her article with a rousing battle cry for her female comrades to join in the emergent women's art movement in order to seize power and authority within the art world for themselves, invoking the imagery of a golden key (*jinyao* 金鑰) as the prize that promised equality for her sisters.

> Now the time of the Women's Art Movement has arrived! Happily, holy sounds are already calling in the air! Venus has already descended before us! . . . My fellow women! If you are determined to study art, hasten to root out the weeds of vanity from your hearts. Start afresh and labor earnestly for the sake of developing women's skills. Do not watch quietly from a distance, letting men alone exert themselves in the struggle of opening up a path for the arts. We should use [our] innate talents to grasp the golden key of art.[55]

"Women and Art" is a vibrant call for action; its author speaks with energy and authority. The passion with which Jin writes was certainly equal to other art critics of her generation—such as Ni Yide, who receives much discussion throughout this book. Yet, while Ni is accepted as a leading Republican-period art theorist today, Jin has been largely forgotten. Little has been written about her in art history texts and even less has been noted concerning the many women to whom she called to arms.

A comparison of Jin Qijing's impassioned mission and the actions of early twentieth-century *nühuajia* with the careers of modern women artists in France illuminates striking parallels. The collective Union des Femmes Peintres et Sculpteurs, founded by Madame Léon Bertaux in 1881, staged annual exhibitions and grew to include well over 400 members.[56] Ten years into her presidency of the Union, Mme Bertaux published a cry for action from her sisters of the brush and chisel. Like Jin's solicitation, Bertaux's article reasons that women have an innate connection to the arts and asserts that the invention of a civilizing and uplifting art is a "feminine mission." Sounding much the same as Jin's plea to her own contemporaries, Bertaux declares, "Yes, let us, women, create, we must do it and we can do it, this new art which is ahead of us, *l'Art feminin*."[57] Like Jin's "golden key," art for Bertaux represented a way for women to advance not only their own cause but that of all of society as well. Though the women of the Union predated their counterparts in China by half a century, both groups actively staked their claim on an emergent professional field.

But if Tamar Garb's enlightening analysis of the widely overlooked Union "tell[s] a story that has never been told" while simultaneously "rewrite[ing] an old narrative from a new perspective," a study of Chinese women artists of the Republican period is even more disarmingly familiar and yet, from a Western perspective, unexpectedly new.[58] The women of the Union fought against oppression and ridicule, challenged the preconceptions of the entrenched fraternity of their art world, and campaigned for admittance to the leading art schools. For its many members, the Union offered professional support while simultaneously maintaining a culturally conservative view of women's inherent nature and place in late eighteenth-century French society.[59] In many ways, the reality faced by the women of this book could not have been more different. The feminism we encounter in China is informed by but stands apart from its European counterpart and the historical context in which *nühuajia* worked starkly broke with tradition.[60] Republican-period modernizers, a strong sociopolitical contingent since the May Fourth Movement, vehemently opposed conservative social norms and encouraged women to take up new societal roles. Popular discourse largely celebrated female artists, as well as women who pursued other creative occupations, such as writers and actresses. By pursuing educations and productive careers, women artists contributed to social progress and upheld the ideology of the state. Yet, despite the positive ways in which their activities were perceived at the time, today the career accomplishments and artworks for Chinese women as artists remain just as obscure as those of the women of the Union.

THIS BOOK

If art historians struggle to fully consider the roles of women as artists—by either lamenting female artists and their works as untraceable or simply forgetting to consider them entirely—that is in part because we are left with so very little information to analyze. China's long twentieth century was not kind, and many artworks, ephemera, correspondence, and even artists disappeared among the ravages of numerous military and political campaigns. In search of clues about a largely forgotten era, recent scholars from a range of disciplines have turned sharp eyes to the Republican-period's robust publishing industry. Mass printed materials offer the richest and most detailed period information for analysis available to us today. However, contemporary periodicals present, as Joan Judge observes in her latest book, "not simple truths but complex dialectics that reflect tensions both within and beyond the pages."[61] Add to this the problem that few women seem to have recorded or published writings about their views on art. Over the years their textual silence has exacerbated a progressive amnesia about their contributions.

To be frank, from today's perspective the impact women had on the Chinese modern art world appears negligible. Though the women of the early twentieth century held faculty positions at major art schools and circulated in prominent artist societies, it is challenging if not impossible to isolate their imprint in the longer narrative of Chinese art. The scarcity of extant artworks and documentation offers limited visual and textual evidence of their activities. Western-style painting in China in the first decades of the century was a mad hodgepodge of imported styles with little evidence of a domestically produced artistic lineage. Written accounts seldom confirm the extent of an artist's influence in the contemporary art scene; if a Chinese artist was to credit his or her artistic influence, that influence was more often a Western artist, not Chinese peer. Analysis of the art market provides even less insight. There were no major collectors of modernist art in China and artists working in Western styles primarily lived on their teaching salaries rather than artwork sales. But these vexing circumstances hold equally true for most male artists as well. In truth, it can be challenging to prove the lasting impact of *any* Republican-period modernist artist, male or female!

It is possible, however, to more accurately document and reassess female artists' contributions during the brief flowering of modernist art. Thus, I am not making bold claims about women's dominance in the art field; instead I am uncovering forgotten accomplishments and correcting arbitrary exclusions so as to reinsert women artists as equal participants in the development of modern art in China. The primary objective of this book is to demonstrate that women were not tangential to modernist art in China (as has been usually assumed to date), but, to the contrary, they situated themselves at the heart of its formation.

To trace the activities of women artists, this book delves frequently and deeply into the artifacts of Republican print media, as the printed page supplies the richest insight into the work and lives that remains accessible today. In my research I make use of a variety of primary sources, many of which have been previously overlooked or little discussed in scholarship to date. These resources include editorials in women's magazines, such as *The Ladies' Journal*, and Shanghai pictorials, such as *The Young Companion* (*Liangyou huabao* 良友畫報); art journals and theoretical essays published by leading art societies and artists, such as the Storm Society and its cofounder Ni Yide; public announcements that appear in major newspapers such as *Shenbao*; and newspaper clippings that feature articles on artists of the day and their work, such as the many miniature exhibition reviews and biographies of Guan Zilan that appear in several serials. The multitude of these materials affirm that female professional artists were once a growing force and valued as contributors to the art world and the nation and that popular culture of the time celebrated *nühuajia* both individually and as a phenomenon. My investigation concentrates on biographical analysis and historical contextualization—recovering these women's since forgotten accomplishments and reasserting the significance of their contributions—to document women's participation in the emergence of modern Chinese art.

But what was modern Chinese art? What made China's modern art different from that which preceded it?[62] Certainly, in the case of *guohua* artists, who often produced paintings of conventional subjects using traditional media, the modernity of the artwork might not be found in the physical object.[63] Rather, for modern Chinese art, just as important as the created image was the conceptual role of the artist and the social context in which the artist worked. For this reason, the first two chapters begin with a focus on these two essential signifiers of the modern in modern Chinese art, the artist herself and the art society.

Chapter 1 examines media portrayals of artists in Republican-period periodicals and evaluates how women used their public personas to invent and then define through performance these new occupational roles. This investigation pays particular attention to profiles of the oil painter Guan Zilan, which preserve clues about the professional standards set for women in early twentieth-century China and the ways in which Guan chose to present herself to the public. China's popular magazines of the 1920s and 1930s abound with material on contemporary artists. Within these brief introductions, traditional and imported stereotypes amalgamated into a new conception of the artist as social reformer with the power to construct a modern Chinese society. Contemporary depictions of women artists additionally document rapidly changing perceptions of modern womanhood. Outlining the parameters within which female artists operated, I examine how women like Guan Zilan used public personas to define and perform the new social role of professional female artist (*nühuajia*). Through reproductions of portrait studio photographs and painted self-portraits, women artists deliberately emphasized their visuality in collaborations with the media, performed as confident protagonists in the public sphere, and played to societal notions of the new occupational role of professional *nühuajia*.

In other words, Chinese women artists of the early twentieth century forged their own identities just as much as they were defined by the art establishment.

Chapter 2 centers on the ways in which the dynamics of group image and gender politics shaped the development of women's careers. As a case study, I examine Qiu Ti's still life titled *Flower*, which was publicly awarded an exhibition prize and was acclaimed in print as an example of non-representational artistic expression. My investigation traces the painting's legacy as a controversial artwork and ties its portrayal in the news media to the avant-garde art group's modernist ideology and the active dialogue in the larger art community about the role of art in society. I also examine Qiu Ti's publicized status as a prominent painting society's only official female member and assess how art groups' public presentation of women painters satisfied the varied intentions of these collectives. Although Qiu Ti is often considered exceptional for her membership in a modernist art society, in fact women's participation in artist associations and institutions—such as Pan Yuliang's connections to the Yiyuan painting society and the Shanghai Academy of Art and Guan Zilan's links to the Dawn Art Society and the Zhonghua Fine Arts Academy—were the norm. Reevaluating the nature of women's membership to such prominent art societies allows a clearer perspective of their participation in Republican China's art world.

The intersection of artistic practice and modern art theory is the subject of the third chapter. I look at women artists' engagement in the modernist discourse surrounding the newly popular genre of the nude, which was embraced as the antithesis of traditional Chinese painting. I explore in detail three factors in early 1930s China that encouraged numerous female artists to paint and exhibit images of female nudes: the widespread exposure and acceptance of nude imagery, the prevailing modernist art ideology espoused by influential theorists, and the feminist aspirations of the women in the field as revealed in their published articles. For women artists, painting the female nude represented an opportunity to attain parity with their male counterparts. This chapter analyzes the early work of Pan Yuliang, the only Republican-period female artist typically recognized today and who, when she is remembered at all, is best remembered for her penchant for painting the female nude. This chapter challenges conventional gender theory—which assigns to the nude the role of passive object of the male gaze and product of the male hand—by examining women artists' equally zealous participation in one of the most definitive artistic practices of China's modern art movement.

No sooner had women grasped at the "golden key" of professional careers in the arts, however, than it slipped through their fingers. As China anticipated and then entered war with Japan, the very practice of modernist art waned under an onslaught of public debate. The consensus of the art community shifted away from modernism and toward realism and art's social obligation, thus limiting the professional development for all modernist artists. But for women, the late 1930s delivered additional blows to their careers as professional artists. Chapter 4 explores the political campaigns and wartime hardships that forced most women to abandon their careers. First came the Nationalist government's New Life Movement that demanded women perform as Good Wives and Wise Mothers within the confines of the home so as to create a unified front of homemakers and caregivers. Later, impoverished living conditions and the constant threat of air raids reduced many women's activities to supportive roles while male artists monopolized professional resources and recognition. At this time, a handful of female artists turned to activism, maintaining their careers by reinventing themselves as willing martyrs for the national cause. The first half of this chapter pays special attention to the female artist Fang Junbi and finds that, although the Nationalist campaigns undid the vocational advances of many of her female peers, in the role of grieving widow Fang was able to subvert the conservative rhetoric to the advantage of her career. The second half of this chapter examines the wartime careers of Liang Baibo and Yu Feng, who served as cartoonists on the front lines. I emphasize the battles in which these women actively engaged: both their participation in the war effort and their struggles at the end of their careers as modernist artists. Ultimately, the *nühuajia*'s movement from margins to the center ended with her return to the periphery of professional recognition, where she has remained until the present.

This book will bring her back to the center, where she belongs. In it, we trace the arc of women artists' professional careers during China's Modern Art Movement—from their distribution of laudatory introductions to the wider public, to their fervent activities at the height of modern art in the Republican period, and finally to their struggles against the social and economic pressures that were to constrain and ultimately extinguish their careers. Although war and the limping demise of modernist art in wartime China effectively strangled their access to the profession, during the decade or so when modern art was its most vibrant women alongside their male peers directed its progress by joining influential art groups, staging public exhibitions, and producing equally innovative artworks. As Jin Qijing asserted, a golden key of opportunity in the art world truly did appear before them, if momentarily, and many women readily seized it.

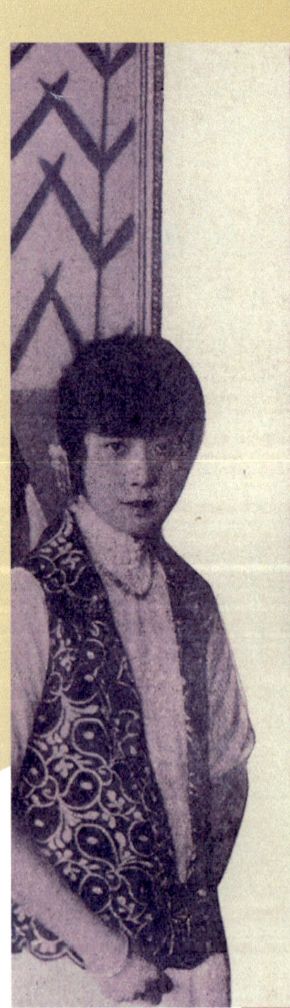

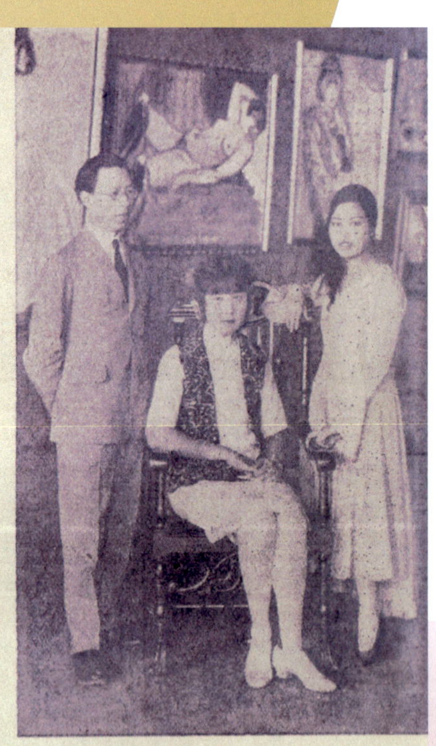

關女士與其藝友陳抱一君及鍾獨清女士在會場之合影

陳氏在上海洋畫界歷史甚久，爲關女士之導師，此次關氏個展，得其幫助極多，鍾女士留法研究音樂多年，關女士之好友也。

I

A Beacon in the Distance

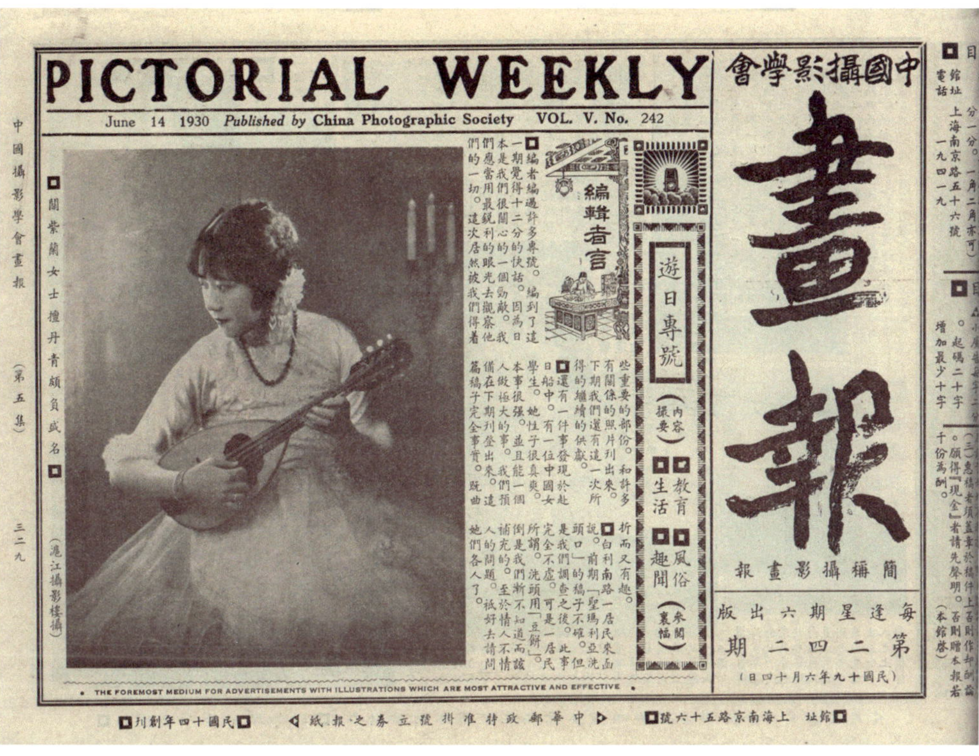

1.1 Cover photograph featuring Guan Zilan, China Photographic Society's *Pictorial Weekly*. Wou Kong Photography Studio, "Guan Zilan nüshi shan danqing po fu shengming [Famous Painter Miss Guan Zilan]," *Pictorial Weekly* 5, no. 242 (1930): cover.

In a large, black-and-white photograph commanding the front page of a 1930 issue of the China Photographic Society's Pictorial Weekly, a young Chinese woman plays dress up (fig. 1.1).[1] She wears a flower in her hair, a necklace of dark-toned beads, and a lace tulle gown. In her hands she cradles a mandolin as she gazes dreamily off to one side. A painted backdrop with a candelabrum burning in the shadows completes the thoroughly romanticized image of the Occident. The photograph's caption identifies the sitter as Miss Guan Zilan 關紫蘭 (1903–85) and adds that she enjoys a great reputation for her skill at painting. As

"Guan nüshi yu qi yiyou Chen Baoyi jun ji Zhong Duqing nüshi zai huichang zhi hexiang [Group photo of Miss Guan and her artist friends Mister Chen Baoyi and Miss Zhong Duqing at the event space]" (detail of fig. 1.8).

distinctive as Guan Zilan's photograph remains, paging through Chinese magazines and journals of the 1920s and 1930s it becomes apparent that her profile is but one example of the veritable fad of news coverage on contemporary painters that swept through China at that time.

A handful of recent studies have begun to investigate media portrayals of Republican-period women artists and analyze the common characteristics of such coverage, as well as question the impact it had on women's careers.[2] In general, scholars note that periodicals' presentations of female artists were different from those of men, emphasizing the women's femininity and physical appearance over their professional skills. One of the closest readings of Republican-period print media coverage of women artists is an essay by Lesley Ma in the anthology *Liangyou: Kaleidoscopic Modernity and the Shanghai Global Metropolis, 1926–1945*.[3] Examining *The Young Companion's* treatment of female artists, Ma affirms that pictorials placed greater emphasis on their visages as well as their relationships to men (such as male family members and teachers) than on their actual artistic output. She argues, "mass media nature and editorial decisions reinforce certain gender stereotypes" and undermined women artists' parity with their male peers. Finding that editors framed female artists as modern embodiments of classical feminine virtues, Ma theorizes that the publication steamrolled over the professional aspirations of women in favor of conventional commercial practices that focused primarily on their pretty appearance. Ma's assessment places responsibility for the content and style of news coverage squarely on the shoulders of press editors. Rather than considering the possibility that female artists enthusiastically contributed to their public personas, she assumes these women to be mute or complacent in a hostile work environment: "Due to the lack of first-hand accounts, we can only speculate that the silence, or complacency, suggests that for women artists, opportunities to be reviewed by critics on the same public platform as male artists trumped the issues of gender bias they encountered." From Ma's perspective, it would seem that the women artists profiled in the news media were unwilling participants with little alternative but to play along in a system that undermined their intentions.

Certainly, it can be challenging to ascertain the extent of a woman's agency in her public portrayal via the news and entertainment media, even in today's media coverage. Images of Guan Zilan discussed above threaten to render the intentions of the sitter nearly invisible. The fanciful treatment of the artist's portrait—her trendy makeup and hair, delicate pose, and distinctive dress—hinges on her sophisticated feminine beauty. Apart from the brief identification of her occupation, the publication provides no evidence of Guan's artistic ability. A highly affected portrait manufactured by a professional photography studio and circulated in a society newspaper, what can this image tell us about the woman pictured—the early twentieth-century oil painter Guan Zilan? To what extent did this artist wield control over her own image?

Whereas scholarship to date concentrates on inequities in the news coverage for women artists as opposed to men, the status of female modernist artists and their stake in the operation of the professional publicity media machine is more complicated than previously acknowledged. This chapter analyzes a rich assortment of news media coverage on Guan Zilan. The material assessed offers a lens through which to better understand the professional ambitions and social mobility of early twentieth-century Chinese women artists. Through a close reading of her profiles and comparison with those of other female artists, I excavate the nature of Guan Zilan's engagement with the press. As a female artist, Guan's image and identification in the mass media positioned her at the intersection of two trends in China's early twentieth-century periodical press: coverage of contemporary artists and coverage of modern women. Moreover, print media coverage of female modernist artists of the Republican-period, which is remarkably abundant and positive in tone, indicates that women were understood to be contributing to the advancement of visual art in modern China.

GUAN ZILAN'S DEBUT

As her introduction in *Pictorial Weekly* attests, Guan Zilan was indeed a talented painter. She specialized in oil on canvas and excelled at figure paintings and landscapes composed of bold colors and strong forms. Guan inherited her artistic skills from her parents, both of whom designed fabric patterns for the textile industry.[4] Her parents used the great wealth they had derived from ties to the booming textile trade to support the formal education and extended artistic training of their only child. Born and raised in Shanghai, Guan Zilan attended the Shanghai Shenzhou Girls' Picture Training Course (Shanghai Shenzhou Nüxiao Tuhua Zhuanxiuke 上海神州女校圖畫專修科). There she worked with teachers Chen Baoyi and Hong Ye to develop a broad base of artistic skills, including *xihua*, *guohua*, color theory, perspective, and life drawing. Under the mentorship of Chen Baoyi, she transferred to the Chinese University of the Arts (Zhonghua Yishu Daxue 中華藝術大學), where she continued to study under him and Hong Ye, as well as Ding Yanyong.

In her artistic studies, Guan Zilan trained with leading figures in the contemporary art scene. An early proponent of modernist art, Chen Baoyi 陳抱一 (1893–1945) took a leadership role in multiple art societies and had cofounded the Eastern Painting Society (Dongfang Huihua 東方繪畫)—one of China's first Western-style artist organizations—as an art student in 1915.[5] The following year, he left for studies in Japan and trained under Fujishima Takeji (1867–1943), an advocate of modernist art and the head of the Western Painting Department at the Kawabata Art School in Tokyo. Hong Ye 洪野 (1886–1932) from early on took interest in cultivating the careers of women artists; as a neighbor of the young Pan Yuliang, he first introduced her to oil painting in 1917.[6] Later, he would become the director of the Correspondence Department for the Shanghai Academy of Art.[7] Ding Yanyong 丁衍鏞 (1902–78) had also studied with Fujishima Takeji at the Kawabata Art School and later transferred to the prestigious, if more conservative, Tokyo School of Fine Arts. Upon returning to China in 1925, he initially found employment at the Shanghai Academy of Art, but at the end of that year he left to found the Chinese University of the Arts with Chen Baoyi. The private art academy formally opened its doors to students in 1926, and Guan Zilan was among the first students to study at the school. Under the tutelage of Chen Baoyi and the other faculty, she received instruction in the most avant-garde styles and artistic practices of the day.

When Guan graduated with honors from the Chinese University of the Arts, once again her mentor Chen Baoyi suggested her next course of action and, following his advice, she left for study abroad in Japan.[8] Shortly after her arrival, Guan Zilan staged a solo exhibition and began studying with Kametaka Fumiko, an established female painter and president of the Sekiso-sha Girls' School for Painting in Kobe. She later enrolled at the Tokyo Academy of Culture (Nihon Tōkyō Bunka Gaku-in) and exhibited in several prestigious exhibitions, including the Nikakai Art Exhibition, the Ueno Fine Art Exhibition, and the Hyogo Prefectural Art Exhibition in Kobe. Thus, Guan enjoyed the requisites for a successful career as a female artist in the Republican period: she possessed a talent at painting and, equally important, she benefitted from the advantage of a family that encouraged her pursuit of a career as a painter and provided the financial means to support her study and professional advancement.

Guan Zilan's debut in the press began with her graduation from the Chinese University of the Arts in June 1927, and a frenzy of publicity spanned the following five years. The assortment of coverage—a mix of biographic profiles, exhibition reviews, and captions accompanying personal photographs—documents both her own interaction with the news media and the development of a persona that equally emphasized her gender and her professionalism. Guan's repeated interactions with the press—at one point an embedded reporter even joined the artist on an overseas excursion—affirms her endorsement of the news coverage she provoked.

At the time of her graduation, Guan joined an exhibition of over two hundred artworks produced

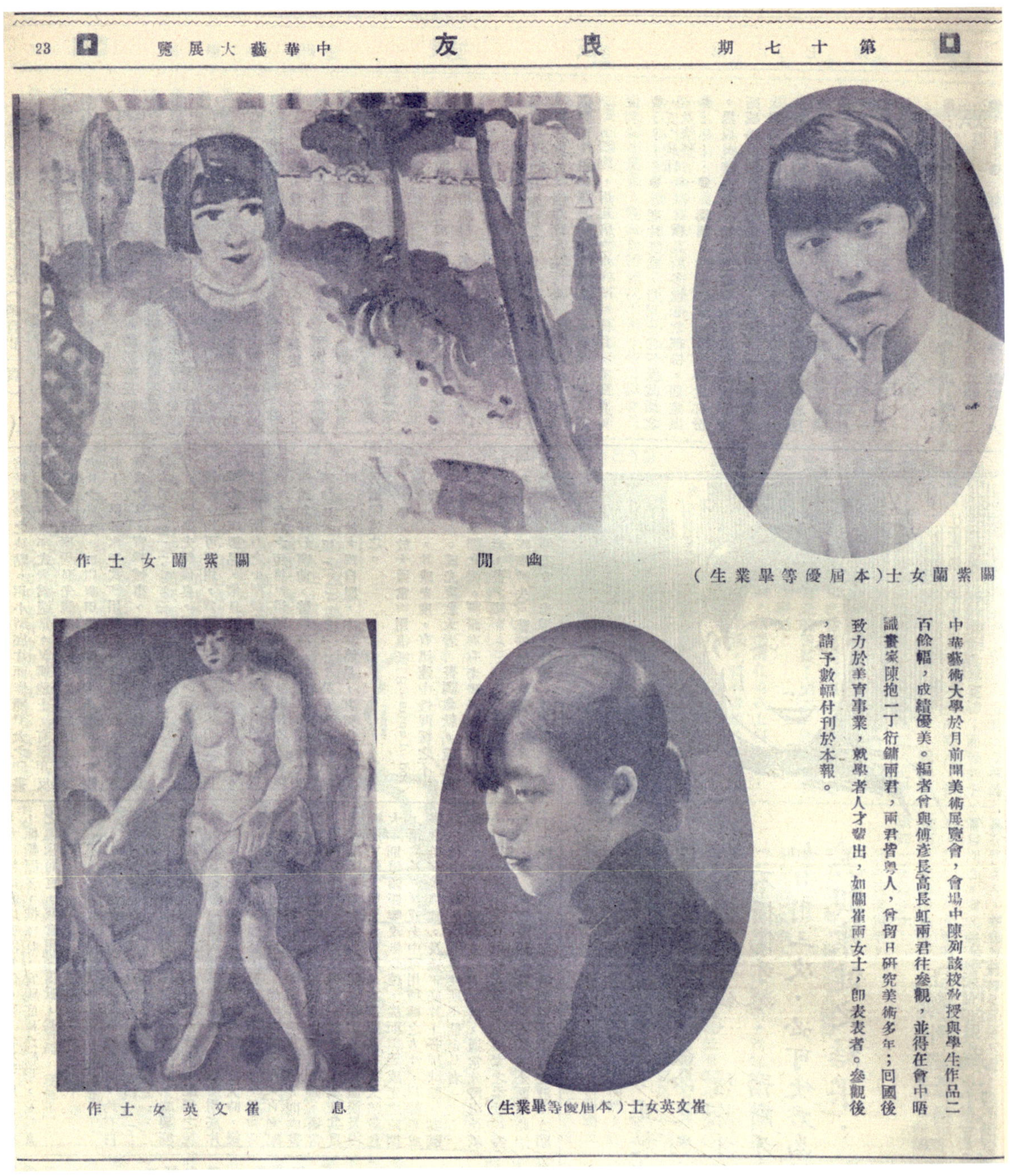

第十七期　良友　中華藝大展覽　23

幽閒　關紫蘭女士作

關紫蘭女士（本屆優等畢業生）

中華藝術大學於月前開美術展覽會，會場中陳列該校教授與學生作品二百餘幅，成績優美。編者曾與傅彥長高長虹兩君往參觀，並得在會中晤識畫家陳抱一丁衍鏞兩君，兩君皆粵人，曾留日研究美術多年；回國後致力於美育事業，就學者人才輩出，如關崔兩女士，即表表者。參觀後，請予數幅付刊於本報。

息　崔文英女士作

崔文英女士（本屆優等畢業生）

1.2 Coverage of the Chinese University of the Arts' exhibition, *The Young Companion* 17 (August 1927).

by the students and professors of the Chinese University of the Arts. When the editor of *The Young Companion*, Liang Desuo 梁得所 (1905–38), visited the exhibition, Chen Baoyi and Ding Yanyong recommended two star pupils for special attention, both of whom were women. Consequently, the next month's issue included artwork reproductions by and photographs of the professors as well as the two exemplary graduates, Guan Zilan and Cui Wenying 崔文英 (n.d.) (fig. 1.2).[9] While the two-page feature provides no additional information about Guan, an illuminative detail may be teased from the visual evidence of her portrait photograph. The product of a professional photography studio rather than an onsite snapshot, its appearance in *The Young Companion* piece suggests that Guan Zilan voluntarily gave the photograph to Liang Desuo for the express purpose of public distribution. From this first interaction with the press, Guan intended to present her best face to the public. This professional studio portrait depicts a young woman with modishly cropped hair and bright, inquisitive eyes; her face is confidently directed toward the camera and she holds one hand thoughtfully (but delicately) tucked under her chin.[10] This self-assured but elegant demeanor was to become a trademark characteristic of Guan's public identity. No less significant, Guan Zilan's representative painting, *Leisure* (*Youxian* 幽閒), is a self-portrait and the sitter's nearly identical appearance and demeanor reinforces the persona cultivated by the photograph. In the painted image, the artist sits in the foreground, poised but relaxed, while a lakeside landscape recedes over her shoulder. The juxtaposition of the painting and the photograph invites comparison of the artist and her work and thus an evaluation of her aptitude vis-à-vis the verisimilitude and painterly expression of the image. The pairing also allows an assessment of her identity—her social status and her comportment as a member of the first generation of female art professionals—creating an infinity mirror of sorts, as the viewer looks from one to the other for confirmation.

Not long thereafter, *The Eastern Times Photo Supplement* published the very same photograph in an artist introduction exclusive to Guan Zilan (fig. 1.3).[11] Again the photograph appears directly next to the artist's self-portrait. The woman in the oil painting wears the same hairstyle and expression. She also poses in a similar manner as before, except that this time she gracefully rests her arm in her lap while holding in her hand an impressive fan made of peacock feathers. An English-language caption accompanying the images states, "Miss Kuan Tzu-lan is noted for painting. At the left is her masterpiece 'Peacock.'" The Chinese portion of the text observes that she is "known as the Marval of the East" ("*shizhe yu wei dongfang* Marval 識者譽為東方 Marval") and is even more glowing in its appraisal of the artist.

The word "Marval" might be a simple misspelling of marvel, but more likely it refers to the French painter, Jacqueline Marval (1866–1932). Part of the School of Paris, Marval had studied under Gustav Moreau in the École des Beaux Arts, collaborated with Matisse, and exhibited at the Salon des Indépendants and the Salon d'Automne. The *Supplement's* comparison with Marval clearly flattered Guan, but it also exposes two aspects of the social context in which she operated. In the first, the newspaper relied on the likelihood of a rather sophisticated audience with a knowledge of contemporary Western artists. With no transliteration or discussion of Marval provided, the supplement assumes its readership not only knew the word referred to a painter but to a female painter at that. Second, the reference draws on the cult of artistic celebrity to elevate China's own accomplished female painter by means of comparison with an even more widely renowned female painter. It is precisely this cultivation of celebrity that led to a proliferation of news coverage of Guan Zilan and other artists in diverse formats and across a wide variety of print media outlets.

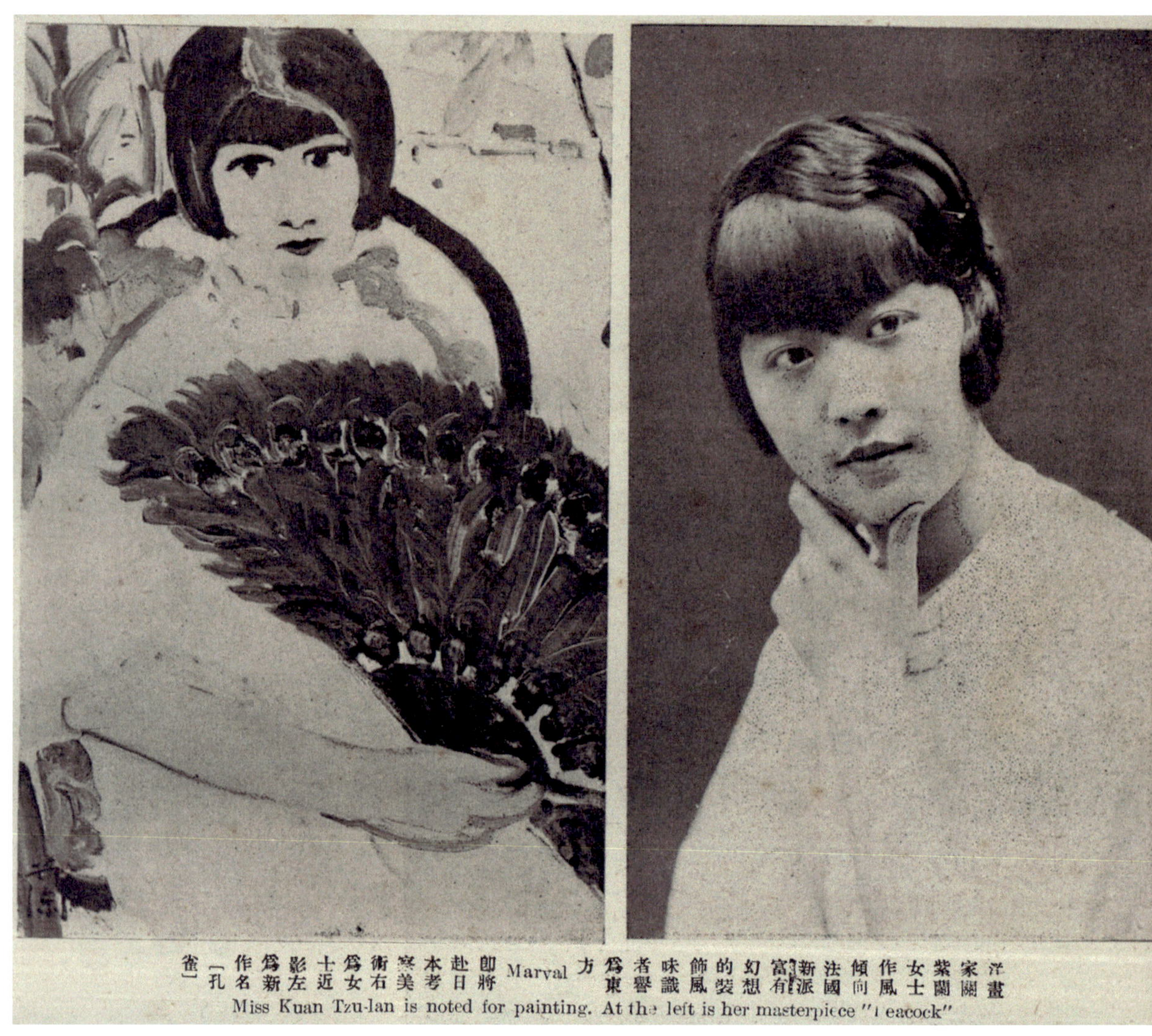

1.3 "Miss Kuan Tzu-lan is noted for painting. At the left is her masterpiece, 'Peacock'," *The Eastern Times Photo Supplement* 375 (1927): 3.

WOMEN ARTISTS AS MEDIA CELEBRITIES AND GUAN ZILAN'S ENGAGEMENT WITH THE PRESS

The same unrelenting preoccupation with physical appearance seen in news coverage of Guan Zilan may be observed in any number of other publications, including a special issue of the popular Shanghai magazine *The Ladies' Journal*.[12] Dedicated to women artists, this issue was coedited by Jin Qijing, who in the same issue published her call for women to rise up and seize the golden key of career opportunities in the arts (as discussed in the Introduction). Jin tenaciously vocalized her fight for equal consideration of women artists, but in the special issue that she coproduced the reader finds the standard editorial choices encountered in other publications. Certainly, the formatting of the artists' biographies is virtually identical. In 1920s China, such biographical sketches were by far the artist's most expedient means to fame. The practice was an outgrowth of China's millennia-old hagiographic tradition and what Jonathan Hay has termed the "social mechanism for artistic celebrity" that coincided with the rise of a thriving print culture in the late Qing.[13] The biographies published in Republican-period print media, which were critical to the careers of artists, tended to be brief and superficial assessments of artists' professional qualifications. But whereas men's biographies often omitted images of the artist in favor of including reproductions of his work, in women's biographies the photo is paramount.

Simultaneously, then, *The Eastern Times Photo Supplement* publicized Guan Zilan as a masterful and modern painter along with images emphasizing her physical appearance. The consistency between the visual offerings found in the publications suggests that Guan Zilan selected the images herself and submitted them to the press. Guan's direct relationship with *The Eastern Times Photo Supplement* is all the more apparent in three subsequent news reports. Bao Zhenqing, named as the newspaper's correspondent in the coverage, evidently spent a substantial amount of time with Guan and sent back to his editors photographs and information regarding her recent exploits. In one photograph he poses with her and two Japanese news reporters, providing visual evidence that the artist had made the news abroad as well.[14] A few weeks later, Bao is credited as the photographer for a group photo of Guan Zilan hosting a reception of Japanese painters.[15] In a third photograph, which occupies more than half of the paper's front page, he is listed as one of four nearly indistinguishable male figures in a boat with Guan Zilan at the prow.[16]

What a staggeringly modern impression this last photograph must have provided to its intended audience. By today's standards, the image might be mistaken as a conventional rendition of a familiar subject: a beautiful woman in a pleasant setting. In actuality, the photograph employed a visual vocabulary that radically defined the new social parameters of the female professional artist. The artist, an unmarried woman from a respectable family, sits comfortably in a boat in the middle of a vast and picturesque lake, but her companions are men, not one of whom is identified as a relation of hers![17] She is labeled a "famous Chinese painter," and the newspaper not only chronicles her independent journey in a foreign land, but—thanks to the marvels of modern technology—did so practically in real time. As part of the ongoing coverage on Guan Zilan, this news bite effectively served to the readership a serialized update of the artist's progress. Its daring presentation of a Chinese debutante—which would have been unthinkable even a few years prior—must have cemented Guan's reputation as a modern woman unafraid to break with social conventions.

Similarly, artist introductions in other periodicals commonly present Guan Zilan as a modern artist of the highest caliber. If few of these profile pieces discuss the specifics of Guan's paintings in much detail, that does not appear to detract from the press's opinion of Guan as a modern artist. *The Morning Post Sunday Picture Section* (*Chenbao xingqi huabao*晨報星期畫報) offered its readers a glimpse of both Guan and her exhibition.[18] In the

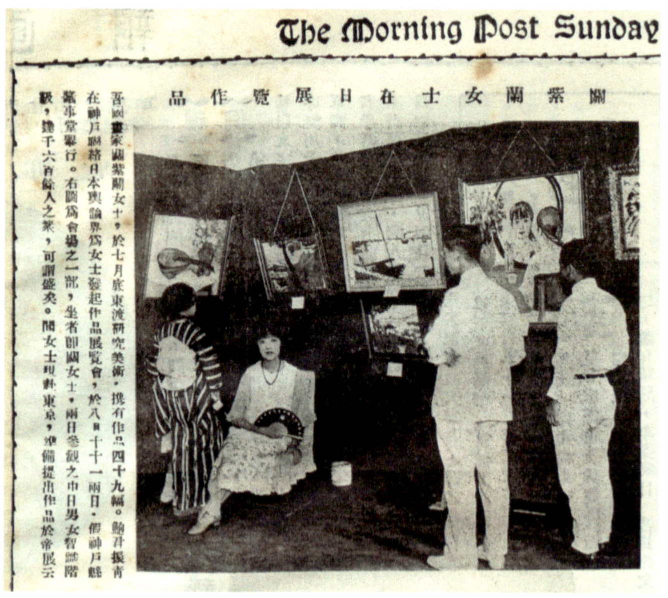
The Morning Post Sunday

關紫蘭女士在日展覽作品

吾國畫家關紫蘭女士，於七月底東渡研究美術，携有作品四十九幅。鮑君振青在神戶聯絡日本輿論界為女士發起作品展覽會，於八月十十一兩日，假神戶縣議事堂舉行。右圖為會場之一部，坐者即關女士。兩日參觀之中日男女智識階級，幾千六百餘人之衆，可謂盛矣。關女士現赴東京，準備提出作品於帝展云

1.4 "Guan Zilan nüshi zai riben zhanlan zuopin [Artworks from Guan Zilan's Exhibition in Japan]," *The Morning Post Sunday Picture Section* 2, no. 100 (1927): 2.

snapshot, Guan sits in a corner of the exhibit (fig. 1.4). She stares unflinchingly at the camera and takes no notice of three exhibition attendees in her close proximity. A woman in a kimono directly by Guan's side completely ignores her and edges close to the framed paintings. In contrast, the two men standing before Guan direct their gaze straight at her rather than the artwork on the wall to their side. The figures' arrangement within the scene produces a surreal composition, as if Guan herself was one of the many objects on view at her exhibition, much like a wax figure in a museum.

Although the image suggests the artist is on display as much as the artwork, the accompanying text explicitly frames her as an internationally renowned modern artist. The paragraph-long biographic passage concentrates on the hallmarks of Guan's success—her study abroad and exhibition, her professional link to Japan's educated elite, and the popularity of her work—and matter-of-factly describes the female artist in terms equal to those used for her male contemporaries. The text precisely notes that she carried forty-nine paintings with her to Japan, which she then displayed in a two-day solo exhibition in Kobe that was attended by more than 1,600 members of the Japanese intelligentsia. It also notes that Guan was readying to travel to Tokyo, where she would participate in the Teiten Exhibition (Japan's Imperial Fine Arts Exhibition). Not only do Guan Zilan's actions—her overseas travel and participation in international solo and juried exhibitions—represent a radical departure from traditional activities for women, they also undeniably linked her to the modernization of China's twentieth-century art world.

Thus, to focus on Guan's triumph in Japan was to equate her with China's enthusiastic implementation of modern institutional practices. Her acceptance into an international art community stood as a victory in the advancement of Chinese culture and represented the strengthening of the nation. An article that renders such an interpretation explicit ran in the August 29, 1927, edition of the Shanghai newspaper *Shenbao*. Titled "View of Guan Zilan's Solo Exhibition (Guan Zilan gezhan de guan'gan 關紫蘭個展的觀感)," the review explicates the national significance of Guan's artistic undertakings abroad.[19] Taking Japan as model for civilization, the article lauds Japanese state-implemented reforms, particularly for the incorporation of the Arts (*yishu* 藝術) in its nation-building efforts. The Arts are credited with having transformed Japan into a new nation, and this line of thought corresponds with the discourse of China's New Culture Movement and Cai Yuanpei's invocation for the populace to rely on the Arts in order to build up a modern Chinese morality. The article, having linked the Arts to Japan's ascendency, reminds the reader that China likewise should manifest its "beautiful national character" (*meide guominxing* 美的國民性) and suggests that Guan Zilan's exhibition works toward that end. Thus, Guan Zilan's artwork is held up as a source of national pride, with the positive reception of her exhibition in Japan cited as the realization of China's worth on a global stage.

In light of the importance attached to the international exposure of Chinese artists, it is not surprising that introductions for Guan Zilan that circulated in the print media the following year continued to emphasize her activity in Japan. Guan made the cover of the October 1928 issue of *The Modern Lady*, a product of *The Young Companion's* publishing house (fig. 1.5a).[20] Inside the issue, a full-page artist introduction features four reproductions of her paintings and a reprint of the cover photograph sized down to correspond with the scale of the painting reproductions (fig. 1.5b). In the photograph Guan strikes a demure pose. Although her face is directed toward the camera, she tilts her gaze downward and gracefully positions her hands near her neck. Perhaps Guan included her hands in her portrait shot because she wished to spotlight the tools of her trade. More likely, however, the young and affluent artist intended to show off her expensive, cutting-edge wristwatch.

Even with the journal's doubled printing of Guan Zilan's urbane portrait photograph, *The Modern Lady* coverage cultivates Guan Zilan's persona as a serious modern artist. The diverse genres of the four paintings—a still life, a house, a landscape, and figures in a domestic setting—spotlight Guan's artistic versatility.[21] The short passage of text identifies her as an outstanding female painter and highlights her still life *Narcissus* (*Shuixianhua* 水仙花) for its inclusion in the selective Nikakai Exhibition in Tokyo the previous year. In a similar vein, *The Young Companion* reproduced yet another photo studio portrait.[22] Its extraordinary size—occupying a full page—would seem to indicate that the publication fixated solely on Guan Zilan's physical appearance, but the accompanying artist introduction reveals otherwise. Noting the artist's home province and college education, the pictorial calls her an expert on Western painting (*xiyanghua*) and shares that her solo exhibition in Japan was highly praised by the art world. The profile also directs the reader to a reproduction elsewhere in the issue of her landscape painting *West Lake* (*Xihu* 西湖). In fact, readers of the periodical were already familiar with her artwork as the October issue of the previous year had run a reproduction of *Peony* (*Shaoyao* 芍藥). In both of these profiles, as well as the many others, Guan Zilan likely suggested the tenor of the text and certainly provided the reproductions of her artworks and photographic portraits of herself to the press. That is to say, Guan worked with the press to shape her public image.

At the same time that she publicized herself within the news media, Guan Zilan advanced her career, and by 1930 she had held teaching positions at multiple art schools in Shanghai.[23] That same year she also staged a solo exhibition at the Hua'an Building (Hua'an Dasha 華安大廈) in Shanghai. Guan's artistic activity prompted a flurry of interest and that year several publications ran short profiles introducing her to the public. One example, *The Young Companion's* full-page "Art Exhibits: By Miss Violet Kwan," provides a photographic review of Guan Zilan's solo exhibition (fig. 1.6). The largest reproductions are portraits of women from the artist's social circle: *Miss L* (*L nüshi xiang* L女士像), which depicts a young lady holding a small dog in her lap, and *The Green-Dressed Girl* (*Lüyi shaonü* 綠衣少女), in which a little girl wears a dress with an oversized bow. These two images anchor the upper left and lower right corners. Two medium-sized landscapes appear in the upper right corner. The

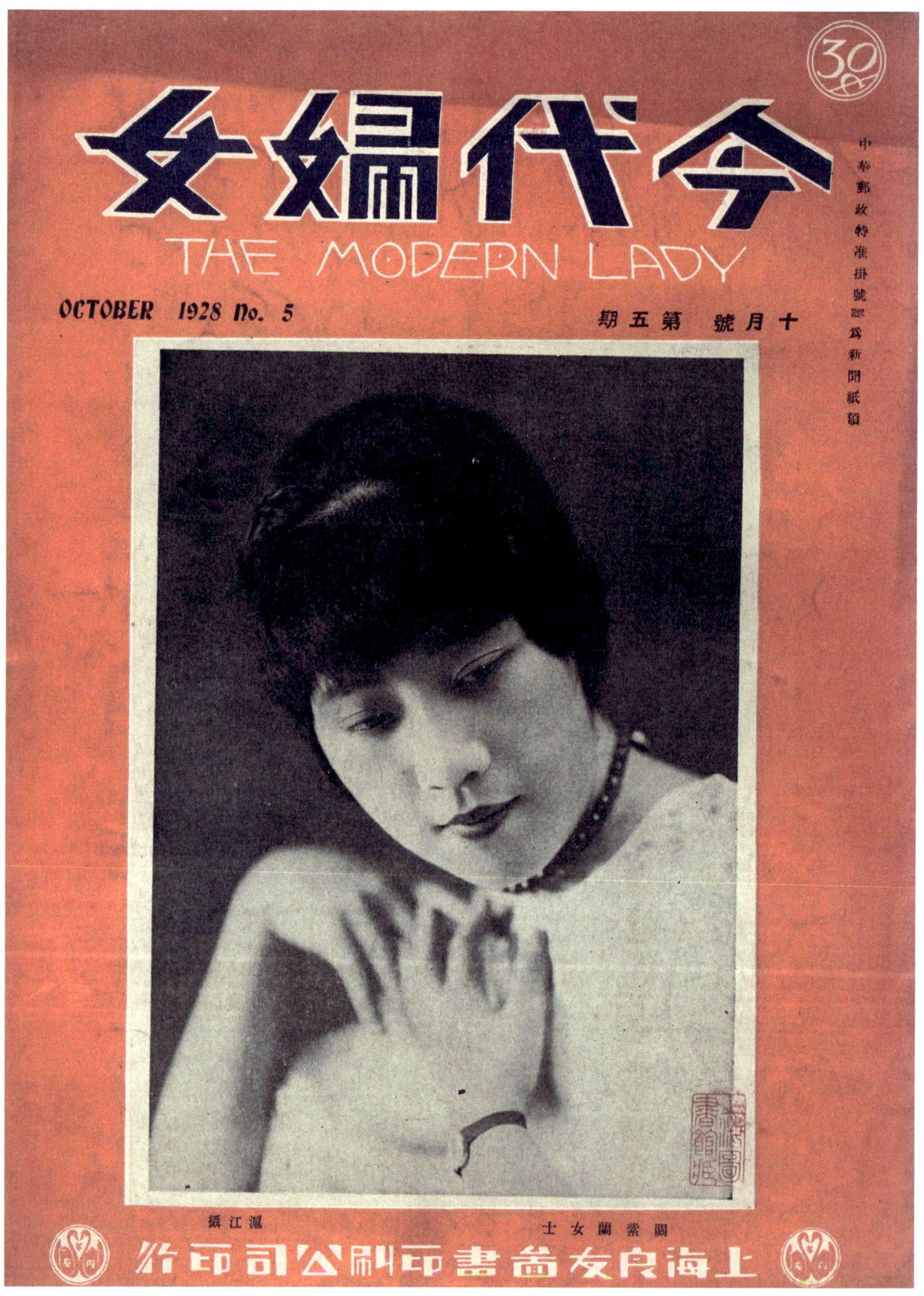

1.5a Wou Kong Photography Studio, "Guan Zilan nüshi [Miss Guan Zilan]," *The Modern Lady* 5 (1928).

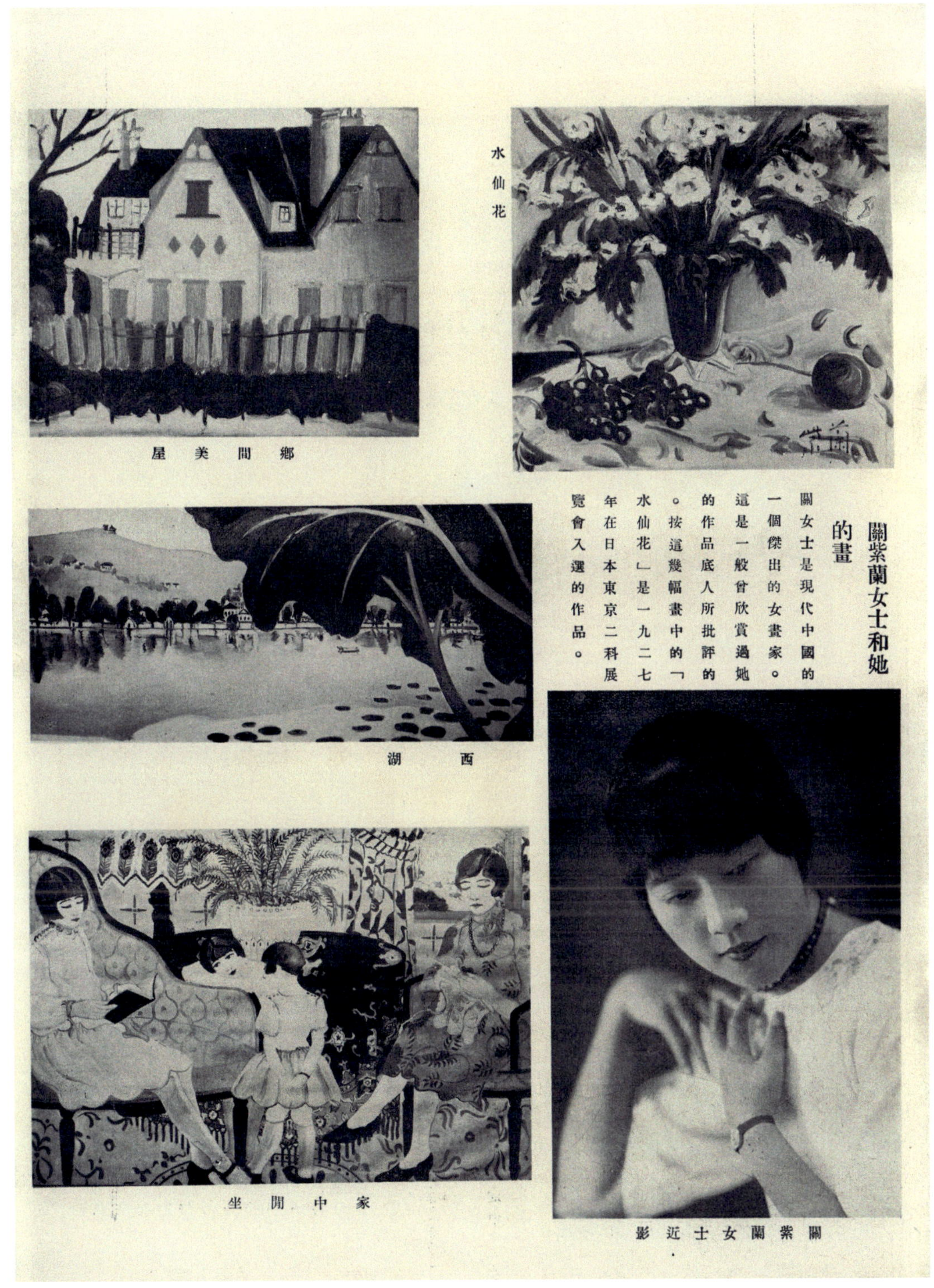

關紫蘭女士和她的畫

關女士是現代中國的一個傑出的女畫家。這是一般曾欣賞過她的作品底人所批評的。按這幾幅畫中的「水仙花」是一九二七年在日本東京二科展覽會入選的作品。

水仙花

鄉間美屋

西湖

家中閒坐

關紫蘭女士近影

1.5b Biography for Guan Zilan. "Guan Zilan nüshi he ta de hua [Miss Guan Zilan and her paintings]," *The Modern Lady* 5 (1928).

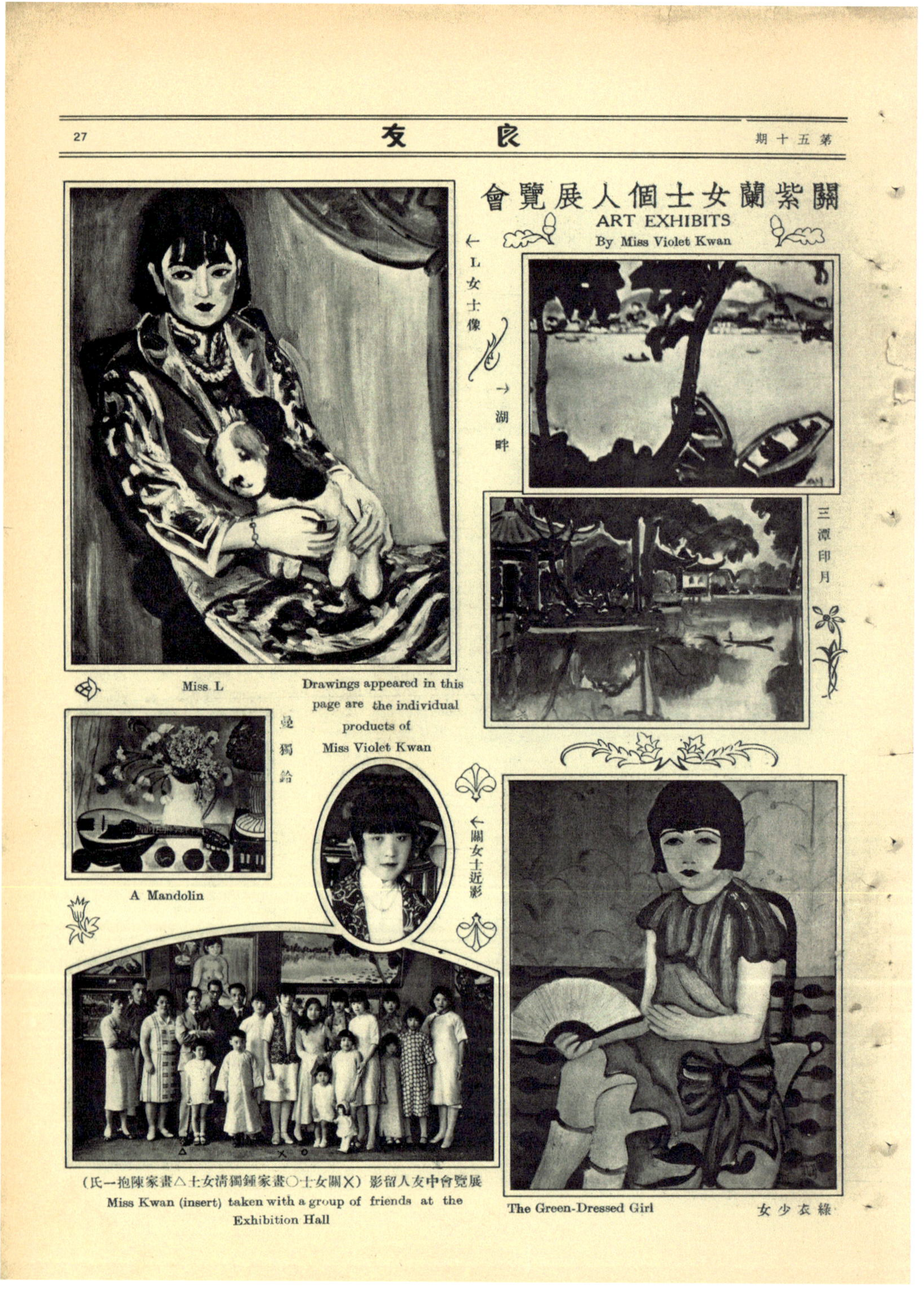
27 良友 第五十期

關紫蘭女士個人展覽會

ART EXHIBITS

By Miss Violet Kwan

←L女士像

→湖畔

三潭印月

Miss L

Drawings appeared in this page are the individual products of Miss Violet Kwan

曼獨鈴

A Mandolin

←關女士近影

展覽會中友人留影 (X關女士○畫家鍾獨清女士△畫家陳抱一氏)

Miss Kwan (insert) taken with a group of friends at the Exhibition Hall

The Green-Dressed Girl 綠衣少女

1.6 Coverage of Guan Zilan's solo exhibition. "Art Exhibits: By Miss Violet Kwan," *The Young Companion* 50 (1930): 27.

smallest of the reproductions, a still life titled *A Mandolin* (*Manduling* 曼獨鈴), shares the lower left corner with a group photograph in the exhibition space and an inset of Guan Zilan. Taken as a whole, the variety of mundane subjects open a window onto Guan's world, letting the viewer peer at the assorted objects and individuals encountered in her daily existence as if through the artist's own eyes.

The photograph of the exhibition is a conspicuously staged group portrait that depicts Guan posing with her support network. Two individuals identified in the Chinese-language caption are her mentor Chen Baoyi and her former classmate and fellow female artist Zhong Duqing. Guan Zilan's biographies commonly refer to Chen, the man who was most instrumental to her occupational success. For Guan, the persistent reference to her friend and mentor served as a form of endorsement from a much more established member of the art community. In this way, the regular association of Guan Zilan with a male figure did not indicate the editors' lack of confidence in the female artist's expertise but, rather, the continuation of conventional Chinese artistic practices in which a better recognized artist promoted the work of a protégé. Zhong Duqing, on the other hand, was not a senior member of the art world, but her study-abroad experience in France lent Guan an extra air of credibility.

GUAN ZILAN AS CULTURAL ICON

Throughout her publicity campaign, Guan Zilan embraced a feminized professional persona. She coded herself in the social role of a young lady of means and her artworks unhesitatingly offer her perspective as such; reproductions of her work attest that she was particularly fond of depicting beautifully attired young women and girls at leisure. In image after image, Guan provides glimpses into her elite world. She painted self-portraits with luxurious props such as European mandolins and peacock feather fans; she captured the likenesses of her well-dressed female friends, young and old, singly and in groups; and she depicted the types of locales enjoyed by gentlewomen (*guixiu* 閨秀) of the upper class, from the exquisite parlors where she might socialize to pleasure trips on the shores of the West Lake.

And yet, Guan's self-referential subject matter bears no relation to her painting style. The dynamic brushwork of her artworks refuse classification as products of a "feminine hand." Instead of a soft and delicate handling of the brush, as perhaps some might expect from a well-heeled lady, Guan attacked her canvases with a riot of brilliant colors, layering them with thick, bold strokes. In her compositions, she pares down details, letting silhouetted shapes and textured brushstrokes take over. Guan's style is every bit as vigorous and avant-garde as that of any of her male contemporaries, including art school founder Liu Haisu, carefree genius Pang Xunqin, and Guan's own mentor Chen Baoyi.

Unlike works by men, however, Guan Zilan's paintings visually present the disembodied experience of the Modern Girl.[24] Her canvases meld subjects of a stereotypically feminine nature—that is, objects and environments associated with the ladies of China's upper classes or outright depictions of women, such as female nudes and portraits—with a style that asserts the modern artistic sensibility of the twentieth century. Confronted with both the paintings and the artist in an exhibition, or with Guan's paintings alongside her photographic likeness in the pages of a magazine, the viewer encountered the Modern Girl in the flesh, while simultaneously experiencing a privileged view of the world through her eyes.

A consummate performer, Guan Zilan not only painted images of an affluent Modern Girl's life, she additionally tailored her own self-presentation for public consumption. A *Modern Miscellany* (*Shidai huabao* 時代畫報) feature from 1930 that praises Guan's feminine characteristics affirms her mastery at cultivating a persona of elegance and refined beauty. Her biography appears as part of a double-page feature titled "Trying on a Bit of Makeup" (*Qing zhuang jiu shi* 輕妝就試).[25] The photograph is identical to the one on the front page of the China Photographic Society's *Pictorial Weekly*. The biographical sketch pays greater attention to Guan

Zilan's feminine charms and her status as a fashion icon than to her professional career. The reader is told that Guan is skilled at both music and fashion, that she picks her outfits with care, and that she selected the dress she wears in the photo for its fluffy appearance. On the same page, a full-length studio portrait depicts another socialite, who wears an asymmetrical dress with an ebullient plaid and floral pattern. The fact that this particular image of Guan Zilan holding a mandolin appeared in at least two venues—and a similar shot from the same photography session made the cover of *The Young Companion* that same year (fig. 1.7)—strongly suggests that the artist personally worked with the press in the commercial distribution of her image.[26] Unlike the paparazzi shots purchased by the tabloids today, Guan's photographs—as those accompanying most of the published biographies on women artists discussed in this chapter—were professional studio photographs paid for and likely submitted to the press by the artist herself.[27] She was a loyal patron of Wou Kong Studio (Hujiang Sheying Lou 滬江攝影樓), a professional photography studio that specialized in the production of glamour shots for Shanghai's socialites and movie stars, at least thirty of which appear in issues of the women's magazine *Lin Loon*.[28]

A series of Guan Zilan's informal drawings suggests—particularly when considered in conjunction with her penchant for romanticized portrait photographs—that the artist internalized the popular interpretation of modernized femininity presented in her photographs. Among her extant artworks are more than a dozen sketches of sultry-eyed Hollywood starlets.[29] Unpublished in her lifetime and presumably never exhibited, these sketches are not preparatory drawings for finished paintings but personal studies of modern fashion and a globalized feminine beauty ideal. As if seeking to layer the glamour of the silver screen atop her own already fashionable countenance, she also produced self-portrait sketches that employ the same intense gaze and idealized facial features as her renditions of Western beauties.[30]

Guan's desire to harmonize her personal appearance with the images that she created is perhaps most easily discerned in a color photograph from the artist's personal estate, also apparently unpublished in her lifetime.[31] In it, the artist sits gracefully on the floor with her legs to one side, while three large painted canvases rest against the wall behind her. Although the top half of the upper canvas is cropped out of the photograph, enough remains visible to determine all three paintings are images of young women. Most likely all three are self-portraits. Certainly, Guan's self-presentation in the photograph seeks to emphasize the living Modern Girl's visual affinity to the painted image: her hairstyle and pose is identical to one of the paintings, and her attire is quite similar in pattern and cut. Thus, her paintings and sketches, coupled with the photographs for which she sat, capture an inner process of identity formation in which Guan reimagined herself as a cultural icon of modern femininity and glamour. Moreover, Guan's self-conscious identification with the contents of her paintings, and her desire to manifest her lived experiences within the public space of her exhibited artworks, profoundly impacted her portrayal in the news media.

Given Guan Zilan's intense involvement in the refinement of her own image, *Modern Miscellany's* coverage of her in "Trying on a Bit of Makeup"—a feature dedicated to fashion rather than professional accomplishments—does not indicate a dismissive view of her career as a painter. Even in a biography rather frivolously dedicated to her sartorial interests, Guan Zilan is described as "enthusiastically engaged in painting's New Art Movement" ("*wei rexin congshi yu huihua de xin yishu yundong* 為熱心從事於繪畫的新藝術運動"). Indeed, the pictorial was quite sympathetic to Guan Zilan's position as a modern artist. Founded by cartoonists and managed by Shao Xunmei 邵洵美 (Zau Sinmay, 1906–68), *Modern Miscellany* was a high-quality periodical with an emphasis on the arts.[32] In just one issue prior to the fashion profile, the pictorial had run a one-page photographic review of her exhibition and its "masterworks." (fig. 1.8). All of the reproduced paintings are depictions of young women—including two captured in the background

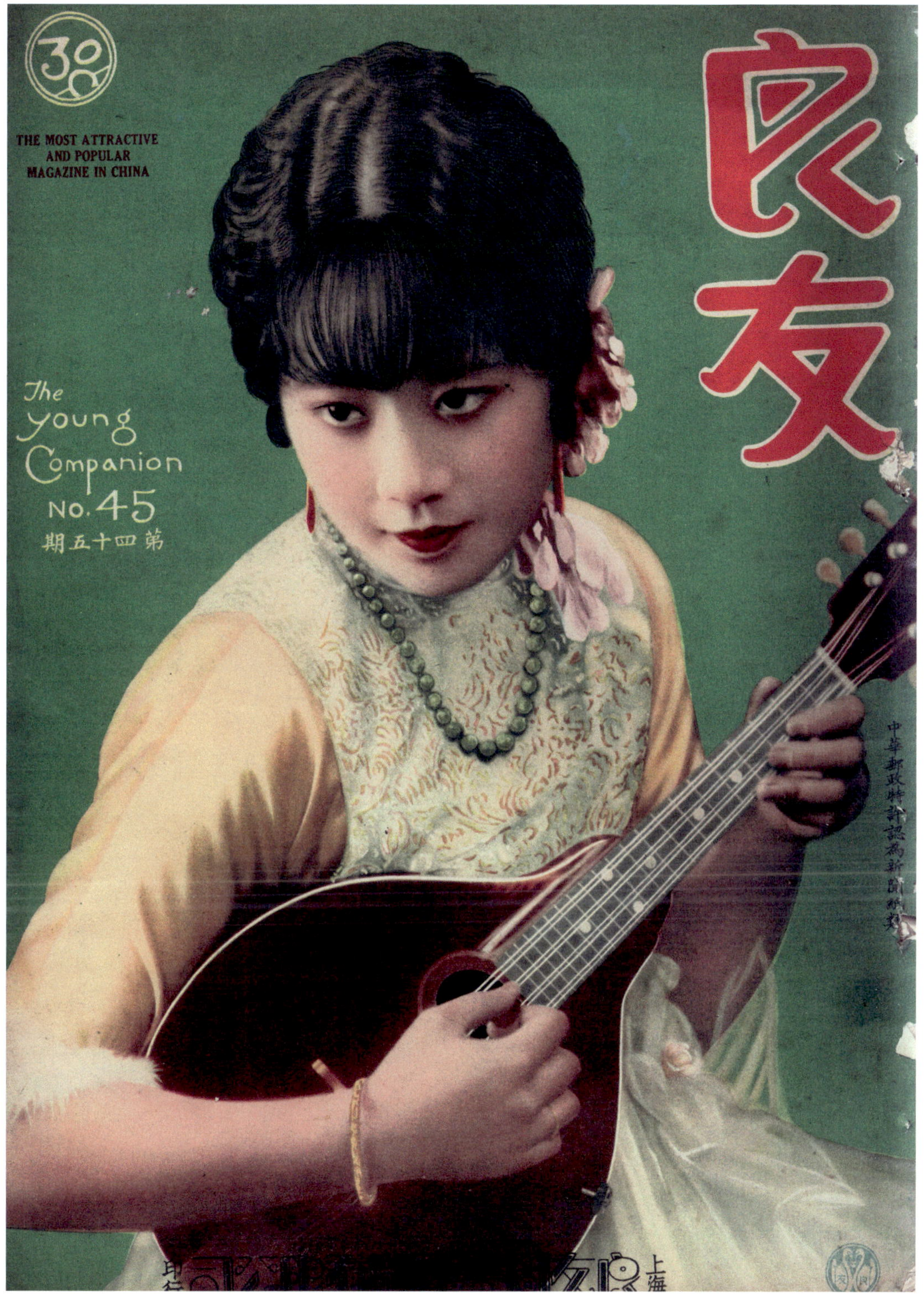

1.7 Cover image of Guan Zilan for *The Young Companion* 45 (1930).

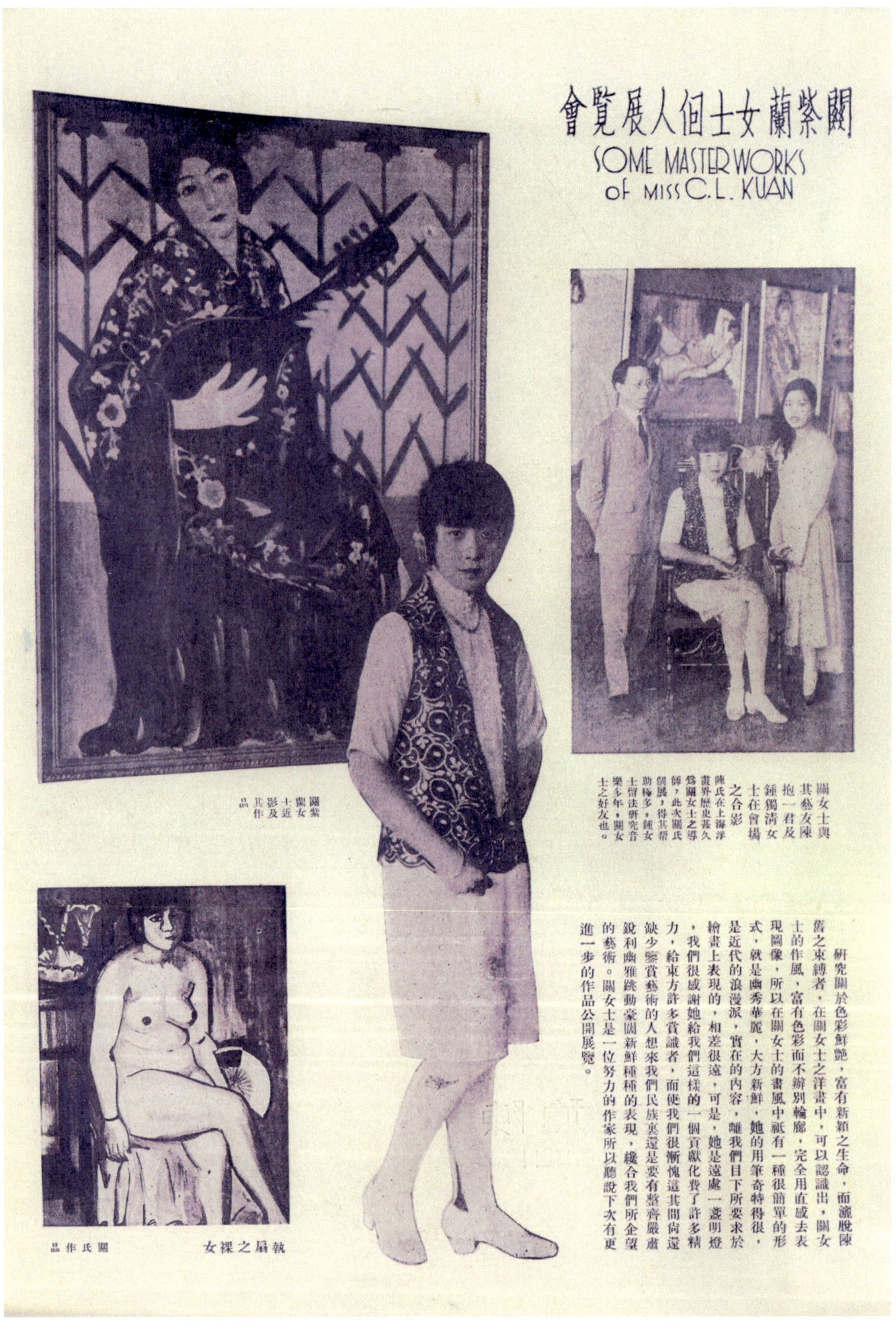

關紫蘭女士個人展覽會

SOME MASTERWORKS of MISS C. L. KUAN

關紫蘭女士近影及其作品

關女士與其藝友陳抱一君及鍾獨清女士在會場之合影

陳氏在上海洋畫界歷史甚久爲關女士之導師，此次關氏個展，得其幫助極多，鍾女士留法研究音樂多年，關女士之好友也。

研究關於色彩鮮艷，富有新穎之生命，而灑脫陳舊之束縛者，在關女士之洋畫中，可以認識出，關女士的作風，富有色彩而不辨別輪廓，完全用直感去表現圖像，所以在關女士的畫風中祇有一種很簡單的形式，就是幽秀華麗，大方新鮮，她的用筆奇特得很，是近代的浪漫派，實在的內容，離我們目下所要求於繪畫上表現的，相差很遠，可是，她是遠處一盞明燈，我們很感謝她給我們這樣的一個貢獻化費了許多精力，給東方許多賞識者，而使我們很慚愧這其間尚還缺少鑒賞藝術的人想來我們民族裏還是要有整齊嚴肅銳利幽雅跳動豪闊新鮮種種的表現，纔合我們所企望的藝術。關女士是一位努力的作家所以聽說下次有更進一步的作品公開展覽。

執扇之裸女　關氏作品

1.8 Exhibition coverage and brief biography for Guan Zilan. “Some Masterworks of Miss C. L. Kuan,” *Modern Miscellany* 1, no. 6 (1930).

of an onsite photo—one of which rather self-referentially pictures a woman stroking a mandolin. A photograph of Guan in the exhibition space singles out her support network; this time the significance of Chen Baoyi's and Zhong Duqing's relationship to the artist is clearly outlined in the caption below. An exceptionally long profile for Guan Zilan provides the most probing discussion of her work heretofore.[33] The text identifies her as an avant-garde artist and discusses her style in detail, noting in her paintings an abundance of color, the absence of outlines, and a fresh use of form. The discussion of the artist regards her as a expert and repeatedly remarks on her diligence. Calling her a "beacon in the distance" (*yuanchu yizhan mingdeng* 遠處一盞明燈) the pictorial asserts that more exhibitions of art such as hers are necessary for the advancement of the arts in China. As a female artist, Guan Zilan is once again linked to social change and the fate of the nation; the passage intertwines her public performance of the profession with the realization of national progress.

What can account for the dramatically divergent presentations of this artist within a single publication, who in one issue is designated a fashion plate and in another a beacon of Chinese modern art? These two profiles in particular capture the seeming conflict found within many portrayals of the *nühuajia*, whose photographic portraits stress her physical attractiveness at the same time that her professional credentials dominate the text of her biographies. For Republican-period audiences, however, the tension—created from this perpetual vacillation between objectification and professionalism—merged seamlessly into a singular persona. The two sides of her public presentation transformed Guan Zilan into a cultural icon: the celebrated female professional artist. She was not the nameless Modern Girl found in countless calendar posters and magazine advertisements but a self-possessed female artist who exhibited successfully on the world stage and was simultaneously confident in her femininity.

Persistent in her self-promotion, Guan Zilan constructed a persona that relied on her social prominence as an artist and her status as a media darling. An outgoing socialite from a wealthy family, Guan possessed a love of fine clothes, Parisian perfume, and the public display of photos of herself through mass media.[34] As a daughter of high society she not only had access to the considerable wealth required for her much-publicized overseas trips and exhibitions, but she also held name recognition that promised to boost the popular periodicals' sales figures. Yet for all of her newsworthy artistic exploits, the impetus for such coverage was initiated (and perhaps funded) by Guan Zilan herself. And in the media coverage that she unquestionably condoned and potentially intimately involved herself with, a clear picture of Guan emerges. In her media presentations, Guan was both admired as a beautiful and fashionable young woman and valued greatly—as a beacon amongst her peers, no less—as a modern artist.

REASSESSING MEDIA PORTRAYALS OF WOMEN ARTISTS

Guan Zilan's biographies present hyperfeminized images of a woman artist, and the press's portrayals of her sister artists routinely accentuate gender as well. Although the biographies of these New Women appear in the modern format of mass-marketed magazines and document their newly recognized professional roles, the sustained influence of old models is readily apparent. The biographies found in Republican-period popular magazines perpetuated the formulaic biography of tradition. If magazine editors and members of the art community advocated the modernization of society and the reformation of gender roles, *why* did artist introductions approach the genders differently and privilege the women's physical appearances over their artistic productions?

Scholarship has noted the perplexing incongruities in modernist rhetoric and the social discourse as recorded in Republican-period print culture. These recent studies tend to fixate on the contradictory dimensions of the press's presentations of women and argue that editors mediated these portrayals. Joan Judge in the opening of her recent, authoritative book on *Women's Eastern Times* (*Funü shibao* 婦女時報) observes that although women contributors "discreetly challenged" masculine cultural norms, "the journal's agenda was largely set by its male editor, male publisher, and many male contributing authors."[35] Another scholar concludes that *The Young Companion* was more interested in "presenting women artists as modern—and 'model'—women than as modern artists."[36] Certainly, coverage of female artists differed from that of male artists in many respects, but perhaps to some extent our current view of Republican women's relationship with the press serves as an apologetics—by reasoning that outside forces overrode the ambitions of these daring, modern female visionaries we are able to more comfortably shift responsibility for the ultimate failure of women's equality away from the women themselves. The assumption that women artists minimally involved themselves in the construction of their professional image, however, threatens to undercut these women's professional activities and accomplishments.

This chapter chooses to reframe the discussion. Refocusing attention onto women artists' involvement in the production of artist biographies and the roles those biographies played within Republican-period society allows for recognition of the women's autonomy, however limited. Publicity for women artists may have been moderated by a publishing industry that profited from the women's sexual appeal, but women were far more than helpless pawns. They actively manipulated press coverage for their own professional gain, just as men did, and smartly employed the same "mechanism for artistic celebrity," the mass-distributed biographies, if by different means. Buoyed with a sense of newly won agency and immersed in the social practices of their generation, women enthusiastically generated biographies that entwined their public personas with their gender. Just as it would have been inconceivable for her grandmother to have abstained from the pervasive and self-perpetuated footbinding culture of late imperial China, so too was it impossible for the career woman of the Republican period to fully separate the physicality and visuality of her gendered body from her professional persona. In her definitive study of the material culture of the much-vilified tradition of footbinding, Dorothy Ko points out that, "[h]owever dominant, male desires and tastes cannot account for the longevity let alone the geographical and social scope [of the practice]."[37] Ko's challenging counteranalysis reminds us that throughout the centuries generations of Chinese women, of their own volition, practiced footbinding on themselves and pressed the tradition onto their daughters. From within the confines of her own social reality, Guan Zilan similarly perceived the tangible benefits of her heightened feminine allure and she deliberately tied her professional status as a *nühuajia* to her physical appearance. We may shake our heads today at the futility of her endeavor, but for the women artists faced with promises of professional advancement and societal liberation, what could make more sense than pointing out that she was an artist *and* female?

Chinese women artists are not alone in their conflicted presentations of self; female artists across the world have grappled (and continue to grapple) with the daunting task of constructing a socially condoned public image.[38] In her analysis of the nineteenth-century French painter Rosa Bonheur, feminist art historian Linda Nochlin wonders that the stridently independent female artist felt compelled to defend her own femininity and to denounce women who overstepped their gender roles.[39] Bonheur—who wore men's trousers and refused to get married—felt the strain of societal expectations in an inner conflict only resolvable through blatantly contradictory assertions. For Nochlin, Bonheur's hypocritical rejection of other women's non-normative lifestyles was "somewhat pathetic" and signaled a surrender to the "demands of her own conscience," which "condemned her for not being a 'feminine' woman." But it is in the contradictions that Bonheur found and defined her gendered identity. As Judith Butler informs us,

"Gender is what is put on, invariably, under constraint, daily and incessantly, with anxiety and pleasure."[40] Just as Bonheur anxiously kept a stock of frilly dresses in her closet to assuage fears (perhaps that of others or perhaps her own) of her gender transgressions, so Guan delighted in the positive assessment of her conspicuously feminine fashion choices. On a daily basis, both women—consciously or not—assessed and defined what it meant to be a female artist. In Bonheur's lived experiences we find a mirroring of the same antithetical thought process that drove Chinese women artists to mimic the laudatory biographies of female exemplars while simultaneously flaunting their modernity.

Indeed, by readjusting our perception of women's involvement in the construction of their public image, a new view of Republican-period female artists emerges. From this revised perspective, we see women engaged in a savvy process of self-mediatization by cultivating professional identities that would appeal to the Chinese art world and the larger contemporary society. Manipulating the system to their advantage, they disseminated public personas predicated on gender and professional qualifications. Prominent portrait photographs visually emphasized the gender of the artist, thus forcing the acknowledgement of a new age in which women were career artists and painted professionally rather than as leisure activity. Biographical texts underscore this distinction by brandishing the professional credentials that separated each woman from the casual hobbyist—because it was in the performance (more than the artwork) that female artists best fulfilled their roles as productive members of modern society. Despite the gender discrimination, media portrayals of women artists consistently herald them as legitimate artists capable of genius.

It was this professionalization of women's careers that was crucial to China's modernity project, and the very concept of a female career artist emerged as inextricably enmeshed with contemporary notions of modernity and model behavior. Correspondingly, reportage on women artists emphasize the most revolutionary aspect of women's new social roles as professional artists: their gender. The female artist's identification with her gender, which was to undermine her access to the occupation just a few years later (discussed in chapter 4), offered her social and professional visibility. At a time when the mobilization of a female workforce held the promise of China's positive reformation, women artists' unfolding performance in the reform of gender and occupational roles made them and their biographies an indispensable component of the modernity project. Unlike men, who chose to work in modern media and styles and who could affect a modern lifestyle, *nühuajia* became the literal embodiment of advances in Chinese society. It was the very existence of the female professional artist that made China modern.

While media portrayals provided crucial stepping-stones for the career development of artists of both genders, printed publicity was just one tactic for advancement in the art world. Equally essential, participation in modernized artist societies helped artists secure professional recognition. Women artists participated as founders and primary members of several of the most influential art organizations. But, as will be explored in the next chapter, the dynamics of their participation were more complex than previously recognized.

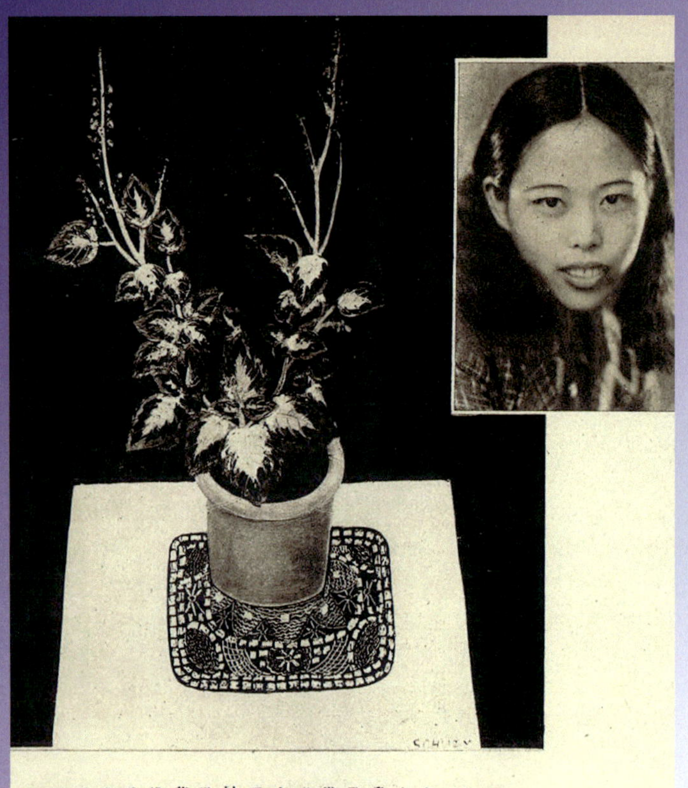

決瀾社獎

決瀾社為滬上有數之繪畫團集前曾發起獎勵新進努力作家辦法于十月在世界學院舉行第二屆展覽中以丘堤女士之「花」尤稱佳構遂由該社社員之評定獲得「決瀾社獎」云上為丘堤女士近影及其作品

2

By Any Other Name

When Qiu Ti 丘堤 (1906–58) exhibited *Flower* (*Hua* 花), a painting of a potted plant on a table, at the Second Annual Storm Society Exhibition, she won the sole prize presented in the history of the group (fig. 2.1).[1] The original painting was lost decades ago and all that remains of it today is a black-and-white photographic reproduction and a couple of brief textual references. Nonetheless, today *Flower* is Qiu Ti's most heralded work.[2] The painting is also frequently cited as justification for Qiu Ti's inclusion in the painting society as its exclusive female member.

While scholarship of the past two decades has come to recognize the pivotal role the Storm Society played in the development of modernist painting in 1930s China, research focused on Qiu Ti remains limited.[3] In the few instances where Qiu Ti's artistic career has been considered, she is primarily identified as a progressive member of one of Republican China's most avant-garde art groups. As evidence of this identity, such scholarship typically cites the award she received, but what do we really know of the award or of her status within the group? Is it merely coincidence that the group's so-called only female member was also the recipient of its only award?

"Juelanshe jiang [The Storm Society Award]" (detail of fig. 2.6).

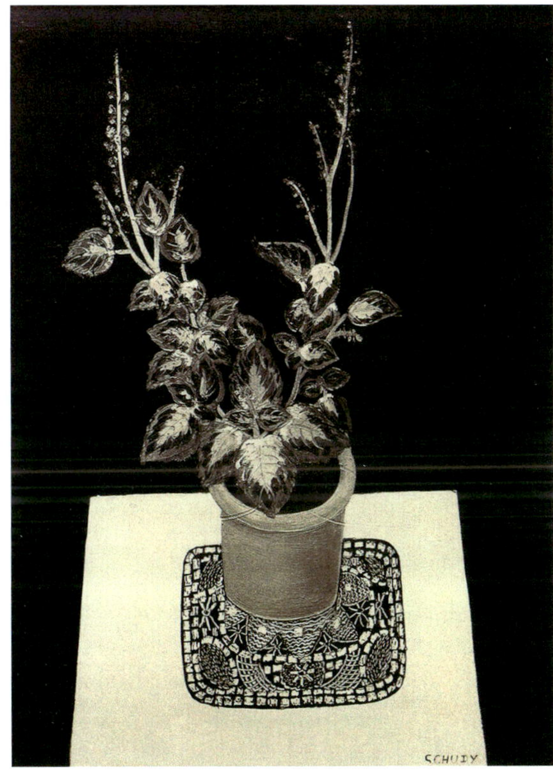

2.1 Qiu Ti, *Flower (Hua)*, ca. 1933. Oil on canvas. Lost. Reproduction from Pang Tao, ed. *The Storm Society and Post-Storm Art Phenomenon* (Taipei: Chin Show Publishing Co., Ltd, 1997): 35. Courtesy of the Schudy [Qiu Ti] Archives at The Li Ching Cultural and Educational Foundation.

This chapter presents an overview of Qiu Ti's personal history and her involvement with the Storm Society. It also considers how she was received in the Storm Society and how her contribution to the group is understood by art historians today. Exploring the circumstances surrounding the exhibition of *Flower* and the group's selection of Qiu Ti to receive the award, I analyze the painting, as well as a controversy that has been attributed to it, and compare it with works by her peers. I then question prevailing beliefs that Qiu Ti was the only female member and won admittance to the group based on this painting. Rather than scrutinize Qiu Ti's own motives or intentions behind the creation of *Flower*, this chapter focuses on challenging and reframing perceptions of her role within the group. By taking *Flower* as a case study, I assess how the presentation of women could satisfy the needs of an art association and how subsequent scholarship inadvertently misconstrues and diminishes women's participation in China's modern art societies.

While a detailed and unflinching discussion of the particulars of the Storm Society Award may at first appear to negate Qiu Ti's professional accomplishment, the main goal is to construct a more nuanced account of her participation in the group. As such, it falls in line with the recurring theme of this book, which is the exposure and correction of misassumptions about Republican-period women artists and their careers. In chapter 1 I argued that, though scholarship has concentrated on how they were restricted and pigeonholed by popular media, female artists chose to empower themselves by embracing and promoting their gendered identities. In this chapter, I critique intimations of exclusivity and declarations of exceptionalism undergirding a particularly influential contemporary essay, as well as recent scholarship on Qiu Ti. Here again, things are not as they might at first seem, and this chapter uncovers a set of mischaracterizations concocted by the writer of the essay, Storm Society spokesperson Ni Yide 倪貽德 (1901–70). Just as chapter 1 argues that women leveraged the gender bias of media portrayals to their advantage, so too this chapter finds that, though Ni's disproportionately influential characterization has been taken to suggest otherwise, female modernist painters such as Qiu Ti were foundational members of art organizations. Reevaluating Qiu Ti's position within the Storm Society reframes *Flower* as a painting with evolving significance and provides a detailed examination of the impact of group identity and gender politics on the development of women's careers.

FORMATION OF QIU TI'S CAREER AND THE STORM SOCIETY

At the same time the Storm Society was forming in the early 1930s, Qiu Bizhen 丘碧珍, a young woman from the small town of Xiapu in northeastern Fujian Province, was busily reinventing her life. It was around this time that she took Qiu Ti as her new name and briefly adopted a romanized rendering of it, Schudy, as a signature. She soon joined the high-profile Storm Society, won an exhibition award, and had her image and profile published in several popular magazines. A whirlwind romance with her colleague Pang Xunqin 龐薰琹 (1906–85) quickly led to the start of a family. Meanwhile, previous episodes in the young artist's life—including her time spent in Japan and a prior romantic attachment—quietly slipped into the past.[4]

Whether deliberately suppressed or simply forgotten, aspects of Qiu Ti's upbringing indicate her early interest in progressivism and a natural inclination toward the modernist stance later embraced by the Storm Society. Born at the end of the Qing dynasty in 1906, Qiu Ti enjoyed the new social equalities extended to women in the Republican period. As a child, she attended primary school and a middle school for girls, and it was during this time that a thirteen-year-old Qiu Ti was particularly struck by the radical ideals of the May Fourth Movement and participated in social reform actions.[5] In 1920 Qiu Ti entered Fuzhou Women's Normal School (Fuzhou Nüzi Shifan Xuexiao 福州女子師範學校) and while there she and three of her friends showed early artistic promise. Attaining regional recognition for their talents in the arts, they collectively became known as the Four Talented Women of East Fujian (*Mindong si cainü* 閩東四才女).[6] During this time Qiu Ti cut her hair short in a dramatically modern style, and in the summers of 1923 and 1924, she returned to her hometown to lead door-to-door campaigns aimed at teaching women and children to read.

Following her graduation from Fuzhou Women's Normal School in 1925, Qiu Ti's personal history becomes much less transparent. Eventually, she moved to Shanghai and enrolled in the Western Painting Department in the Shanghai Academy of Art (Shanghai Meishu Zhuanke Xuexiao 上海美術專科學校).[7] While school records confirm that Qiu Ti graduated in the second class of the Western Painting Department at the Shangai Academy of Art in 1928, the exact time of her entry into the program is unknown. Like Guan Zilan, Qiu Ti continued her postgraduate studies in Japan, where she graduated from Tokyo East Asia Japanese Language Professional School (Tokyo Tōa Nihongo Senmon Gakkō) and attended the Tokyo Pacific Ocean Art School (Taiheiyō Bijutsu Gakkō).[8] Returning to Shanghai around the end of 1929, Qiu Ti secured a position as researcher in the oil painting department at the Shangai Academy of Art.[9]

A dramatic sequence of changes that redefined Qiu Ti's life began in the fall of 1932. In September of that year, she attended Pang Xunqin's solo exhibition and met the artist. As a modernist oil painter intent on reforming China's art world and himself recently returned from abroad, Pang Xunqin impressed Qiu Ti greatly.[10] By the following year the two were in a relationship and Qiu Ti had become a high-profile member of the Storm Society.

As a member of the Storm Society, Qiu Ti contributed to the leading modernist art group in Republican Shanghai. When she joined in 1932, the organization had already existed for a year and had recently staged its first annual group exhibition. Pang Xunqin and his friend Ni Yide spearheaded the society—Pang provided the energetic impetus while Ni contributed his expertise as an established art critic. Pang Xunqin had returned in 1929 from four years of study at the Académie Julien in Paris. At the time of his return, Shanghai was known as the "Paris of the Orient," but Pang still felt that it lacked the lively atmosphere and worldly sophistication of the French capital. Hoping to vitalize the Shanghai art scene, he opened a Parisian-style art salon, and it was in this short-lived venture that Pang Xunqin first made the acquaintance of Ni Yide. Ni, for his part, had studied at the Shanghai Academy of Fine Art, graduating in 1922, and later spent a year studying in Japan. A good five years older than Pang Xunqin, Ni Yide had already established himself as an oil painter and art theorist with important connections in the local community by the time the younger artist arrived in Shanghai. Although the two struck up an immediate friendship, they did not launch their avant-garde painting society until two years later. At that time Ni Yide had returned from a temporary teaching position at the Wuchang Art School, and Pang Xunqin's Parisian salon had already proved a financial failure and closed. The two hoped that their art association's exhibitions and publications could promote the modernist art movement and further its members' careers. Even still, a career in *xihua* was not as lucrative as one in *guohua* and the opportunities for Storm Society members to sell paintings were few and far between.[11] For financial means, most modernist artists depended on teaching positions and the members of the Storm Society were no exception.

At the time of its first meeting in the winter of 1931, the Storm Society consisted of only seven initial members including Pang Xunqin and Ni Yide. The group chose the name Juelanshe (决澜社), which refers to a storm-caused wave with destructive power, to serve as a metaphor for the energy with which the members hoped to modernize the Shanghai art scene.[12] Its members recognized its position beyond the pale of standard art practice, and the Storm Society battled to shift the art scene to a modernist terrain modeled on that of Europe. The group held annual art exhibitions, which several popular Shanghai magazines covered with photographic reviews.[13] Initially, group members hoped to publish a journal to advocate their cause but could not afford the expense.[14] Ni Yide's role as editor-in-chief of the short-lived art journal *L'Art* (*Yishu xunkan* 藝術旬刊), however, gave Storm Society members the opportunity to publish several articles about their group.[15] In these writings the Storm Society repeatedly trumpeted its radical status.

Like many artists' associations of its day, the Storm Society penned a manifesto, which it published in *L'Art* in 1932, around the time that Qiu Ti joined the group.[16] An audacious declaration, the manifesto is filled with melodramatic prose that pulses with a defiant spirit as it calls out the "countless morons" and "shallow minds" responsible for the "mediocrity and vulgarity" that was smothering China's art scene. The vivid language and metaphoric imagery of the manifesto addresses the factionalism of the Chinese art community and proclaims the Storm Society's opposition to the other groups. Declaring a hatred of the old and conventional, the society aligned itself against traditionalism and suggested resistance to new *guohua* as well.[17] The manifesto also rails against the techniques of literal reproduction employed by Western academic realism. Chastising the blasé state of the current art scene in China and promising to bring a sweeping wave of avant-garde art trends fresh from Europe, the manifesto singles out a few particularly inspirational European stylistic movements, namely, fauvism, cubism, dadaism, and surrealism. Arguing against the need for mimesis or socially relevant subject matter in art, the Storm Society advocated the self-expression of the artist. As did other art societies, the Storm Society intended to reenergize and reconstruct the ailing nation through art, but its admiration of a wide range of European art movements underscored the group's encouragement of artistic diversity and independence. Above all, the manifesto makes it clear that the members of the group planned to lead by example, using their own lives to demonstrate the sincerity of their aims. To emphasize this point, the text ends with the second iteration of the manifesto's refrain, "Let us rise up! With our raging passion and iron intellect, we will create a world interwoven with color, line and form!"[18] In its concerns, the group's manifesto responds to earlier developments in the art community, in particular a heated debate initiated by Xu Beihong's scathing critique of the 1929 First National Art Exhibition. As Ralph Croizier explains in his article on the Storm Society, the manifesto and modernist dialogue forwarded by the members of the group meant that, "it was now a contest between westernizers over who possessed the real essence of Western art and supposedly the future of China."[19]

Ni Yide's role as an art critic and his connections in the publishing world meant that many of his theories on art were published, and these provide insight into the views held by the Storm Society membership in general.[20] In his essays, Ni Yide derides Chinese society, arguing that his country harbored vulgar tastes and, being oblivious to global developments in modern painting, was inhospitable to the development of "genuine" art. The passion of his views comes across in his declaration:

> Art! Art! We have talked a great deal about it in China for nearly 20 years. What have we accomplished? Speaking of the overall art scene, despite today's large number of art schools, where are the new talents they have trained? Although quite a few people have returned from studies abroad, where are their works? . . . This is the current state of our art scene, neither dead nor alive. Thus the young and more avant-garde painters among us should band together and create a new art movement. In China, the earlier Western painting movement has come to an end. Now is the dawning of a new era.[21]

The other members of the Storm Society shared this ideological vision. A good deal older, Wang Jiyuan 王濟遠 (1893–1975) nevertheless spoke of the group's goals with equal enthusiasm, declaring, "We want to hit the rotten art of contemporary China with a powerful wave."[22] Seventy years later, the youngest member of the group, Yang Taiyang 陽太陽 (1909–2009), restated this intent when asked about the society's artistic goals in a television interview.[23] Pointing to a collective desire to obliterate conservativism, Yang described the group's aim to forcefully introduce modernism through their pursuit of innovation and individuality in art. Yang's words underscore how avant-garde the Storm Society, with its idealistic proclamations and youthful bravado, strove to be.

Despite the manifesto's call for a "world of pure shapes," some of the paintings of Storm Society cofounder Pang Xunqin do, in fact, invite political readings. His most controversial painting, *Son of Earth*, was a highly charged criticism of ineffectual government. Its sympathetic depiction of a peasant-class family of flood victims supports a left-wing political view and Communist ideology.[24] Not all of Pang Xuqin's paintings contain such blatant ideological content, but the political commentary apparent in this painting certainly was not lost on the audience when the artist displayed his painting at the Third Annual Storm Society Exhibition.[25] As discussed below, however, the group members' artistic output was not quite as radical as the essays of Ni Yide, the group's primary spokesman, envisioned.[26] For all his vibrant talk of revolutionizing art in China, Ni Yide's own art leaned toward the conservative, and it is hard to imagine that his paintings could have been considered radical.[27] Arguably, Ni Yide contributed more to the Storm Society through his dynamic and eloquently worded theoretical essays than through the stylistic choices presented in his paintings. The gap between artifice and reality—that is, Ni Yide's presentation of the group and the praxis of its members—becomes distinguishable with a closer look at Qiu Ti's engagement with the group.

QIU TI'S PUBLIC PERSONA

Around the time Qiu Ti began to interact with the Storm Society, she also began to actively craft her public persona. She stifled certain episodes from her personal history by concealing her age and avoiding discussion of her past, and she distributed artist introductions via multiple Shanghai pictorials.[28] As a member of the Storm Society, she participated in an artists' organization that proudly agitated the Chinese art world with its progressive ideology. The decisive actions that Qiu Ti took at this stage of her life—rewriting her own narrative and joining a radically modernist painting society—suggest her continued commitment to the reform movement and her identification with the emergent social role of the "New Woman." Media coverage portrays her in this light. Just as seen with Guan Zilan in chapter 1, Qiu Ti is simultaneously admired for her feminine qualities and promoted for her professionalism.

The earliest published photograph of Qiu Ti known is in the photographic review of the Second Annual Storm Society Exhibition published in the November 1933 issue of *Modern Miscellany* (fig. 2.2).[29] The two-page spread consists of eleven black-and-white, variously sized reproductions of artworks featured in the exhibition. A small strip running across the bottom of both pages contains the photographs of eight Storm Society members taken at the exhibition, with each artist positioned in front of one of his or her works. Only a small portion of the framed painting behind Qiu Ti is visible, but it is enough to identify it as *Flower*. Qiu Ti's portrait photograph is equal in size and composition to those of her male colleagues and is neither placed next to nor otherwise related to that of her husband. Like the others, she has a representative painting reproduced in the news feature; hers is a lively rendition of female nudes in a landscape (fig. 2.3). The equal treatment suggests a perception—on the part of the editor as well as of the members who collectively submitted publicity materials—that Qiu Ti contributed as much to the group as the others.

Two profiles of Qiu Ti the following year similarly characterize her as a practicing artist of merit; both herald her marriage to Pang Xunqin but present Qiu Ti as his equal. The first, from the July 1934 issue of *The Young Companion*, includes a photograph of the newlyweds, which captures the couple sitting together in warmly intimate proximity (fig. 2.4). Qiu Ti wears a fashionable *qipao* and looks out toward the photographer. Pang, dressed in a traditional *dagua* robe, rests his gaze on her, making Qiu Ti the focus of the picture. The accompanying text reads: "Artist Mr. Pang Xunqin, famous for his excellent paintings, recently married Ms. Qiu Ti. Ms. Qiu is also considered accomplished among

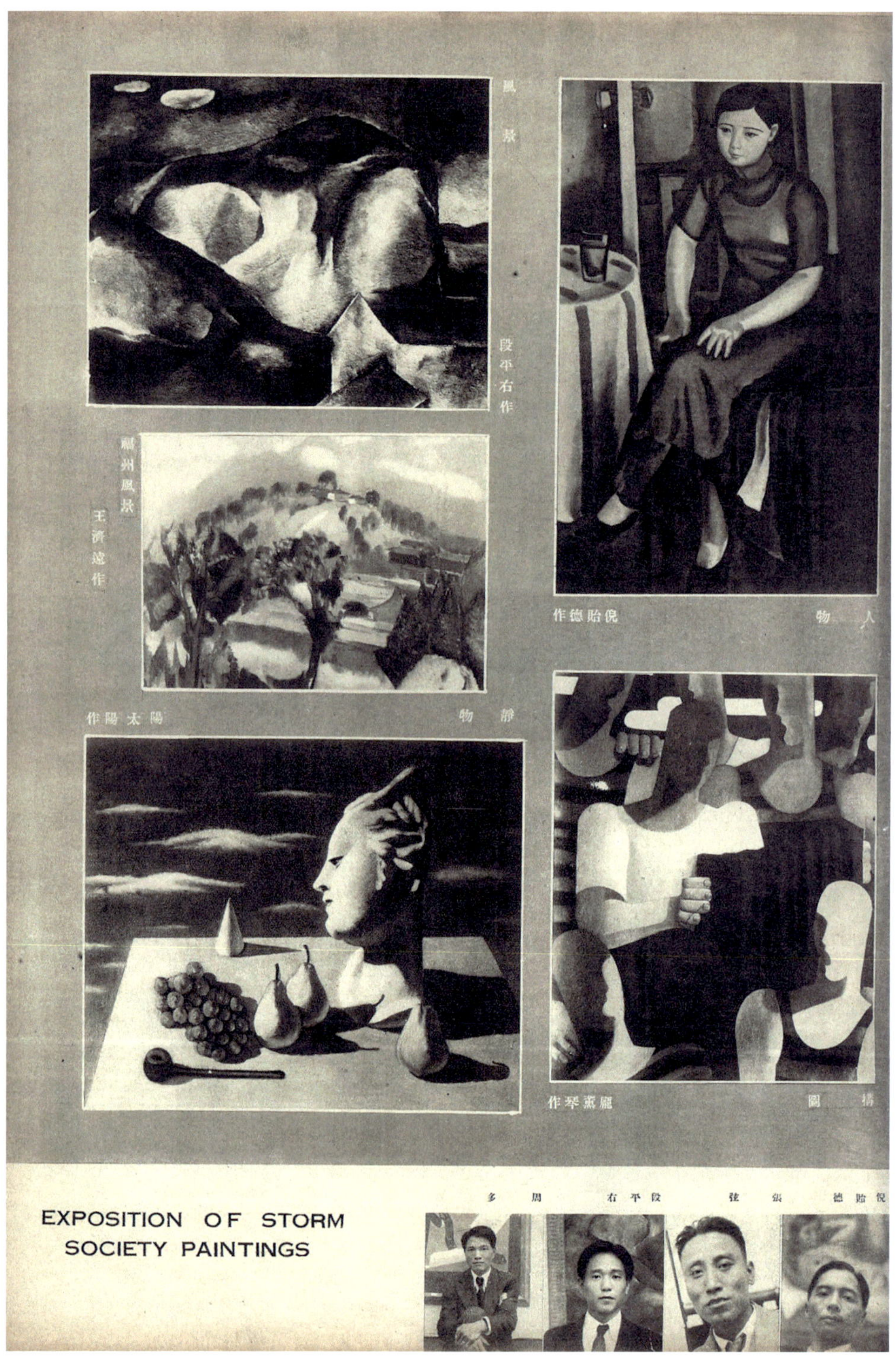

2.2 “Exposition of Storm Society Paintings,” *Modern Miscellany* 5, no. 1 (November 1933): unnumbered page.

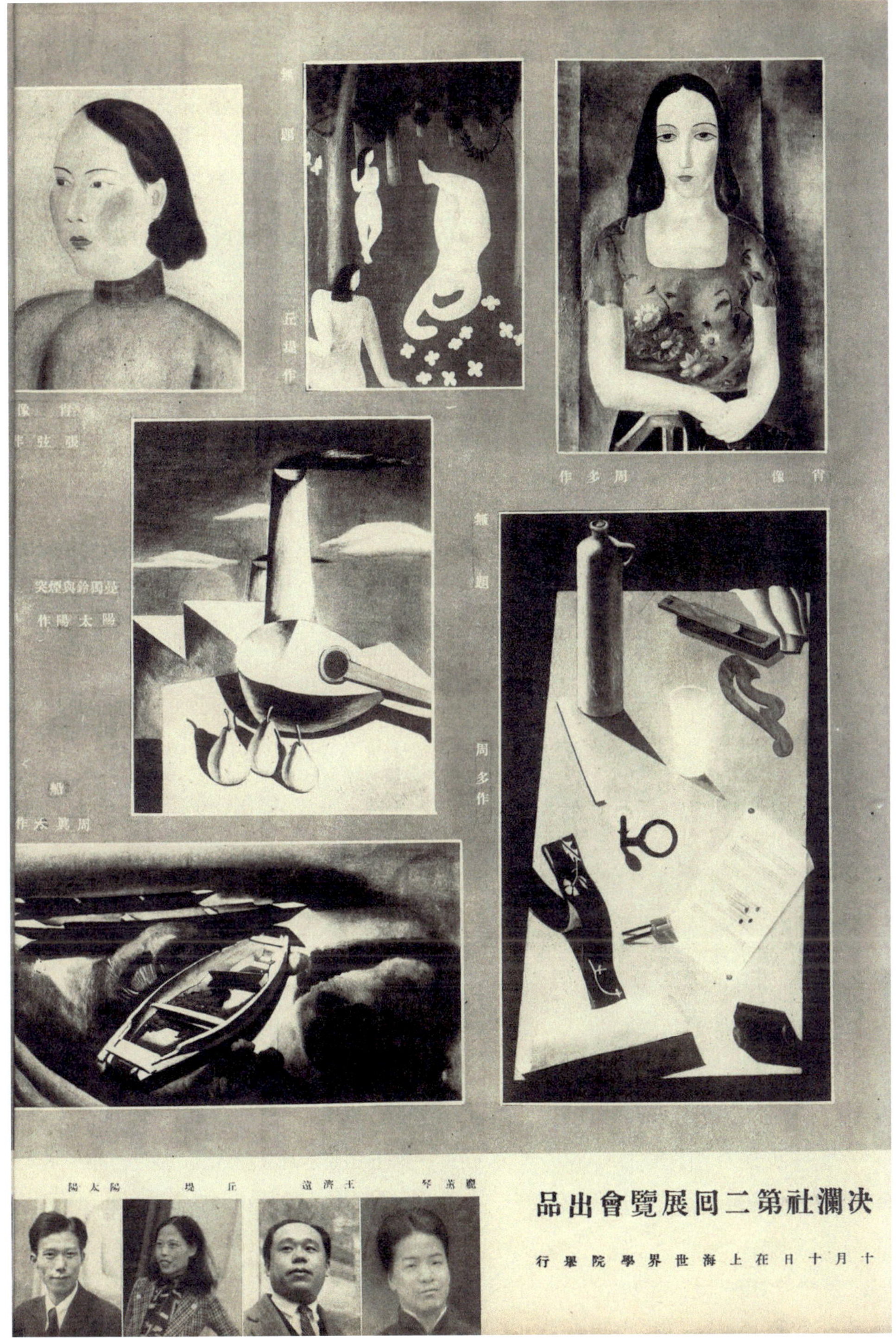
無題 丘堤作
肖像 周多作
肖像 張弦作
曼陀鈴與煙突 陽太陽作
無題 周多作
船 周真太作
龐薰琹
王濟遠
丘堤
陽太陽
决瀾社第二回展覽會出品
十月十日在上海世界學院舉行

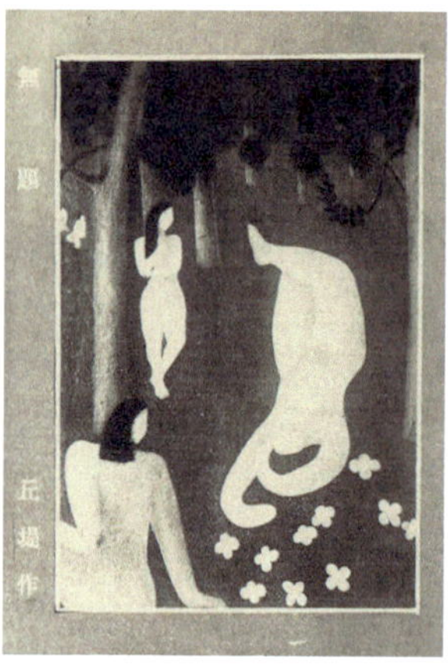

2.3 Qiu Ti, *Untitled (Wuti)*, 1933 or before. Oil on canvas. Lost and presumed destroyed. Detail from "Exposition of Storm Society Paintings," *Modern Miscellany* 5, no. 1 (November 1933): unnumbered page.

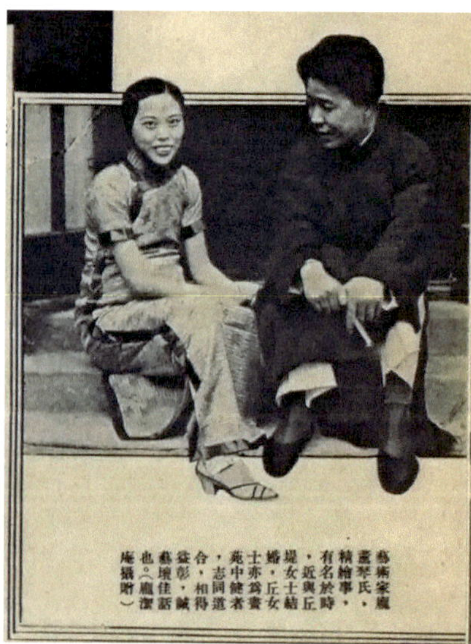

2.4 Profile of Qiu Ti and Pang Xunqin. *The Young Companion* 90 (July 1934): 14.

the art set. Like-minded and bringing out the best in each other, they are the talk of the art scene."[30]

Despite its brevity and tabloid-like focus on the social scene, the media profile portrays Qiu Ti's occupation in an overwhelmingly affirmative light. Pang Xunqin takes precedence by virtue of his relative fame, but Qiu Ti is also described as a significant presence in the art community. The idioms used to describe the two—"like-minded" (*zhitong daohe* 志同道合) and "bringing out the best in each other" (*xiangde yizhang* 相得益彰)—indicate a mutually beneficial relationship. Rather than casting Qiu Ti as a wife playing a supportive role, the announcement suggests both artists were equally intent on advancing their careers.

A second profile the same year also mentions the marriage and likewise portrays Qiu Ti as an artist in her own right. The small news feature combines a photograph of Qiu Ti with a short caption and a black-and-white reproduction of her painting of a nude figure (fig. 2.5).[31] The pleasantly phrased caption has the ring of a marriage announcement, but it also includes information standard for artist introductions, such as the name of her home province, her professional affiliation, and her study-abroad experience. As expected in light of the analysis of female artists' media portrayals in chapter 1, Qiu Ti's biography makes note of her ties to a prominent member of the art community, in this case her husband, whose career was relatively established and who presumably needed no other introduction. As with historical examples of women artist's biographies, the caliber of Qiu Ti's work is described in predictably feminine terms, which are extended to assess the artist's own character.[32] The text also recycles the same stock phrase used in *The Young Companion* to indicate the couple's notoriety ("the talk of the art scene" *yitan jiahua* 藝壇佳話) as it announces that the two had recently married.

In this second profile, as with the first, the newlyweds are celebrated for being a thoroughly modern couple—a reader of the day would have immediately perceived that the couple had married for love and mutual respect as opposed to familial obligation. Although these two media portrayals

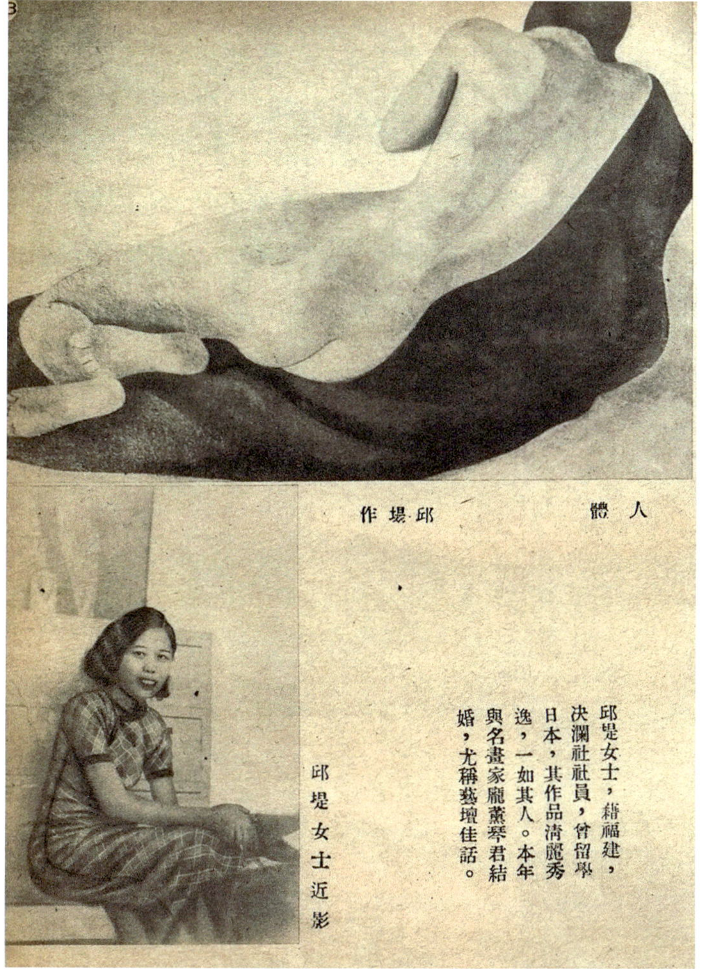

人體　邱堤作

邱堤女士，籍福建，決瀾社社員，曾留學日本，其作品清麗秀逸，一如其人。本年與名畫家龐薰琹君結婚，尤稱藝壇佳話。

邱堤女士近影

2.5 Qiu Ti's biography, *The Cosmopolitan*, no. 13 (November 1934): 33.

emphasize Qiu Ti's married status, she is presented as a wife who is her husband's equal in the professional field. Thus, just as was the case for Guan Zilan, Qiu Ti's artist introductions proclaim her embrace of modern womanhood in her assumption of the new social role of professional artist. Yet no matter how positive and validating these portrayals of Qiu Ti are, they give us little by which to evaluate her artwork—most of which is no longer extant—or her contributions to the society. Qiu Ti published no writings of her own, meaning that the little information we have about her today comes primarily from journalistic remnants such as these. As discussed below, however, an overreliance on two particular instances of media coverage generates a common misinterpretation of Qiu Ti's position within the society.

A COLEUS BY ANY OTHER NAME

What most dramatically colors current perception of Qiu Ti's career are two mentions of her winning an award, one published a month following the exhibition and the other a full two years later. The first, an announcement of the "Storm Society Prize" in the November 1933 issue of *Modern Miscellany*, notifies the public of Qiu Ti's accomplish-

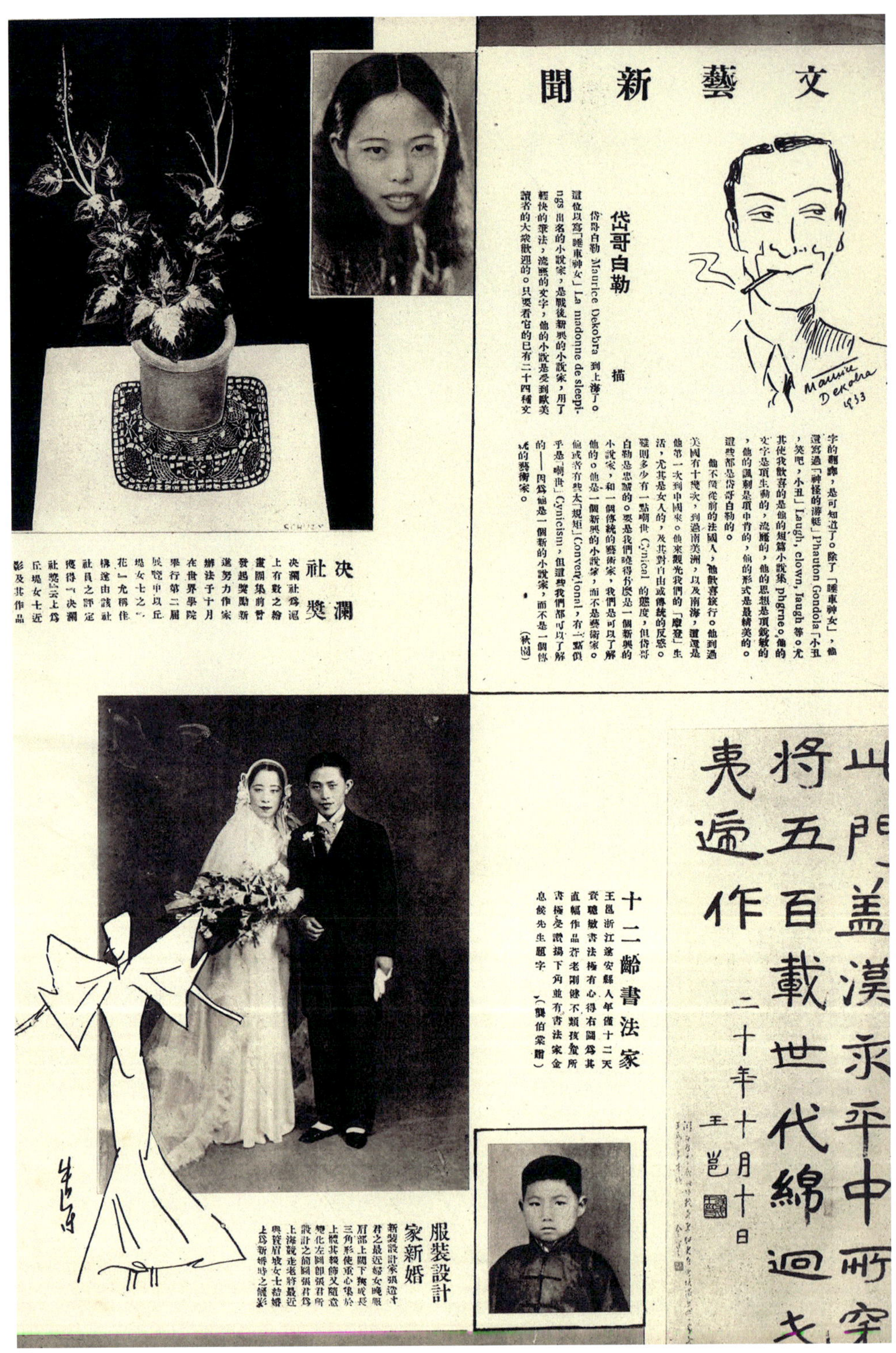

決瀾社獎

決瀾社爲滬上有數之繪畫團集前曾發起獎勵新進努力作家辦法于十月在世界學院舉行第二屆展覽中以丘堤女士之「花」尤稱佳構遂由該社社員之評定獲得「決瀾社獎」云上爲丘堤女士近影及其作品

文藝新聞

岱哥白勒 描

岱哥白勒 Maurice Dekobra 到上海了。這位以寫「睡車神女」La madonne de sleepings 出名的小說家，是戰後新興的小說家，用了輕快的筆法，流麗的文字，他的小說是受到歐美讀者的大衆歡迎的。只要看它的已有二十四種文字的翻譯，是可知道了。除了「睡車神女」，他還寫過「神怪的游艇」Phauton Gondola「小丑，笑吧，小丑」Laugh, clown, laugh 等。尤其使我歡喜的是他的短篇小說集 phgrne。他的文字是頂生動的，流麗的，他的思想是頂銳敏的，他的諷刺是頂中肯的，他的形式是最精美的。這些都是岱哥白勒的。

他不像從前的法國人，他歡喜旅行。他到過美國有十幾次，到過南美洲，以及南海，這還是他第一次到中國來。他來觀光我們的「摩登」生活，尤其是女人的，及其對自由或傳統的反感。雖則多少有一點嘲世 Cynical 的態度，但岱哥白勒是忠誠的。要是我們曉得什麽是一個新興的小說家，和一個傳統的藝術家，我們是可以了解他的。他是一個新興的小說家，而不是藝術家。但或者有些太「規矩」Conventional，有一點似乎是「嘲世」Cynicism，但這些我們都可以了解的——因爲他是一個新的小說家，而不是一個傳統的藝術家。

（秋園）

十二齡書法家

王邕浙江遂安縣人年僅十二天資聰敏書法極有心得右圖爲其直幅作品蒼老剛健不類孩童所書極受讚揚下角並有書法家金息侯先生題字（龔伯棠贈）

服裝設計家新婚

新裝設計家張道才君之最近婦女晚服肩部上闊下狹成長三角形使重心集於上體其裝飾又隨意變化左圖即張君所設計之簡圖張君爲上海競走老將最近與寶眉娥女士結婚上爲新婚時之儷影

2.6 “Juelanshe jiang [The Storm Society Award]” *Modern Miscellany* 5, no. 3 (December 1933).

ment (fig. 2.6). The news report features a large black-and-white photograph of *Flower* partially obscured by a smaller-sized headshot of the artist and the following statement:

> The Storm Society, one of the notable painting organizations in Shanghai, recently initiated the practice of rewarding up-and-coming, hardworking artists. During the Second Exhibition at the World Society in October, Miss Qiu Ti's *Flower* was especially praised as an exceptional work. Based on their evaluation, members of the organization presented her the Storm Society Award. Above is a recent image of Ms. Qiu Ti and her work.[33]

This brief caption describes the Storm Society as a reputable art association and confirms the date and location of the Second Exhibition. Nothing is said, however, about the artist's training, professional career, or her relationship with the Storm Society. For her portrait photograph, which was clearly captured in a professional sitting, Qiu Ti poses like many women depicted in the magazines of the day, in a three-quarters view with her gaze alluringly directed at the camera. In the arrangement of the images, Qiu Ti's feminine visage takes precedence over her artistic accomplishment: overlapping *Flower* with Qiu Ti's portrait disrupts the visual integrity of the painting to focus on the artist's gender.

Just as the award announcement provides no insight into the credentials of the artist, neither is anything written about the properties of the artwork which led the society to declare it exceptional. The black-and-white reproduction of *Flower* accompanying the announcement, though, reveals the painting's skillfully balanced tone, texture, and shapes to form a lively study of contrasts—light and dark, rough and smooth, geometric and organic. A dark hue served as the background of the painting. Stretching to all four corners of the canvas, this flat, even color appears as an impenetrable blanket, separating the subject of the picture from any recognizable environment. In contrast, a trapezoid as light as the background is dark and equally flat occupies most of the lower half of the painting. The large potted plant and patterned mat mark the geometric form as a table; while the mat is slightly off center, the pot is precisely in the center of the table and the canvas. The pot is a smooth cylindrical form, from which the asymmetrical plant grows dynamically upward. The lower half of the plant is a bushy mass of serrated tricolored leaves remarkable for the complexity of their vivid patterns; above, plant stems thrust dramatically upward and end in inflorescences that stab into the abstract ground at the top of the picture. These sparsely covered spears are sprinkled with tiny flowers and buds as thin and fragile as the body of the plant is bushy and vibrant. These vivid contrasts in hue, texture, and shape create a tension that is intensified by the distortions of space. The surface of the table is sharply tipped, creating a sense of instability; the objects on the table look as if they might slide off the bottom of the picture. She then heightened the spatial ambiguity by adding her signature, "Schudy," to the lower right corner of the tabletop. Overall, the mastery of Qiu Ti's hand is easily apparent in the intensity and vigor of the artwork, notwithstanding the limitations of the black-and-white reproduction.

Despite its spatial ambiguities and coarse brushwork, *Flower* is remarkably descriptive, so much so that the variety of plant is quite obvious.[34] Qiu Ti faithfully portrayed the distinguishing characteristics of the coleus (in Chinese, *wucaisu* 五彩苏), an ornamental plant cultivated for its distinctive leaves of brilliant reds and greens. Several varieties of coleus bear large leaves with the same serrated edges and variegated patterning as the plant seen in the painting. The coleus plant is typically appreciated for its full and bushy form, but such a growth is only achieved by pinching off the flower stems when they begin to sprout upward from the mass of the plant. If left to its own devices, the coleus grows spindly stems that reach up toward the sky and produce tiny vertical rows of flowers, just as seen in the painting.

Although *Flower* depicts a common coleus, Qiu Ti's painting has been repeatedly recognized in the scholarly community for its supposed radical color scheme. This curious present-day interpretation of the painting results from recent readings of the second reference to Qiu Ti's winning of the award, Ni Yide's essay, "Juelanshe de yi qun 决澜社的一群 [The Storm Society's Group]."[35] Published in 1935, two years after Qiu Ti exhibited the painting and received the award, the essay promoted the painting society in anticipation of its Fourth Annual Exhibition.[36] Ni Yide begins his article with a lengthy and romantic description of his good friend Pang Xunqin and the circumstances surrounding the founding of the Storm Society; he then introduces individual members of the group. In the last paragraph he comes to Qiu Ti:

> If our memory serves well, we may still remember the autumn of 1933 Second Storm Society Exhibition award winner Qiu Ti. She is the Storm Society's only female artist. Her masterpiece *Flower* was at that time the main feature and special feature in many illustrated publications, yet at the same time was by one know-nothing critic censured for its mistake of red leaves and green flowers. Regardless of whether among flowering plants there is or is not a red-leafed green-flowered variety, sometimes for the sake of decorative effect, there is no harm in even changing natural colors. That painting *Flower* was done entirely in a decorative style. Based on this award-winning painting she was recommended for membership in the Storm Society.[37]

Based on this brief description, most recent scholars infer that *Flower* stirred up great controversy. For example, in his groundbreaking 1993 study of the Storm Society, Ralph Croizier draws heavily from Ni Yide's essay to inform his analysis of Qiu Ti's painting and its impact on the art world at the time of its public display. Discussing the entries in the Storm Society exhibition of 1933, Croizier writes that *Flower* was the most interesting entry to the exhibition and he intuits that the painting generated the exhibition's "biggest controversy," due to its coloration having "disturbed critics and casual onlookers" alike.[38] Quoting the essay, Croizier uses Ni Yide's theoretical argument in support of altering color to achieve decorative results to tie *Flower* to both the rhetoric of the group's manifesto and to the larger debate between realism and modernism that was roiling in the Chinese art world at the time.[39] Five years later, Kuiyi Shen's essay for the canon-making Guggenheim show *A Century in Crisis: Modernity and Tradition in the Art of Twentieth-Century China*, similarly reasons that the critical reception of *Flower* provoked Ni Yide's words about the painting and cites Croizier as its source.[40] Over the past several years, additional discussions of Qiu Ti's *Flower*—presented by both American and Chinese scholars—more or less follow Croizier's initial interpretation of Ni Yide's logic.[41]

Whereas recent scholars have built up Ni Yide's report of a critic, in reality *Flower* was probably not that controversial. Tame postimpressionistic oil paintings of still lifes were indeed commonplace in 1934, including two paintings of lilies from Ni Yide's own solo exhibition, but some of his contemporaries created artworks starkly avant-garde in comparison.[42] Also published that year, Lin Fengmian's 林風眠 (1900–1991) experimental painting *Cockscomb*, a boldly brushed composition of ragged black outline and prismatic colors of yellow, green, blue, and vibrant red in abstracted shapes, begs comparisons to primitivist and fauvist works (fig. 2.7).[43] In the Storm Society's 1934 exhibition, several equally provocative paintings hung alongside Qiu Ti's award-winning *Flower*. The bold composition and the sharp delineation of objects in Zhou Duo's 周多 (1905–1989) still life give his painting a modernist feel, while Yang Taiyang exhibited at least two surrealist still lifes. Duan Pingyou's 段平右 (1906–?) composition of bold geometric shapes is barely recognizable as a landscape. Pang Xunqin exhibited a minimalist painting of a crowd of streamlined figures so puzzling that one publication printed it upside down.[44] A second exhibition entry by Qiu Ti herself, a painting of nudes in a landscape, is more daring than the artwork that Ni Yide had singled out as controversial. The female nude was not startling per se, as it had emerged as a popular subject of modern art in China by the 1930s (see chapter 3), but Qiu Ti's painting takes the theme into new territory with her innovative compositional arrangement and abstracted style. Altogether, these artworks suggest that *Flower*—a depiction of a plant that was accurate to life not just in physical dimensions but also in selection of color—though indeed a striking image, could not have been the most provocative painting of its time. Despite Ni Yide's protestations against a mystery critic, for anyone familiar with this plant the colors of the painting would not have been unsettling.[45]

We have no way of confirming whether Ni Yide's understanding of Qiu Ti's painting was shared by the artist herself, but it seems unlikely that *Flower* was meant to be as complex and subversive as he suggests in his essay. In the case of this painting—for which the group's professional art theorist and most vocal ideological firebrand functioned as the artist's mouthpiece—the essay is more revealing of Ni Yide's own views on art theory than Qiu Ti's personal artistic motivations. Rather than concentrate on Qiu Ti's use of color, then, it is more pertinent to examine how Ni Yide's discussion of *Flower* ties into the popular dialogue and trends of the Shanghai art community at that time and to explicate the objectives that underlie his words.

In light of the intentions professed in the Storm Society's manifesto, Ni Yide's discussion of *Flower* confirms the group's ideology. As already noted, Ni Yide made a point of emphasizing the prerogative of the artist to create an image in a "decorative style" (*zhuangshi fengde* 裝飾風的). This sounds like a defense of "art for art's sake," but it can be assumed it was more than that given the group's professed desire to use revolutionary creations of "pure design" to shock Chinese society into a new awareness. In positing the painting as a challenge to the status quo in its flagrant reversal of a conventional color scheme, Ni Yide links Qiu Ti's painting to the pursuit of group objectives. *Flower* not only bucked traditionalism, but as a purely decorative object it also divorced itself from any dogmatic content. Thus, according to Ni Yide's interpretation, *Flower* supported the Storm Society's insistence that art be received on individual merits—instead of serving ideological or literary themes slavishly—while offering a revolutionary approach to painting in the form of progressive spirit and

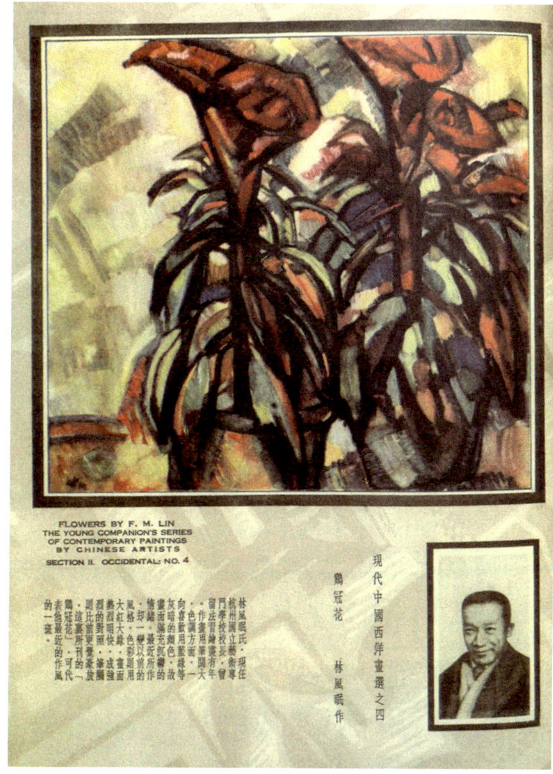

2.7 "Flowers by F. M. Lin: *The Young Companion*'s Series of Contemporary Paintings by Chinese Artists. Section II Occidental: 4," *The Young Companion* 87 (1934): 18/19.

pure design. Ni Yide's reading of the painting as a defiant reversal of color is suspect, however, and the very motivations behind the bestowing of the award verge on the opportunistic and point to a calculated attempt at media publicity.

First mention of the award appears just over a month before the exhibition in an announcement that the group submitted to the September 4, 1933, issue of *Shenbao*. The notice records pertinent details, in particular that the Storm Society's Second Annual Exhibition was to be held at the World Society from October 10th to 18th, as well as the group's eagerness to increase participation in the event.[46] To this end, the Storm Society welcomed nonaffiliated artists and encouraged their involvement by holding a competition open only to them.

The prize of 100 yuan, a substantial amount in 1933, served as a means of drawing attention to the group and generating curiosity about the show. This seems to be the award that Qiu Ti received at the exhibition in the following month.

Despite the publicity scheme, Pang Xunqin's memoir, *Jiushi zheyang zouguo lai de* 就是这样走过来的 [*It Happened Just Like This*], indicates that the attendance at the Second Annual Storm Society Exhibition was disappointing.[47] The venue, provided free of charge through personal connections, turned out to be an inconvenient location that drew few visitors outside of the tight-knit artist community.[48] Though the popular pictorial magazines *The Young Companion* and *Modern Miscellany* reproduced a handful of the exhibited paintings for a wider audience following the close of the event, at the time of the exhibition neither magazine published a photograph of *Flower*.[49]

Nearly two months after the exhibition, *Modern Miscellany* ran its quarter-page announcement of the award bestowed on the painting. The wording of the announcement implies that the newly established prize would be a reoccurring event for the purpose of encouraging new artists. *Flower* is noted for having received special acclaim, but the announcement leaves it to its readers to determine the outstanding merits of the painting. Notably, the award announcement neither mentions any controversy surrounding the painting nor addresses the artist's use of color. Apparently, Qiu Ti's choice of colors for the plant was not deemed remarkable enough to be newsworthy.

Rather, the Storm Society's decision to award Qiu Ti the prize appears to have been at least partly motivated by financial circumstances. The call for exhibition submissions that the Storm Society had posted in *Shenbao* stipulated that the award would be a cash prize and was reserved for a work by an unaffiliated artist. While all recorded members of the Storm Society were automatically disqualified from the competition the following year, Qiu Ti remained a candidate; she had begun interacting with members of the group around the time of its first exhibition, but the second annual exhibition was her first public showing with the Storm Society and her affiliation had yet to be officially recognized in print.[50] Qiu Ti was most likely already married to Pang Xunqin by this time, thus by placing the cash prize in her hands, the group ensured the sum benefited two core members of the Storm Society.[51] Publicizing Qiu Ti as an *official* member after she received the award both legitimized the society's actions and also provided a media opportunity in which the group heralded a professional female artist joining their ranks.

Thus, Ni Yide could stress in his 1935 essay that she had gained entry to the group by virtue of her award-winning painting.[52] In so doing, he amends the particulars of Qiu Ti's participation in the Storm Society to conform to the ulterior interests of the group. Stating that the award earned her a spot in the group, in a bit of circular logic, qualifies Qiu Ti for the award by implying that she was not a member beforehand. In explaining why she was given the award, Ni Yide focused on the innovativeness of *Flower* and provided a theoretical basis for the painting's formal properties. At the same time, he advanced the group's artistic agenda by characterizing the painting as a product of pure artistic license, echoing the group's strong expression of similar artistic ideals in its manifesto published three years earlier. However, unlike the original award announcement, Ni Yide's later description of Qiu Ti supplies two significant embellishments. First, as already demonstrated, it fabricates a controversy where likely none existed, and, second, it identifies her as the only female artist in the group. This second embellishment in particular generated lasting repercussions in terms of how scholarship today perceives Qiu Ti's career, as well as those of her female peers. As discussed below, the words of Ni Yide twist Qiu Ti's receipt of the award—which had been a pragmatic decision to conserve financial resources—into a vetting process that, as consequence, transforms her status within the group from equal contributor to token female member.

THE STORM SOCIETY'S "ONLY" FEMALE ARTIST

Just as Ni's essay justifies the group's decision of whom to honor with the award, it conversely validates the awardee and her inclusion in the group as a peer-reviewed and mutually approved member rather than some dilettante wife of a founder. Ni Yide's characterization of Qiu Ti's membership as contingent upon on collective approval of her work simultaneously accomplished two objectives at once: it both emphasized the group's progressive policies and affirmed its exclusivity. Including a female member within Storm Society ranks demonstrates the group's progressive stance in its implicit support of the women's movement and widespread social reform. At the same time, however, Ni cultivates an air of exclusivity by implying that not just anyone was granted membership to the organization. Whereas the early members of the society presumably made independent decisions to join, Ni's essay suggests that the acceptance of Qiu Ti, who also happened to be the Storm Society's only recognized female member, required group approval; only after her work impressed the group was she "recommended" for membership.

Does the public notice of Qiu Ti's vetting process suggest that Storm Society members worried the admittance of underqualified members from the "fairer" sex had the potential to dilute the prestige of their collective? As noted in chapter 1, the notion of female artists was not in itself modern but the social acceptance of women as professionals was. When fine art programs at public colleges became coeducational, young ladies of the upper and middle classes enrolled in no small number. Not all of these women, however, were driven by career aspirations; as in the West, a young woman's studies in the arts could contribute toward her education in the proper comportment of a lady. Some female students' casual approach to their artistic training apparently raised concern among faculty and even prompted Storm Society member Zhang Xuan 張弦 (1901–36), who at the time was professor at the Shanghai Academy of Art, to chide the demeanor of one of his students.[53] Following graduation, these women turned their artistic talents to the enhancement of their status as social butterflies (*jiaojihua* 交際花, "socializing flowers") rather than pursuing careers in the fine arts. So while women's membership could indicate an organization's progressive stance toward women's professional activities, indiscriminate acceptance of "unqualified" or less than serious female artists threatened to reduce the group's image to the level of social club. By 1935, with Qiu Ti's marriage to group cofounder Pang Xunqin then publicly known, her professional intentions would have been doubly suspect. Thus, in linking the award directly to Qiu Ti's admittance, Ni emphasizes that she joined the group by her own merit rather than through a romantic association. In this way, the presentation of the award to Qiu Ti might be read as a gesture of group solidarity. It served as a public proclamation of her equal value to the group and deflated any potential accusations of nepotism.

On the other hand, Ni Yide's essay and his qualifying comments about Qiu Ti's membership may belie his own generally dismissive opinion of women's artistic careers. Overall, there is a striking contrast between his treatment of Qiu Ti and the other members of the group. After Pang Xunqin, Ni lavishes the most attention on Zhou Duo and Duan Pingyou. Calling these two the "Hunan brothers" for their shared home province and friendly exchange of ideas, he spends a lengthy paragraph describing their training, influences, and artistic style. He concludes his enthusiastic endorsement for the two by encouraging interest in whatever future work they might produce. In a shorter paragraph, he concentrates on two painters from Guangxi, Yang Qiuren 楊秋人 (1907–83) and Yang Taiyang. He promotes the two Yangs by praising their talents and highlighting aspects of their styles. A detailed paragraph is devoted to Zhang Xuan. Zhang's artistic training is described at length, with emphasis placed on his two trips to France. His past and present stylistic inspirations are identified, he is recognized for his devotion to his art, and Ni concludes with a description of his current artistic endeavors.

By comparison, Ni's discussion of Qiu Ti makes her career and participation in the group resolutely one-dimensional. Whereas he emphasizes the overall careers of the male members of the Storm Society, his paragraph on Qiu Ti—which perpetuates traditional gender hierarchy with its placement after the men's biographies—fixates on a single accomplishment, her winning of the Storm Society Award.[54] Ni not only neglects her current artistic practice and fails to anticipate the direction of her future work, but he also overlooks her history, training, influences, and artistic interests.

By considering only the circumstances surrounding *Flower*, the paragraph on Qiu Ti serves to promote the group and its ideology more than the artist and we are left with the impression that he did not perceive Qiu Ti as very significant to the group. Ni Yide's discussion of Qiu Ti assigns her a secondary role, more passive recipient than active collaborator. Such an impression is exacerbated by the photographic spread accompanying his essay, which visually reinforces his distinct vision of the Storm Society (fig. 2.8). It includes four paintings by Pang Xunqin, matching the attention lavished on the artist in the essay. Qiu Ti is left artistically mute beside her prolific husband, represented only by a photograph of her face. Not even her award-winning painting is reproduced, much less the artworks that she exhibited in the 1935 group show.

In contrast, a survey of news coverage for this final exhibition facilitates a more measured view of Qiu Ti's place within the group and one markedly different from Ni Yide's. At least four pictorials ran photographic exhibition reviews of the Fourth Annual Storm Society Exhibition.[55] Altogether, the four exhibition reviews feature a combined total of seventeen painting reproductions by ten artists. Space was assuredly at a premium, as no artist has more than one artwork appearing in a single review and some artists are not included in all of the reviews. For example, Yang Qiuren has work in only three of the four reviews and four other artists appear in just one or two of the reviews. Only five artists have paintings reproduced in all of the exhibition reviews, and of these two, Zhang Xuan and Zhou Zhentai 周真太 (?–1936), have the same representative image reproduced all four times. That leaves just three members who were represented in all four reviews and also by multiple works: the two cofounders of the group, Pang Xunqin and Ni Yide, and Qiu Ti.[56] In this choice to accord Qiu Ti the highest prestige of media publicity—with her paintings published identically to the men's and without emphasis on her gender—we may view quite concretely Qiu Ti's equal standing in the group as a core member and observe yet again the divide between the actions of the group and the slanted commentary provided by Ni Yide.

One of the publications documenting the Fourth Exhibition, a review published in *Xinren zhoukan* 新人周刊 [*New People's Weekly*], includes the work of a second female artist affiliated with the Storm Society, which further casts Ni Yide's account of the group's membership into doubt (fig. 2.9). Although Ni designates Qiu Ti as the group's only female member, there was another woman publicly associated with the society: Liang Baibo 梁白波 (1911–ca. late 1960s). Liang is not mentioned in the essay, but she nevertheless participated in the Storm Society activities, including the final exhibition for which Ni Yide's article was published.

Like Qiu Ti, Liang Baibo has been largely forgotten in the narrative of modern Chinese art history.[57] When remembered, she is frequently cited for her romance with married cartoonist Ye Qianyu 葉淺予 (1907–95). More significantly, however, during the Republican period she established a productive, if ultimately brief, career as a cartoonist and illustrator, earning a living through her work for magazines.[58] Her most beloved figure was the frisky protagonist of her *Miss Honeybee* (*Mifeng xiaojie* 蜜蜂小姐) serial cartoon strip, first published in *Li bao* (立報) newspaper in 1935. Initially, Liang Baibo participated in Société de Deux Mondes (Taimeng Huahui 苔蒙畫會), a politically charged artists' society that was even more short-lived than the Storm Society.[59] Pang Xunqin and Zhou Zhentai were cofounders of Société de Deux Mondes, and it is probably through this connection that Liang Baibo decided to join the Storm Society.

In his short article in *L'Art* about the formation of the Storm Society, Pang Xunqin places Liang Baibo first on a list of the twelve members who attended the second organizational meeting for the society.[60]

Media coverage also verifies her continued contributions to the Storm Society until the time of its dissolution. The reproductions of paintings in *Xinren zhoukan* confirm that she had at least one painting, a portrait of a woman, in the fourth and final Storm Society Exhibition show (fig. 2.10).[61] In this exhibition review, Liang Baibo is not only treated as a member of the group, but her painting receives pride of place. The portrait, positioned in the center of the page, intrudes upon the surrounding compositions by four other group members. As Liang Baibo participated with the group from its inception until its final exhibition, it is evident that no award was necessary for women to secure membership.[62] Ni Yide's exclusion of Liang from his essay leaves us to wonder if she was not interested in full membership in the Storm Society or if he selectively forgot her for the sake of emphasizing the group's exclusivity. His pointed labeling of Qiu Ti as the group's only female artist suggests the latter.

Why should a more informed understanding of Qiu Ti's and Liang Baibo's status within the Storm Society, as opposed to Ni Yide's portrayal of their status, matter? As discussed in the Introduction, the proliferation of art groups, which allowed artists to pool resources and stage collective shows, was a crucial aspect of the emergent exhibition culture in early twentieth-century China. Female artists enthusiastically joined these groups and hung their artworks alongside those of their male peers. But although women were participating members of a variety of art societies, the collective atmosphere of these group settings means their individual contributions were often less than transparent to outside observers, particularly now that some eighty years have passed. Though over the years outspoken male group members may have stolen the spotlight, that gradual and surreptitious revision of history should not be mistaken for inactivity or inability on the part of female artists.

Participation by women in Republican-period art groups was more substantial, and their roles more nuanced, than is generally acknowledged in the art historical canon. For example, Guan Zilan participated in the Dawn Art Society (Chenguang Meishu Hui 晨光美術會), a large, progressive art organization dedicated to the advancement of the arts, particularly Western-style painting. Nor was she the first; the Dawn Art Society had included women from its very inception. When it was established in 1920, the group counted at least one woman, Lu Jinglan 陸景蘭 (n.d.), among its roster of founding members.[63] Moreover, the group bylaws explicitly welcome women to membership by clarifying, "... male or female, all may become a member of this Society."[64] An even more prominent artist organization, the Yifeng Art Society (Yifeng She 藝風社), included a number of successful female artists among its ranks: Pan Yuliang, Fang Junbi, Cai Weilian 蔡威廉 (1904–39), and Sun Duoci 孫多慈 (1912–75) all hung paintings in the First Yifeng Society Exhibition of 1934.[65] These women, in turn, represented major institutions of higher learning. Pan Yuliang and Sun Duoci came from Nanjing Central College and Cai Weilian and Fang Junbi came from Hangzhou National Art Academy and Guangzhou University, respectively.

While certain art associations drew a large number of women, some women also participated in multiple organizations simultaneously. Pan Yuliang was tremendously active in the art community, first serving as a professor at her alma mater, the Shanghai Academy of Art, and later at Nanjing Central College. In addition to her activity in the Yifeng Society, she also joined and exhibited with the Yiyuan Painting Research Society (Yiyuan Huihua Yanjiusuo 藝苑繪畫研究所), as did Jin Qijing. Pan cofounded—or at the very least joined as an inaugural member—many other groups, including the Muse (Mo She 摩社) artist group in 1932, the Chinese Art Society (Zhongguo Meishu Hui 中國美術會) in 1933, the Silent Society (Mo She 默社) in 1936, and the National Art Society (Zhonghua Quanguo Meishu Hui 中華全國美術會) in 1937.[66] Other women similarly were widely invested in China's modern art scene.[67] The oil

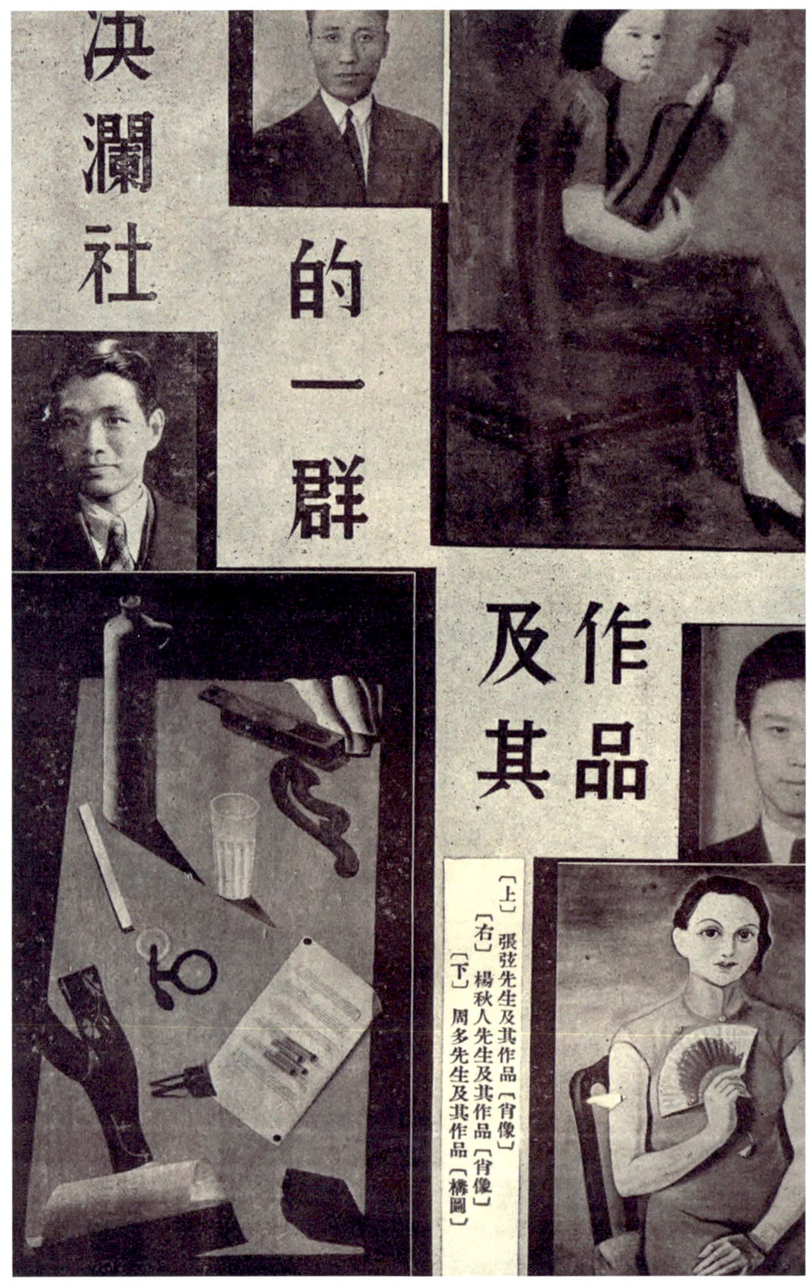

2.8 "Juelanshe de yi qun jiqi zuopin [The Storm Society's Group and Their Works]," *Qingnian jie* 8, no. 3 (October 1935).

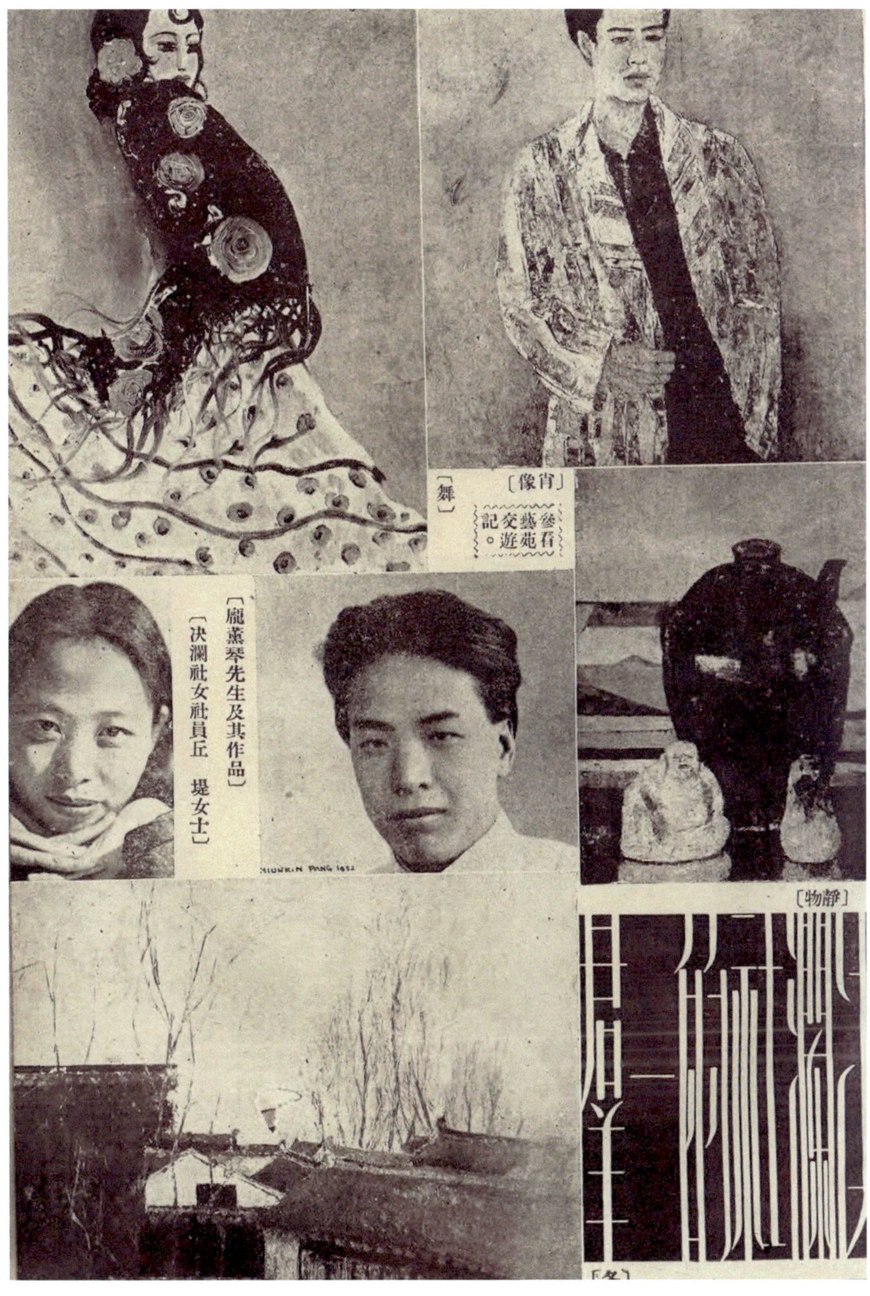
〔肖像〕
〔舞〕
參看藝苑交遊記。
〔龐薰琹先生及其作品〕
〔決瀾社女社員丘 堤女士〕
〔靜物〕

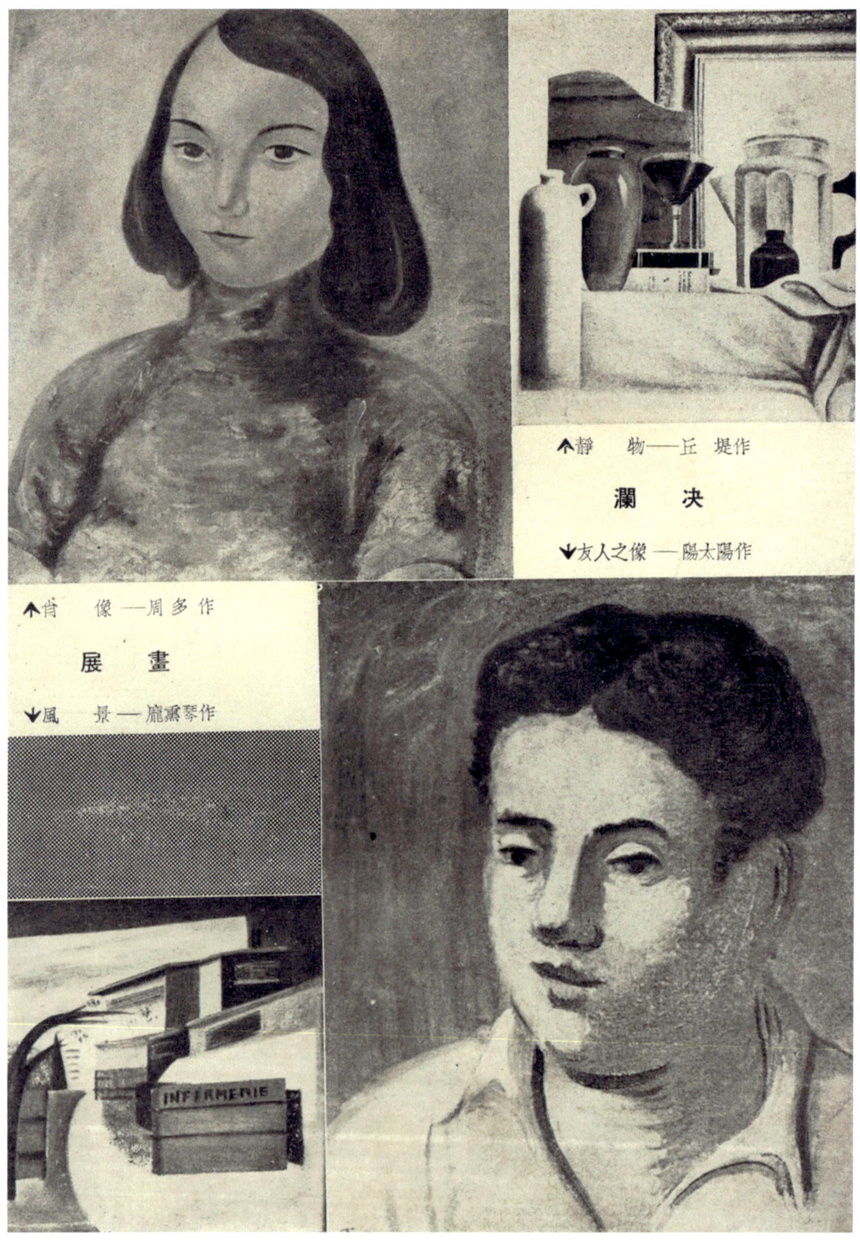

2.9 Artworks from the Fourth Annual Storm Society Exhibition. "Juelan huazhan [Storm Society Painting Exhibition]," *Xinren zhoukan* 2, no. 10 (November 2, 1935).

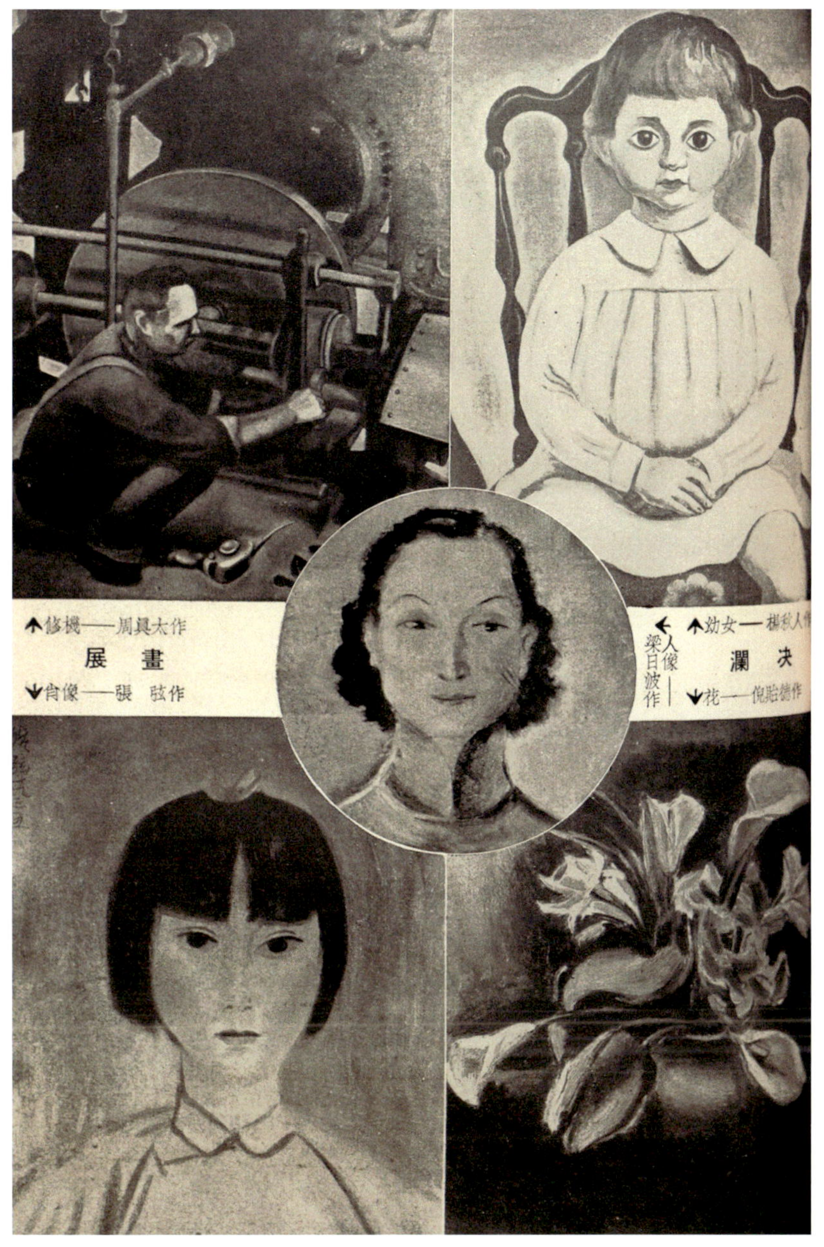
↑修機——周眞太作
畫展
↓肖像——張弦作
↑幼女——楊秋人作
決瀾
↓花——倪貽德作
←人像——梁白波作

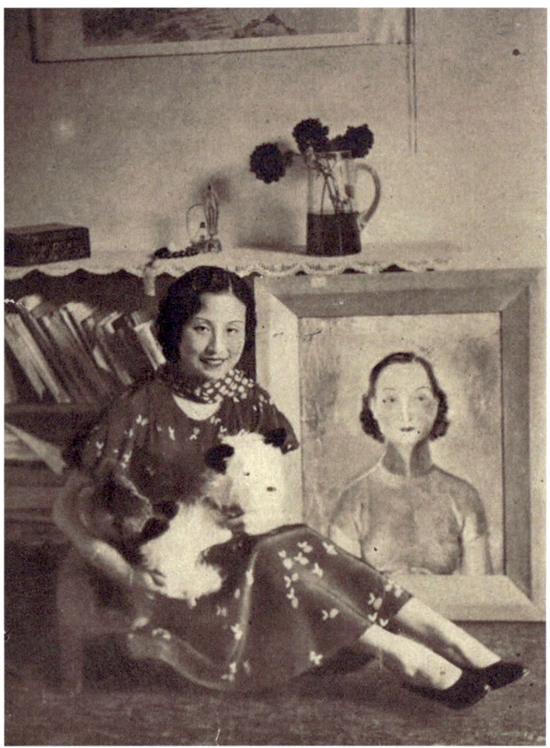

2.10 A photograph of Liang Baibo's *Portrait (Renxiang)* and its sitter. "Chen Yaxian nüshi jiqi huaxiang: Chen nüshi wei guoli yinyueyuan gaocaisheng, xiang wei Liang Baibo nüshi zuo [Miss Chen Yaxian and her portrait: Miss Chen is a top student of the National Conservatory, Liang Baibo painted her likeness]," *Zhonghua* 39 (1935): 24. Source: CNBKSY.

painter Tang Yunyu 唐蘊玉 (1903–67), a Shanghai Shenzhou School for Girls graduate, was a member of the Eastern Art Research Society (Dongfang Yishu Yanjiuhui 東方藝術研究會) and exhibited with the Yiyuan Painting Research Society and the Pegasus Society (Tianma Hui 天馬會).[68] She taught *xihua* at the Shanghai Academy of Art and the Shanghai Art Research Society (Shanghai Yishu Yanjiusuo 上海藝術研究所).[69] Fang Junbi (see chapter 4) taught life drawing at the Shanghai Academy of Art and contributed to the Dawn Art Society and Yiyuan Painting Research Society exhibitions. The examples of just these few women provide a good snapshot of the widespread and lively activity of female artists within China's modern art community.

Given these women's membership to prominent modern art organizations, it is all the more puzzling why Ni Yide chose to misrepresent Qiu Ti as the Storm Society's only female member in an essay that ultimately undermines Qiu Ti's standing within the group. Perhaps he simply intended to sensationalize and legitimatize the award. It may be that he mistakenly assumed that his portrayal of Qiu Ti would be to her benefit. Or perhaps he was truly imperceptive of Qiu Ti's professional activity and his essay provides a glimpse of his own biases.[70] But whether or not Ni personally ranked Qiu Ti equal to the male Storm Society members, his essay manufactures a controversy and provides a problematic account of the painting and its artist. Ni's propensity for hyperbole and dramatics, both in this essay and throughout the entirety of his written works, reaffirms the necessity of the wider range of sources analyzed in this chapter.

TRADING SUPERLATIVES FOR SUBTLETIES

Instead of limiting our perception of *Flower* to Ni Yide's portrayal of a prizewinning subject of controversy, a more nuanced view calls on us to reenvision it as a painting imbued with fluid meaning and multiple functions. At first *Flower*, a relatively literal rendering of a plant common to Qiu Ti's hometown, exhibited as a representative product of Qiu Ti's skillful hand. Later, the group recognized the painting as an outstanding work by an "unaffiliated" artist. Later still, Ni Yide appropriated *Flower* to serve the group's ideological mission by redefining it as an exercise in artistic license, and the painting has been colored by the slant of his theoretical interpretation ever since. Published time and again as an award-winning and provocative artwork, the painting ultimately contributed to the development of Qiu Ti's professional persona, to the expansion of modern art discourse in early twentieth-century China, and even to the present-day understanding of the Storm Society and its objectives.

But at what expense did Ni Yide's praise come? In his appropriation of *Flower* for his own ideological purposes, Ni Yide designates the painting controversial and Qiu Ti as the only female member—whose membership was contingent upon approval—and denies Liang Baibo membership status in the very same gesture. Yet despite Ni's penchant for hyperbole, *Flower* was a coleus, just as Qiu Ti and Liang Baibo were by all other appearances full members. Not only was Ni's characterization of Qiu Ti inaccurate, publicity materials for the group indicate that his view was not shared by the larger group. By questioning the circumstances surrounding the Storm Society Award, this chapter may seem to erode Qiu Ti's primary distinction, but the intent has been to correct the historical record by assigning credit where it is due. Holding Qiu Ti up as an exception—that is, as the only female artist to win a spot in Republican Shanghai's brightest avant-garde association—might seem to honor her accomplishments, just as Ni's praise at first glance appears to elevate Qiu Ti and her role in the group. In actuality, his words have profoundly and persistently eroded her legacy by flattening her professional identity while negating the robust professional activity of women artists of her generation. Perpetuating a narrative of exceptionalism by fixating on an image of Qiu Ti as the only woman artist capable of gaining admittance to an important art group imposes gender qualifications on her accomplishments and minimizes or ignores the professional activities of other women artists. Must we believe it was necessary for Qiu Ti receive a token prize in order to acknowledge her as an equally relevant member of one of China's most influential modern art societies?

Ultimately, Qiu Ti's and Liang Baibo's contested status within the Storm Society confronts us with how easily female artists have been erased from historical record and confirms there is more to be learned about the social interactions and cultural influence of women within the Republican art community. As seen in chapter 1, the occupation of professional female artist carried potent social meaning, no less than the promise of societal reform and national revitalization. Women's activity in art groups not only bolstered the power of the collective, their membership alone could be pointed to as evidence of an art society's progressive ideology. As welcomed members of China's leading art societies, women robustly participated in art societies and made contributions alongside their male colleagues. For these women, membership offered many benefits: the thrill of exchanging ideas and inspiration with colleagues, the opportunity to combine resources for group exhibitions and publications, and career advancement afforded from the increased visibility of the collective. But for Qiu Ti, as for many women artists, membership also entailed subsuming her individual professional identity under the group image.

Although women actively participated in the period's leading art societies, this chapter demonstrates that the dynamics of female artists' participation within these groups remain little understood today. The complexity of interpersonal relationships within professional art associations makes it difficult to track their individual contributions to the collective. However, while the publicity generated by art societies may be suspect for its uneven and calculated presentation of its membership, a focused investigation into the artworks produced and exhibited by female artists helps construct a more nuanced view. The many paintings by women reproduced in the contemporary press document their engagement with the leading discourse and practices of the day. Chapter 3 documents women as artists, whether individually or as members exhibiting in group exhibitions, relishing a subject newly dominant in modern Chinese art—the female nude—and explores the motivations of the artists as well as the reception of their work within the larger community.

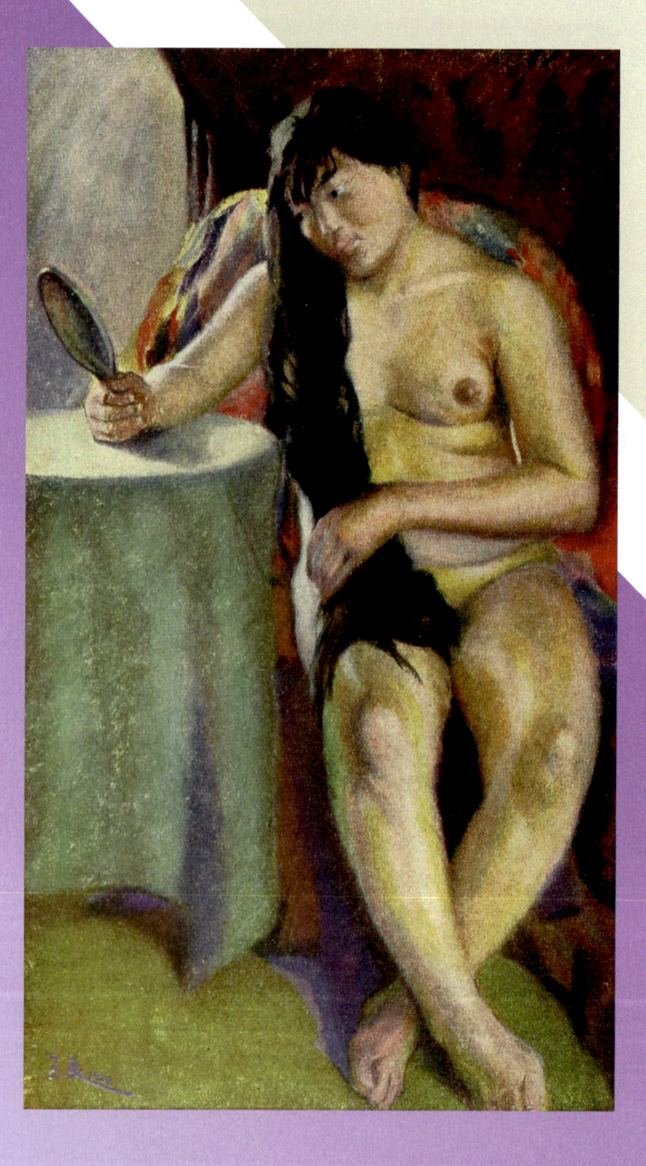

3

Nude Ambition

In 1935, a class from the Shanghai Academy of Art gathered on risers for a group portrait (fig. 3.1). In the black-and-white image, male and female students bundled in coats and scarves crowd together while a starkly naked young woman stands right in their midst. In the act of taking a group photograph with their nude model, the life drawing class followed a precedent established in Europe but with a noticeable divergence: this class is coeducational.[1] The female students smile and stare into the camera with the same confidence as their male classmates.

When it was rediscovered a decade ago, the photograph caused a minor sensation in China and even prompted a CCTV television documentary.[2] It is easy to see why the image generated so much interest: the contrast between the model and the students is jarring. But beyond the juxtaposition of clothed students and a nude paid model, the photograph seems to capture the blatant objectification of the female form. If, as feminist art historians have demonstrated, the artistic depiction of the female nude caters to the heterosexual male gaze, what would prompt these female students to physically place themselves in close proximity to the naked model, much less to be captured together within the same photographic frame?[3] The coeds in the photograph look eager to participate in the class exercise and, as this image attests, women of Republican-period China actively contributed to the production and dissemination of nude imagery. From this realization several questions arise. How did *nühuajia*

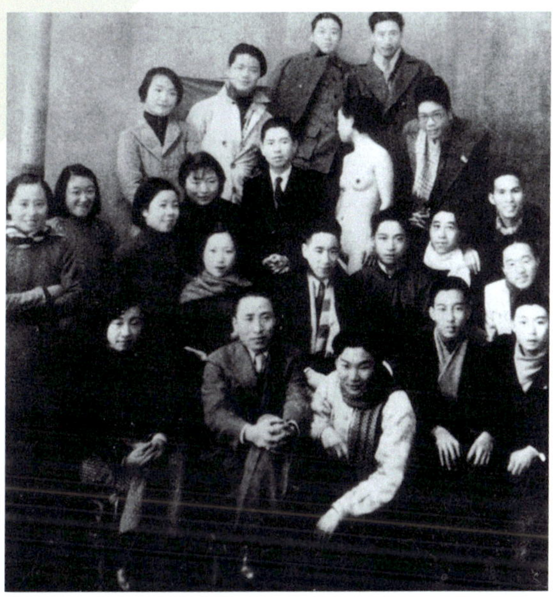

3.1 Shanghai Academy of Art class posing with nude model, ca. 1935. Published widely, including on the cover of Jane Zheng, *The Modernization of Chinese Art: The Shanghai Art College, 1913-1937* (Leuven: Leuven University Press, 2016).

Reflection, Pan Yuliang (detail of fig. 3.5).

approach the subject of the female nude? What did the subject mean to them and what purpose did it serve? When a generation of female artists turns to the female nude for artistic inspiration, what are the implications for the concept of "the gaze"?

This chapter examines the reasons for the prevalence of the female nude in early twentieth-century China, with the aim of better understanding women artists' uses for the genre. I look at the standard modernist art theory propagated by men—which approached the fine art nude as the antithesis of traditional Chinese painting and conservative social values—and also the common portrayal of women's bodies in popular media of the day, to explain the ways in which women's artistic practice acknowledged both. Women as modernist artists produced and exhibited numerous images of female nudes, challenging any reductionist understanding of Republican-period imaging of the female body as consistently catering to heterosexual male desire. Among these women painters of the nude is Pan Yuliang 潘玉良 (1895–1977); today she is by far the best-known female artist of the Republican period but, given her choice of preferred subject, is widely mistook as an anomaly. While identifying how women's contributions to the genre of the nude—one of the most important modernist statements of the day—were equal to those of their male peers, this chapter also analyzes the feminist theories of contemporary female artists and the ways in which their motivations and idealism exceeded that of their male peers.

THE DAWNING OF A CHINESE RENAISSANCE: THE NUDE IN MODERNIST IDEOLOGY

Painting the female nude stood as one of the most definitive artistic practices of China's modern art movement. Elsewhere, I examine Republican China's pseudomedical interest in the female body, the sociopolitical implications of the institutionalization of the life drawing studio, and the ways in which the very act of producing images of nude models from life symbolized national reform.[4] Here, I wish to focus on the ways in which the prevailing modernist art ideology espoused by influential theorists directly linked the genre and its practice to the nation's potential for a cultural renaissance. This ideological connection may be traced back to the introduction of the practice in the first decade of the twentieth century, when China's art educators first advocated life drawing as an essential component of an institutional training in Western artistic styles and techniques. Several institutions of higher learning incorporated nude models in life drawing classes, even when this pedagogy momentarily came under fire in the mid-1920s.[5] Liu Haisu 劉海粟 (1896–1994), the director of the Shanghai Academy of Art and one of the more raucous voices within the modernist art community, famously battled criticism of his school's employment of nude models in the fall of 1925 with a public spectacle of published letters of protest and a radio broadcast voicing his dissent. If anything, his agitation only provoked further action, and nude models were officially prohibited as of the summer of 1926 until a change in government the following year facilitated the revocation of the ban. The ideological fight, however, solidified Liu's reputation as a rebel artist and the simplistic rhetoric invoked in his protestations—that the nude constituted a remedy to the Confucian conservativism that was obstructing national progress—persists to the present.[6]

We find the origins of much of Liu's ideology in "Considering Nude Art," written by influential modernist, art theorist, and Storm Society cofounder Ni Yide. Ni, already much discussed in this book, served as an instructor in the Western Painting Department of the Shanghai Academy of Art until the autumn of 1927.[7] This essay, which was written as a response to the censorship of an alumna's exhibition in October 1924, was published in *The China Times* in December of that year.[8] In it Ni uses much of the same rhetoric later employed by Liu Haisu.[9] Ni was one of the first to proclaim the art nude a signifier of cultural enlightenment and his essay conveys the modernist idealism invested in the act of painting the nude in China.

A rousing polemic on the reception and significance of "nude art" (*luoti yishu* 裸體藝術) in China, "Considering Nude Art" opens with an evocation of its European authority.

> Like other kinds of new doctrines and new ideas, nude art has also infiltrated our land in the wake of contemporary trends. This is one sign of renaissance, a harbinger of an age of rebirth. The aged fragrance of Florence and the spring scenery of the Rhine riverbanks, are about to reappear in our splendid land of China. How we should be thankful and leap for joy at the bright prospect![10]

Ni Yide argues that as a fine art genre the nude held the potential to revolutionize the nation. But, drawing a comparison to socialism, he charges the fine art nude was similarly misunderstood by his countrymen, whose opposition threatened the development of China's art world. He identified three types of opponents: the moralists, who viewed nude images as base pornography; the misguided, for whom life drawings were useful for anatomical study but not finished works of art; and the crass marketers and sham artists, who manufactured crude images of nudes in order to capitalize on the ignorance of young people aspiring to be cosmopolitan. Ni was most offended by the moralists, whom he considered hypocrites despite their espousal of strict Confucian ethics. He pointed to the hypocrisy of the "ancients" of China who proclaimed "free love" (*ziyou lian'ai* 自由戀愛) wrong while indulging themselves in multiple wives and concubines. His interest in the concept of free love and reference to "new ethics" (*xin daode* 新道德) reflect his engagement with the greater modernist discourse of the day. For him, pictures of nude figures were in the same spirit as the new ethics—that is, a modern morality free of Confucian values—in that it was similarly concerned with self-expression and the revelation of true feeling. Inspired by European artists of an earlier generation, Ni Yide embraced primitivism, what he called the "spirit of the primitive times" (*yuanshi shidai de jingshen* 原始時代的精神), when people were happy, naked, innocent, natural, and carefree. Reviving such a mentality, he wrote, offered inspiration and the ability to express true meaning. Ni Yide called on artists to draw stimulation from the moralists' reproaches and intensify their efforts in depicting the human body, maintaining that the fine art nude will prevail in the dawning modern era.

In addition to arguing the need for the genre, Ni Yide's essay illuminates the qualities that he and his colleagues considered essential for proficient paintings of nude figures. Reacting to the sensationalism that greeted depictions of shapely nude models—which he notes led to the fad for using the word "curvaceous" (*quxianmei* 曲線美)—Ni advocated viewing the body through a Western lens as a perfect harmony of form and function. His essay references the formal beauty of ancient Greek art and classicism but calls on Chinese artists to follow modern artists like Cézanne and Matisse and concentrate on the coloration (*secai* 色彩), volume (*yuanwei* 圓味), and voluptuousness (*rougan* 肉感) of the human body. The body was to be composed of round fleshy forms pleasing to the eye and colored with a harmonious play of subtle gradations, which he maintained was desirable because human beings instinctively appreciate soft things.[11] Concentrating his discussion solely on the female form, Ni robustly extols the "body of a luscious young woman in her prime—her high swelling breasts, thighs like jade pillars, large and prominent buttocks"—as "capable of arousing passion for life and eagerness for love!"[12]

While Ni's invigorated discussion of the female body would seem to clothe his own sexual preferences in the guise of reasoned aesthetic principles, his essay goes on to assure the reader of the artist's ideologically pure motives. He pointedly addresses the social position of the life model, dismissing as absurd a commonly held belief that the occupation was akin to prostitution.[13] The model's display of her flesh, in his view, was not only honorable but also a contribution to the creative process for which she should be praised. Moreover, as appreciation for nude subjects increased, so would the prestige of the sitter.[14] He likewise dismissed concerns about artists conducting inappropriate relationships with their models. Artists are preoccupied with more lofty concerns, he explains, and the relationship resulting from their passion for their subjects became that of artist and muse. Although he had not studied in Europe, Ni was well-versed in the romanticized discourse surrounding the subject of the female nude in the West, and his discussion of the relationship between the artist and his model draws heavily from the European tradition.

Ni Yide was also well aware of the artistic ambitions of women; he instructed female students, possibly including Qiu Ti, in coeducational courses.[15] The only gender roles in his essay, however, are those of male artist and female muse. A female model was to be soft and beautiful and inspire the artist to create great art. For his part, the artist was expected to fall passionately in love with his voluptuous subject and transform her into his personal muse.[16] While the male artist is the creative genius, the model's individual identity is effectively erased as she becomes the passive subject of his imagining. As laid forth in his essay, Ni's theories simply do not consider the relationship between a female artist and a nude model. Yet, his apparent oversight did nothing to dissuade women artists from approaching and mastering the genre. As will be discussed in the following section, women were vital and prolific contributors to the production of the female nude in early twentieth-century Chinese art and they shared their artworks widely.

THE NUDE BOOM IN REPUBLICAN-PERIOD PAINTING

Given the obvious enthusiasm with which Ni Yide describes the corporeal qualities of women's flesh, his endorsement of the nude as a painting genre may ring as salaciously subjective, but the fact remains that his ideas were highly influential. A diverse range of print media—from newspapers to popular pictorials to art journals—document Chinese artists' voracious appetite for this subject in the late 1920s and early 1930s.[17] Paintings of female nude figures appeared frequently in exhibitions and in print, particularly in cosmopolitan Shanghai, and provocatively signaled the dawn of a new age of art and culture. In most cases, presentation of the subject is strikingly similar; artists frequently depicted figures in static poses with few or no narrative elements and, through the use of shading, accentuated their three-dimensionality.[18] David Clarke, scholar of modern and contemporary art and theory, argues that these features consistently found in Chinese modernists' paintings of female nudes gave the figures an iconic status that drew attention to the art community's break with China's literati painting tradition.[19] In paintings of staged compositions that clearly represented live models posed in studio settings, modernist artists offered a glaring contrast to a traditional ink painting practice based on the copying of the master paintings of the past.[20] Clarke thus frames the use of the nude as an act of deliberate provocation rather than simply a product of passive reception of the West's cultural influence. Tied to antitraditionalist modernist ideology, working directly from a female life model became a self-reflexive practice through which early twentieth-century artists challenged convention and pointed to their own roles in the modernization of the nation.

Even a quick survey of Republican-period print media demonstrates that women artists produced and exhibited images of female nudes in numbers rivaling their male counterparts, with equal skill, and gained recognition for their work. For instance, the *Jingbao Supplemental* (*Jingbao fukan* 京報副刊) featured Fang Junbi with five of her figure paintings, including two female nudes grouped with her self-portrait, in 1926.[21] In 1934, a color reproduction of Fang's painting of a female nude commanded a whole page of the popular Shanghai pictorial *Arts & Life* (*Meishu shenghuo* 美術生活) (fig. 3.2).[22] More naturalistic and detailed than many paintings by her male peers, Fang's *Figure* (*Renti* 人體) is convincingly proportioned and modeled to impart the tactility of flesh. The artist revels in the precise depiction of the nude in a studio setting; the soft skin of the life model's thigh yields to the foot on which it rests, and the curves of the buttocks conform to the sheet-draped furniture underneath. In

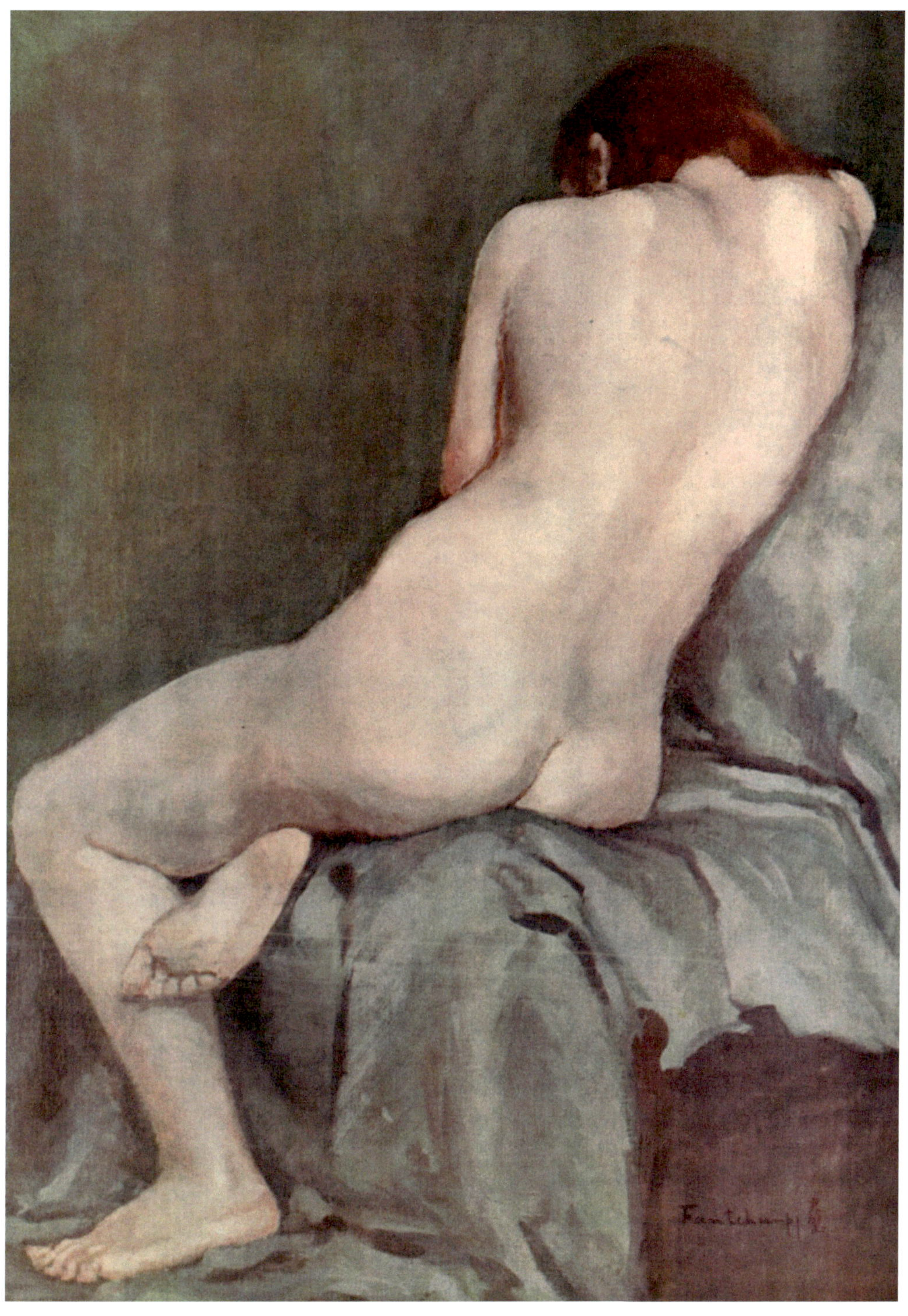

3.2 Fang Junbi, *Figure (Renti)*, *Arts & Life* 4 (July 1934): 5.

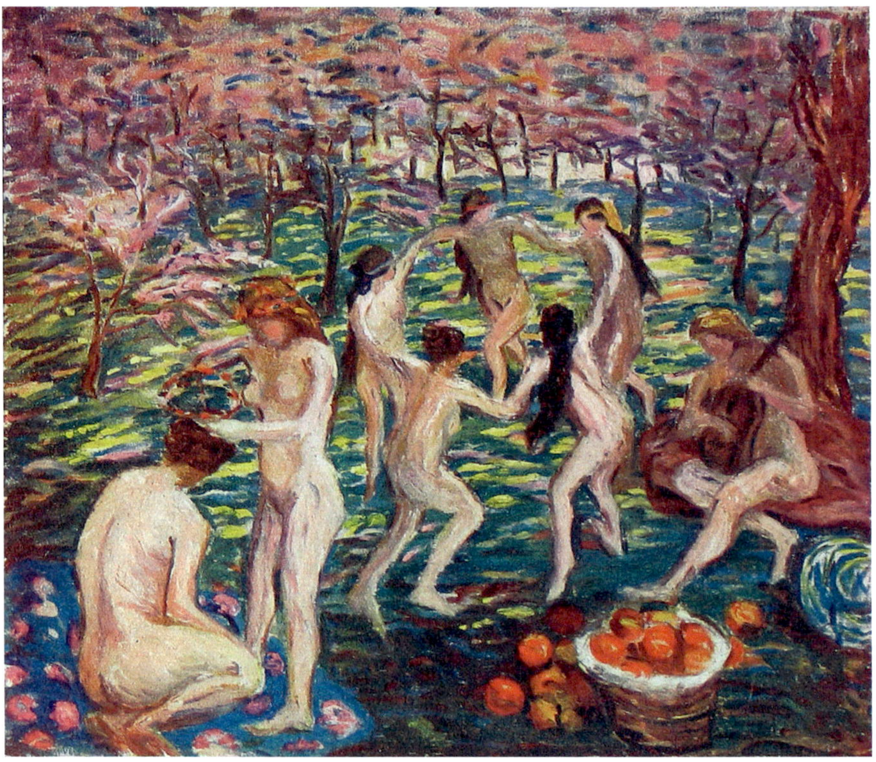

3.3 Pan Yuliang, *Flourish* (*Rong*). *Wenhua* 3 (October 1929). Courtesy of The Li Ching Cultural and Educational Foundation.

The Young Companion's coverage on China College of Arts graduates Guan Zilan and Cui Wenying (see chapter 1), Cui's painting of a seated female nude appears along with her portrait photograph (see fig. 1.2). With *Rest* (*Xi* 息), the artist's volumetric rendering of a model posed in an armchair delineates the anatomy of the figure, clearly indicating her physicality. A photographic review of Guan Zilan's 1930 solo exhibition included two of her paintings of female nudes (see fig. 1.8).[23] Using shading and outlined forms, these, too, create a believable sense of the model's physical presence in the studio space. While Guan's gestural paintings pull stylistic inspiration from fauvism, other women artists employed more naturalistic styles while maintaining sharp focus on the female life model in the studio setting, as seen in Weng Yuanchun's 翁元春 charcoal drawing and Wang Jingyuan's 王靜遠 sculpture, both published in 1929.[24] Though Qiu Ti ventures the furthest from the artist's studio and standard depictions of the life model with her abstracted nudes in a landscape from the second Storm Society exhibition (see fig. 2.3), she also practiced the iconic rendition of the female nude in the studio, as seen in the figure study from her profile in *The Cosmopolitan* (see fig. 2.5).

The number of female nudes published by Pan Yuliang, however, far outnumbers those of her female peers—and perhaps even her male peers. Throughout her career, Pan's preferred subject was the female nude and she published and exhibited many of these images in 1920s and 1930s China.[25] The serendipitous timing of her artistic training no doubt influenced her interest in the nude figure. Pan enrolled in the Shanghai Academy of Art in 1920 and was a member of the young institution's first coeducational class. The year 1920 also marked the introduction of female models to the Academy's life drawing classrooms. The following year, Pan joined the inaugural class of the Sino-Franco College in Lyon, France. Over the next seven years, she took classes at fine arts schools in Lyon, Paris, and Rome.[26]

During her time in France and Italy, Pan studied the European academic tradition firsthand and received a solid training in modeling the human figure in both two-dimensional and three-dimensional media. When she returned to Shanghai in 1928, the cultural climate in China encouraged her to put her skills at painting the female nude to good use.

During Pan Yuliang's absence, proponents of Chinese modernism such as Ni Yide and Liu Haisu had instilled the genre of the female nude as the preeminent marker of a Western artistic training and progressivism. In the decade following her return, Pan applied her artistic training to the images she produced and publicly exhibited. Though her oeuvre from this period includes still lifes, landscapes, and waterscapes, the human form dominates. Contemporary periodicals document her many portraits and figure studies; at least three dozen published reproductions, although some of these are reprints found in multiple serials. Among these, more than half are depictions of nudes, and of these the female nude is predominant.[27] Most of these images of female nudes are straightforward figure studies and firmly locate the model in the studio. A few are flights of fancy, such as *Flourish* (*Rong* 榮), which compositionally quotes Matisse's *La Joie de vivre* (fig. 3.3). Some of the nudes are blatantly seductive, in particular *Meow* (*Mimi* 咪咪), an oil painting of a feline voyeur watching its mistress pull a heavy coat over her nude form (fig. 3.4). The painting—the title of which creates a pun with the word for secret (*mimi* 秘密)—was so titillating that at least at least three magazines published it in the same year. In the 1929 special issue for *The Ladies' Journal*, Pan also published two paintings of nudes that she submitted to the First National Art Exhibition: *Man Lying under Light* (*Deng xia wo nan* 燈下臥男) and *Reflection* (*Guying* 顧影). As discussed below, the editors of the journal exalted *Reflection*, a female nude, with a full-page color reproduction at the front of the issue and a page-long discussion of the image and its artist (fig. 3.5).

The large assortment of female nudes published by Pan and her contemporaries, both male and female, demonstrates a more or less standardized

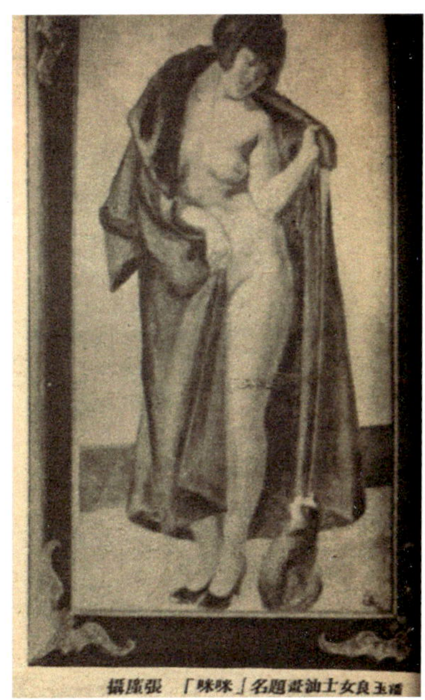

3.4 Pan Yuliang, *Meow* (*Mimi*), *Xinren zhoukan* 1.6 (October 22, 1934). Also published in *Modern Miscellany* 6, no. 12 (10 October 1934).

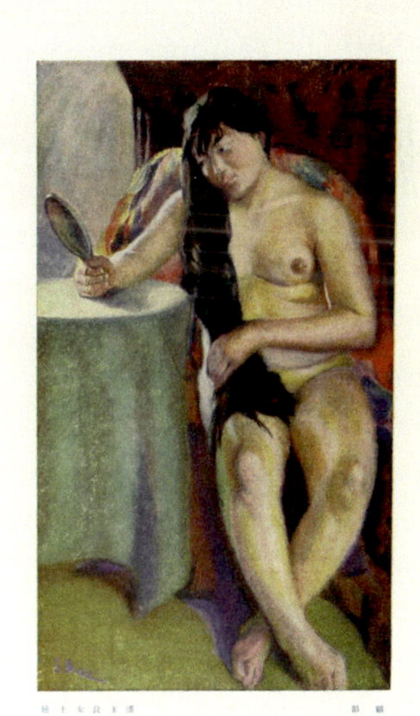

3.5 "*Guying*–Pan Yuliang nüshi hui [*Reflection*, by Pan Yuliang]," *The Ladies' Journal* 15, no. 007 (July 1929): 17.

approach to the representation of the figure that was shared by artists regardless of their sex. As Clarke observes, Chinese modernist artists formulated compositions that made their use of live models obvious. Related to this was their preference for female over male nudes, which came as part of the Western package and in part might be explained, as it is in the West, as catering to the taste of primarily male audiences.[28] Although, something more culturally significant was at work in the packaging and distribution of the female nude as art subject within China, or else why did an image like *Reflection* provoke such high praise from a woman's magazine?

THE NUDE VOGUE AND THE "WOMAN QUESTION"

As it turns out, the nude vogue, however much it satisfied prurient interests, was an expression of Chinese modernity, the aspects of its popularity distinctive to Republican-period society.[29] This modernism played out not only in painting, but even more so in the relatively new medium of photography. Multiple issues of *Arts & Life* featured full-page reproductions of art photographer Lang Jingshan's 郎静山 (1892–1995) black-and-white female nudes—the aesthetics of which, for all they recall erotic photography from the West, were unprecedented in China and thus considered modern.[30] The publishers of Shanghai pictorial *Modern Miscellany* produced mail-order, multivolume sets of photographs of female bodies from around the world purportedly for "scientific study."[31] Photographs of female athletes in *Lin Loon Ladies Magazine*, a Shanghai pictorial with wide distribution during its 1931–37 run, and many other periodicals invited admiration of the physically active body as part of a burgeoning international physical education movement that promoted a modern ideal of a "healthy beauty" (*jianmei* 健美).[32] Within these many examples, the nude or partially clothed female body held the potential to advance modern Chinese civilization—whether in the use of a modern medium to showcase an emergent aesthetic, or in the empiricism of anthropometric comparisons, or simply in the appreciation of the naked limbs and unbound feet of physically active and publicly viewable Modern Girls.[33]

Popular media that included nude figures—specifically, pictures of female nudes printed alongside images of modern young Chinese women—also assuaged deep-seated anxieties about women's expanding roles outside the home. As if a magical looking glass, the nude evoked notions of desirability, femininity, and modernity as viewers' range of cultural sensitivities and personal inclinations allowed, whether simply reminding young women of their own allure and evoking the cultural sophistication of the international art world or on through inviting speculation about the bodies beneath the socialites' clothes. The inclusion of an image of a nude might cast a Chinese woman in a sexual light by its mere proximity to her picture. *Lin Loon Ladies Magazine*, which was marketed to female students and career women of the middle and upper class, juxtaposed pictures of nude or scantily clad Western women with fully clothed modern Chinese women, the obvious depravity of the former making the latter look modest.[34] Confirming the socialite's comparative modesty in the face of a brazen display of flesh, the comparison nevertheless implies an underlying similarity of womanly forms. Such implications underlie *Xinren zhoukan's* pairing of local women's portraits with a classically styled sculpture of a youthful female nude seated upon rocks, the smooth limbs and supple form of the statue inviting comparison with the clothed bodies of the women in the photographs (fig. 3.6).[35] The front and back covers of *Lin Loon Ladies Magazine* typically present a prim Chinese socialite on one and a sultry American vixen on the other, the mirrored positioning underscoring their similarities.[36] The bookending of the images establishes a parallel between the two women—both young, desirable, and celebrated—transforming the socialite into the Chinese equivalent of the Hollywood starlet.[37] Similarly, an issue of *Modern Miscellany* features a double-page spread of Chinese socialites identified by name and described as "Modern Girls" immediately

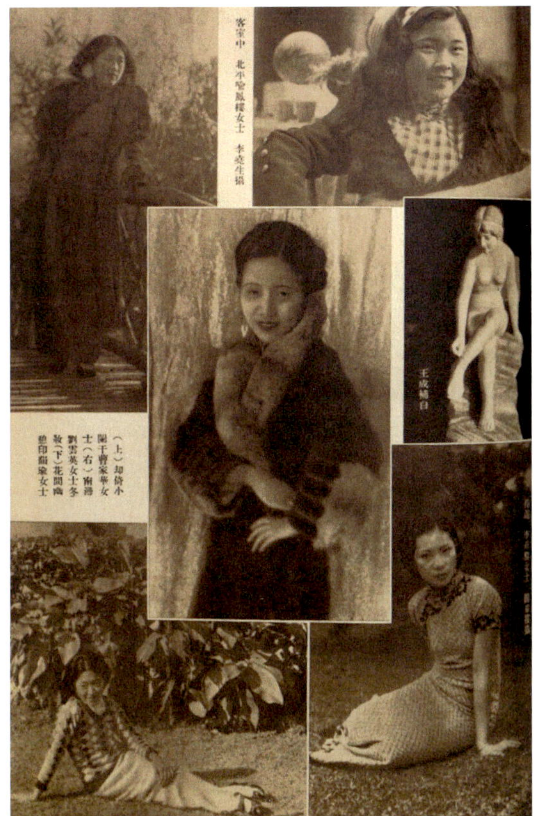

3.6 Photographs of Shanghai's socialites. *Xinren zhoukan* 1, no. 27 (March 18, 1935).

followed by another two-page spread of exuberantly exhibitionist Western women labeled "Nude Beauties in 1933," encouraging titillating speculation about the Chinese women's modern sexuality.[38]

Through this sexualization of Chinese women, magazines sought to address and stabilize gender roles, thereby allaying fears of what the Modern Girl could and should become.[39] Ostensibly, the countless public presentations of the well-heeled daughters of China's urban elite lauded these New Women for their modern accomplishments, which might be viewed as evidence of national progress. Accompanying nude imagery, however, simultaneously reassert the hegemony of the heterosexual male by encouraging admiration of women's physical attributes, thus supporting familiar gender roles with the reassurance that it is men who control the gaze.[40] (Such photographic juxtapositions prompted the conclusion that—were one to strip away their cosmopolitan fashions and college degrees—even China's New Women were still only women, after all.) For their part, the young women of China's middle and upper classes negotiated the parameters of their New Womanhood by submitting their own photographs to be published in these conventionalized photographic features.

The intersection of all of these vested interests results in a continual performance of the hybridization of modern and traditional gender roles across the pages of the Republican-period's popular press. If this period could be characterized by anything, it would be a persistent ambiguity in its peculiarly ambivalent presentations of modern womanhood.

When a woman painted Western-style nudes, her own works provided fodder for such comparisons. For readers accustomed to comparing the provocative covers of *Lin Loon Ladies Magazine* and the like, the experience of viewing a photograph of the artist alongside a reproduction of her painting of a nude must have held the titillating possibility that the painting reflected what the artist knew best, her own body. A cartoon titled "The Convenience of Female Painters," which appeared in *Arts & Life*, imagines the supposed advantage possessed by women painters.[41] It depicts a woman sitting in her studio and looking into a large mirror as she paints herself in the nude (fig. 3.7). The satire hinges on contemporary anxieties associated with women's agency and the willful manipulation of their own sexual allure. Time and again, Republican print media insinuated a similar real-life scenario by placing a painting of a female nude next to a photograph of its female artist. As seen in *The Cosmopolitan* profile (fig. 2.5), traditional Chinese art theory's desire to view qualities of the artist in his or her work encouraged readers to compare Qiu Ti's photographic portrait with the female nude painted by her hand. A connection between the portrait of Cui Wenying and her nude painting in *The Young Companion* layout is emphasized by the similar downward tilt of their heads (see fig. 1.2). In her solo exhibition coverage, Guan Zilan stands in three-

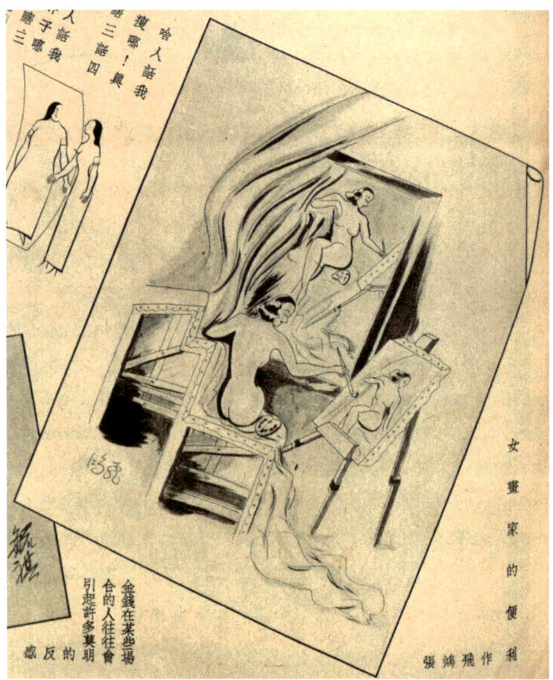

3.7 Zhang Hongfei, "Nühuajia de bianli [The Convenience of Female Painters]," *Arts & Life* 5 (August 1934).

quarter view with her right leg bent and arms down to her sides, subtly echoing the pose of the seated nude in her painting (see fig. 1.8). In another photograph from the same report, Guan Zilan sits directly below a second painting of a female nude, allowing the camera lens to juxtapose artist and painted nude within a single shot. A 1928 feature on Pan Yuliang positions her painted portrait just above her painting of a female nude with similarly short-shorn hair (fig. 3.8).[42] Paradoxically, in each of these examples, the female artist's proficiency at painting the nude bolsters her professional authority. The objectifying gaze created through the visual comparison of the artist to the female nude threatens to undermine that very professionalism but, by visually linking the new career of female artist to a progressive art subject, simultaneously confirms her liberated social role of New Woman.

The abundance of the female nude in Republican-period popular media is well documented today, but women's relationship to these images has been generally ignored. Recent studies of China's early twentieth-century visual culture, assuming a historical context in which men were the cultural agents and women passive objects of "the male gaze," occasionally may raise the question of how women perceived images of female nudes but nonetheless assign the role of creator to men and designate women spectators at best.[43] Such scholarship, while important to our understanding of editorial intent and audience reception, overlooks women artists' contributions to the genre as well as the prerogatives they performed in their choice of subjects and styles. How might we explain the images of female nudes by Pan Yuliang that are rife with sexual innuendo and were painted while she held prominent positions in Shanghai's and Nanjing's leading art societies and institutions? Indeed, the "woman question"—the identification of women's roles in modern Chinese society—that was so potent in the early twentieth century is still open as it pertains to the agency of women like Pan and her "sisters of the brush."

If little has been said of Chinese women artists' handling of the subject of the female nude, a look to scholarship on their sisters in the West yields comparisons of limited applicability. The French painter Susan Valadon (1865–1938) stands out as an exception to the norm in her adoption of the female nude as a regular subject. While academically trained women artists of the upper and middle classes restricted their choice of subjects out of propriety to the production of saccharine images of mothers with children, as did Mary Cassatt, Valadon reveled in the depiction of fecund nude models draped over the sofas and animal skin rugs in her studio. Patricia Mathews argues that Valadon's marginalized social identity—as a member of the working class, she had first entered the art world in the role of artist's model—permitted her an artistic practice in a "basically a male artistic milieu."[44] Mathews's analysis of Valadon's socioeconomic status is constructive in that it reconfirms that artists—both male and female—are to great extent bound by the conventions of their own sociohistorical contexts. But

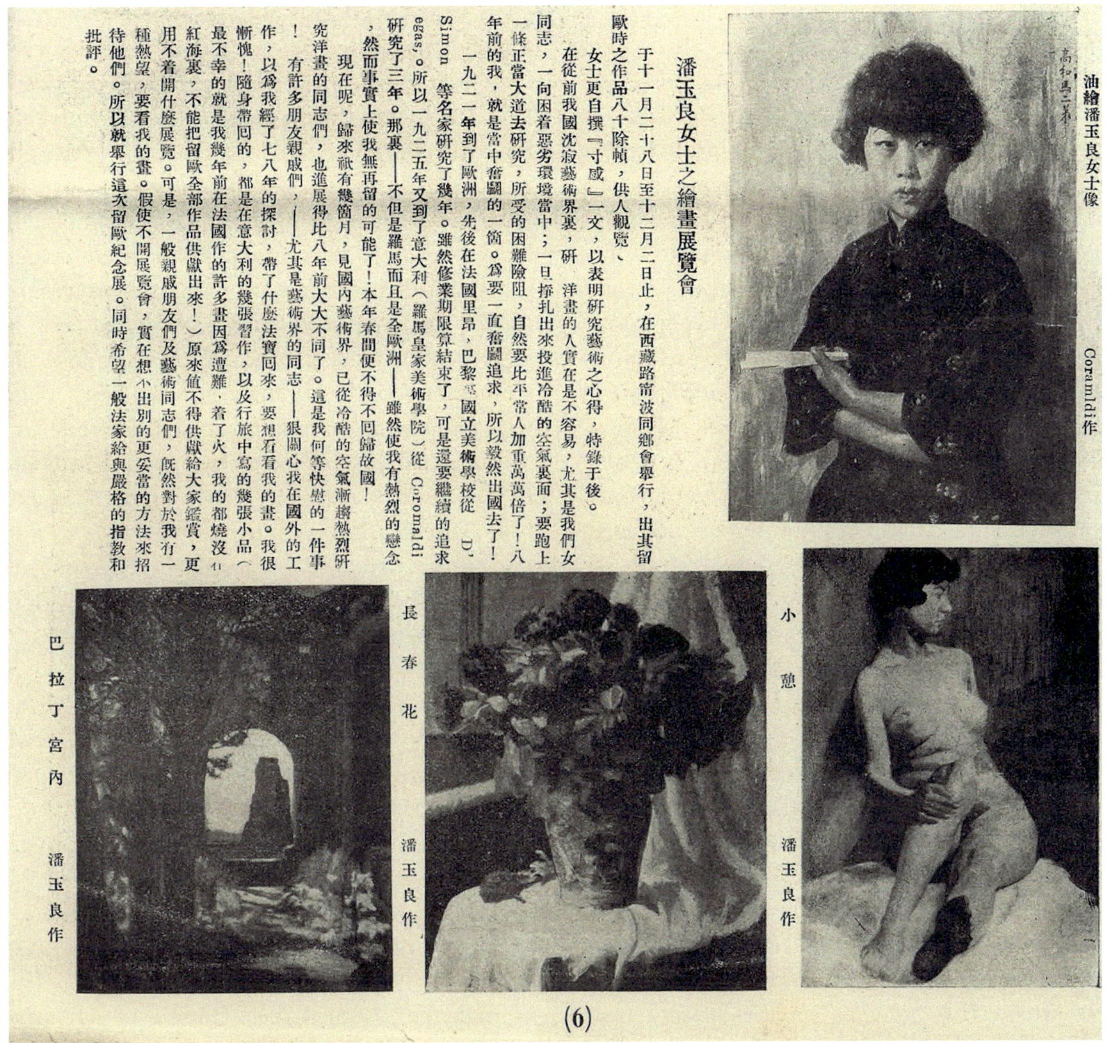

油繪潘玉良女士像

Coromaldi作

潘玉良女士之繪畫展覽會

于十一月二十八日至十二月二日止，在西藏路甯波同鄉會舉行，出其留歐時之作品八十餘幀，供人觀覽、

女士更自撰『寸感』一文，以表明研究藝術之心得，特錄于後。

在從前我國沈寂藝術界裏，研 洋畫的人實在是不容易，尤其是我們女同志，一向困着惡劣環境當中；一旦掙扎出來投進冷酷的空氣裏面；要跑上一條正當大道去研究，所受的困難險阻，自然要比平常人加重萬萬倍了！八年前的我，就是當中奮鬬的一個。爲要一直奮鬬追求，所以毅然出國去了！

一九二一年到了歐洲，先後在法國里昂，巴黎國立美術學校從 D' Simon 等名家研究了幾年。雖然修業期限算結束了，可是還要繼續的追求 egas,。所以一九二五年又到了意大利（羅馬皇家美術學院）從 Coromaldi 研究了三年。那裏——不但是羅馬而且是全歐洲——雖然使我有熱烈的戀念，然而事實上使我無再留的可能了！本年春間便不得不回歸故國！

現在呢，歸來祇有幾箇月，見國內藝術界，已從冷酷的空氣漸趨熱烈研究洋畫的同志們，也進展得比八年前大大不同了。這是我何等快慰的一件事！

有許多朋友親戚們，——尤其是藝術界的同志——狠關心我在國外的工作，以爲我經了七八年的探討，帶了什麼法寶回來，要想看看我的畫。我很慚愧！隨身帶回的，都是在意大利的幾張習作，以及行旅中寫的幾張小品（最不幸的就是我幾年前在法國作的許多畫因爲遭難，着了火，我的都燒沒了紅海裏，不能把留歐全部作品供獻出來！）原來值不得供獻給大家鑑賞，更用不着開什麼展覽。可是，一般親戚朋友們及藝術同志們，既然對於我有一種熱望，要看我的畫。假使不開展覽會，實在想不出別的更妥當的方法來招待他們。所以就舉行這次留歐紀念展。同時希望一般法家給與嚴格的指教和批評。

小憩 潘玉良作

長春花 潘玉良作

巴拉丁宮內 潘玉良作

(6)

3.8 Article on Pan Yuliang that is illustrated with three of her paintings and a portrait of the artist painted by one of her professors, Umberto Coromaldi. *Shanghai manhua* 33 (December 1928): 6. Courtesy of The Li Ching Cultural and Educational Foundation.

here the usefulness of the comparison would seem to end, as the socioeconomic lives of most female professional artists in Republican-period China more closely relate to Cassatt's privileged upbringing than to Valadon's life of hedonistic abandon.[45] The notable difference between the lived experience of the *nühuajia* and those of the lady painters of late-nineteenth-century Europe, however, is the progression of the worldwide women's suffrage movement; from the moment that the female art nude first gained currency in China's art world, Chinese women artists were already operating under the progressive, if at times ambiguous, norms of the modern New Woman.

Comparison to parallel developments in Japan confirms that the timing of the introduction of the nude as fine art genre held utmost significance for women artists. Japan's artistic community first embraced depictions of the female nude as indicative of artistic excellence decades earlier than China when Japanese artists began returning from their studies in fin de siècle Europe.[46] Crucially, this turn of events unfolded before the establishment of a women's rights movement. For a woman in early twentieth-century Japan, establishing a career as a professional artist was nearly impossible.[47] The Tokyo University of the Arts (Tokyo Geijutsu Daigaku), for example, did not even begin admitting female students until 1946.[48] In the early twentieth century, a handful of newly formed women's painting societies existed and the art of some female painters had gained limited exposure in venues such as women's magazines, however, few Japanese women pursued painting as a profession and most of those who did were firmly discouraged from taking up Western-style painting (*yoga*) precisely because of the medium's close association with the nude and overt sexuality.[49] Instead, decorum expected women to restrict themselves to *nihonga*, a modern incarnation of traditional Japanese painting.[50] For the small number of women who dared to pursue *yoga* painting, social pressures and the male camaraderie of the figure painting studio must have been daunting. Thus, when Chinese artists wishing to further their artistic studies traveled to the country to in the late 1920s, as did Guan Zilan and Qiu Ti, women's personal experiences within the Japanese artistic community assuredly differed from that of their male counterparts. While the androcentric culture of the Japanese art world encouraged their male peers to work from the life model, women students from China would have encountered painting practices much more exclusionary than those prevalent in Shanghai.[51]

Far from having the nude shielded from their eyes, as had been the case for women in Japan, Chinese women set up their easels in the life drawing studio and directly engaged the subject in their artistic practice. Female students at art schools such as the Shanghai Academy of Art, a fully coeducational institution since 1920, attended the same classes and studied the same nude models as did their male classmates.[52] Membership organizations such as the Dawn Art Society gave its female members full access to the figure painting studio, where men and women painted from the model side by side.[53] As seen in the photograph opening this chapter, by 1935 women coeds were posing in class photos with their male classmates and instructor—and female nude model—staking their claim on the institutionalized pursuit of enlightenment through the study of figure painting. Female professional artists, such as Pan Yuliang, approached nude figures much as male artists did: they produced life studies of attractive female models. They shared with men a sense of modernist pride in rendering a Western subject in Western mediums, one that promised the realization of a Chinese renaissance. Like Ni Yide, they took the female nude as muse and determined to realize an ideal artistic image of it in the Western sense. Thus, the popularity of the genre rose in tandem with the professionalization of women artists and their admittance to art schools. Whereas Valadon had been an outlier in Europe, for Republican-period female artists who chose to work in modernist styles, painting the female nude was the norm.

NUDE AMBITION: PAINTING THE FEMALE NUDE AS FEMINIST ACTION

It might be assumed that Chinese female artists who painted the female nude simply followed the lead of their male contemporaries, however, these ambitious women found additional incentives. The congruence of their own growing professionalization and the emergence of the nude as fine art not only gave women as artists entry to the practice and its imbricated modernist ideology, it also generated perspectives beyond those supplied by their male contemporaries. Theoretical essays published at this time by women artists themselves attach special significance to the female form and tie their act of painting the female nude to a feminist agenda.

The Ladies' Journal July, 1929, issue in honor of the First National Art Exhibition provides insights into women artists' views on painting nudes. A momentous undertaking for the nation, the exhibition also served as a milestone for Chinese women artists, as at least two dozen earned a spot in the event. As discussed in chapter 1, the special issue features biographies for some of these female artists and reproductions of many artworks by both male and female contributors, including five paintings and one sculpture of female nudes. The issue also includes articles on the arts, and some of these are written by female artists, such as Tao Cuiying 陶粹英 (n.d.), then art director in the School of General Education at Central University (Zhongyang Daxue 中央大學), who expound art theory and practice.

For Tao Cuiying, like Ni Yide, the youthful female was the appropriate subject of figure painting. In her essay "Women's Physical Development and the Techniques of Figure Painting," she concentrates on women's physical forms and the artist's relationship to the model. She provides historical perspective by contrasting ancient notions of beauty in the West and the East—characterizing Western artists as focused on the bodies of voluptuous women while China's artists solely considered the beauty of a woman's face with no concern for the condition of her body—observations with direct bearing on her concern for the physical condition of the model.[54] Tao insists that, no matter how talented the artist, the beauty of a figure painting relies on the healthful beauty of the model. Thus, the first half of Tao's article concentrates on female models and instructs them on the proper cultivation of a healthy physique, though she opined that the fledgling state of Chinese women's [healthful] beauty meant that it was still nearly impossible to find a sufficiently beautiful model.[55] In the latter half of her essay, Tao Cuiying turns from the subject of the painting to its creator and gives the artist concrete instruction on how to render the figure, specifically how to attain proper proportions, coloration, and three-dimensionality—artistic priorities similar to those noted by Clarke in his study of Tao's male peers. These concerns align with those in Ni Yide's essay as well, but Tao's essay diverges from Ni in a major respect—the assumed gender of the reader. Tao Cuiying's article was written for a special art edition of a magazine for women and, as she was herself was an oil painter, we can assume she wrote with female artists in mind. Objecting to traditional Chinese painting's depictions of frail physiques concealed beneath heavy robes, Tao positioned the introduction of the Western figure painting tradition as a means to liberate women from unhealthy body ideals. If an artist such as Tao demanded beautiful models to work from, and the beauty of those models depended on healthy lifestyles, then the practice of painting the fine art nude held the power to improve the lives of Chinese women. Her advice to models on how to cultivate a healthy body could just as easily be directed to any woman, even the female artist. By addressing women on both sides of the easel, female model and female artist, Tao collapses the boundaries between the two.

Jin Qijing's "Women and Art" is equally illuminating.[56] Jin's article, which is discussed in the Introduction, is an appeal to China's female artists that they use professionalization to commandeer their own social progress. In this same essay, Jin argues that women hold a special relationship with the Arts. She credits women with an intuition for art that is rooted in their emotional nature, and to illustrate her point she provides a brief and highly selective survey of the Western world's symbolic imagery of women. She praises the positive feminine traits of Greek sculptures of Venus and proclaims the Renaissance and Leonardo da Vinci's *Mona Lisa* to be the rebirth of feminine charm, equating these images with women's contributions to art. More interesting is her report on women in the exhibition, which encompasses both women artists and images of women. More than one quarter of the eighty Japanese entries depict women, she notes, while all of the Chinese examples of Western-style figure painting feature women.[57] Meanwhile, women artists dazzled attendees, who she describes as shocked to see that the women's brilliance was on par with that of their male colleagues. As outstanding examples, she cites Pan Yuliang, Cai Weilian, and Wang Jingyuan. Jin decides that the content of the exhibition, along with the audience's favorable reception of images of female nudes, illustrates the deep connection between women and art and serves as firm evidence of how essential women are to the field.[58] She declares that, though most people now recognize women's equal standing in society and the arts, in the past women were kept dependent on men and unable to develop their personalities or stimulate their minds. Now that they were entering the public sphere and seeking occupations, women could bloom in the lofty arenas of literature, music, and the arts. Like Tao, Jin also directs women to turn their attention back on themselves, so that they might dispel their inner vanity, rise up, and seize the "golden key" of art.[59]

Invoking Western cultural authority, Tao Cuiying and Jin Qijing link the female nude to the contributions of their gender to art and society. Though Tao focuses on issues of women's health and Jin on women artists achieving parity with men in the arts, both authors turn to the nude painting genre as a means of elevating the position of Chinese women. Thus, in the minds of these two women artists, producing images of nude women was not to be avoided but energetically encouraged. Working to advance the genre in the same way as men, these women understood themselves to be participating as equals and as revolutionizing women's status within their profession. Both discuss the painting of female nudes by women as a reflection of the artists' own accomplishments and ask female readers to consider their own lives in relation to the painted nudes. Blurring the boundary between artist, subject, and female viewer, they see nude paintings as affording their readers mirror-like views and encouraging self-reflection.

The theme of women contemplating themselves is a strong undercurrent in this issue, participating in a global predilection for the motif of the mirror-gazing beauty, but to divergent ends. Among the exhibition's many images of nude figures reproduced within the issue (the majority of which are female) are Terauchi Manjirō's *Mirror (Jing* 鏡) and Ishikawa Toraji's *After the Bath (Yu hou* 浴後), each featuring a disrobed woman seated by a mirror.[60] The male Japanese artists likely intended their paintings of the "woman with mirror" trope to tie into traditional Western symbolism of feminine primping and vanity, but the issue's editors show no indication of sharing this reading of the two images. Instead, recent revived interest in an indigenous, female Narcissus likely colored the Chinese reception of these images. Between 1922 and 1935, prominent social critic, editor, eugenicist, and Confucian revivalist, Pan Guangdan 潘光旦 (1899–1967) produced multiple psychoanalytical studies on the Ming-dynasty poetess Feng Xiaoqing 馮小青 (1595–1612), the first of which was published in *The Ladies' Journal.*[61] In his studies, Pan concludes that Feng, who was only seventeen years old at the time of her death, suffered from a fatal case of narcissism brought on by traditional Chinese culture's social and sexual repression of women. While readers may have thrilled at the suggestion of autoeroticism inherent in Pan's version of Feng's tale, they also would have understood her story as a parable of a woman choosing to value herself in the face of adversity.[62] By repackaging Feng's fate as a defiant act of self-love, Pan lays forth a damning critique of traditional Chinese society's senseless repression of human nature (specifically female sexuality) and its wholesale waste of female talent.

Pan Yuliang's pastel painting, *Reflection*, depicting a seated nude gazing into a mirror, then, is yet another reprisal of the old visual trope of a mirror-gazing woman but to new effect. Her seven-year education in Europe ensures her familiarity with the Western tradition, yet the mirror in her painting suggests neither a woman's vanity nor a voyeuristic eye. Rather, in Pan's reappropriation of the trope we find a personification of the self-reflection beseeched by Tao and Jin. The deflated posture and wistful expression of the figure enact the title, the first half of the idiom *guying zilian* 顧影自憐, which describes the melancholy of feeling unappreciated.[63] The critic Li Yuyi 李寓一 (n.d.), a coeditor of the issue and repeat contributor to *The Ladies' Journal*, supplies a positive interpretation of the painting, however, by reading it as an image of self-affirmation. Li dedicates a separate page of text to the image and its maker, which he opens with the quote, "Others do not cherish me, I cherish myself!"[64] The melodramatic line casts Pan Yuliang's painting as a scene of introspection and confirmation in line with the idiom implied by the painting's title.[65] He further compares the image to the *Mona Lisa* and applauds the artist's ability to convey profound sentiment. His comparison underscores the contemplative nature of Pan's nude but also designates the painting as a masterpiece and affirms its painter as an artist on par with the painting masters of the Italian Renaissance.

Li's analysis of *Reflection* coupled with the articles by Jin and Tao frame the special issue as plea for women to develop an appreciation of their own self-worth and leverages the female nude as a tool for that effort. Woman has become her own muse. As presented in *The Ladies' Journal*, the most popular and enduring women's magazine of the Republican period, Pan Yuliang's female nude turns accountability back onto woman herself, asking her to value herself and determine her own fate. Tao's and Jin's essays instructed Chinese women as to why their well-being mattered and how they could improve their futures. One could well say that, for modernist women painters of the Republican period, the nude signified not only a means to promote progress within the art community and a vehicle for individual female artists' ascent from professional obscurity but also a way to elevate the nation's women as a whole.

DISILLUSIONMENT AND DECLINE

By the late 1920s, an active dialogue on the nude painting genre concentrated on the cultivation of aesthetic appreciation according to modern sensibilities, the achievement of the perfection of form, and by extension the physical health of the model. While the painting of nude bodies may have been a modern gesture for many Chinese artists, for some female artists painting the female nude was also part of their participation in a women's art movement. The potent symbolic value of the female nude—invested with the power to stimulate a Chinese renaissance according to contemporary modernist art ideology—presented women artists with the opportunity to contribute to the modernization of their nation and the liberation of their countrywomen. For female artists of Pan Yuliang's generation, the nude signified their special and authoritative claim to art and could serve as a vehicle for self-reflection and change. For them, the question was not whether to paint the nude but how to create masterful paintings of female nudes, and they accordingly took up the subject matter as a reflection of their talents and a symbol of their parity with their male colleagues.

Judging from a survey of print media, the year 1934 marks the zenith of the female nude in Republican-period popular culture. By the following year, interest in nude imagery had markedly declined.[66] Appearances of nudes in popular media grew increasingly sporadic, although the catalog for the Second National Exhibition of Chinese Art records continued interest within the art world.[67] Outside of the life drawing studios, however, the lustrous promise of the genre had begun to tarnish. Representing an emergent second-generation feminist view of the female nude, satirical cartoons by younger female artists question the genre from a peripheral perspective and work to displace its authority. Liang Baibo's comical depiction of an artist's chagrin at his daughter's mimicry of the artworks lining his studio's walls brings home the hypocrisy hidden in the idealistic rhetoric about the genre (fig. 3.9). Yu Feng's cartoon of a male artist's undue demands upon an impoverished and emaciated female model critiques the exploitative class distinctions underpinning the romanticized artist/muse relationship (fig. 3.10). (See chapter 4 for more information on both of these artists.) Meanwhile, during the protracted buildup to the Second Sino-Japanese War, societal pressure for women to strengthen the nation as "good housewives and wise mothers" led to more restrictive definitions of modern womanhood and reduced tolerance for those who would refuse to conform to conservative expectations. Antithetical to the morality-driven reform movement that was sweeping the nation, the

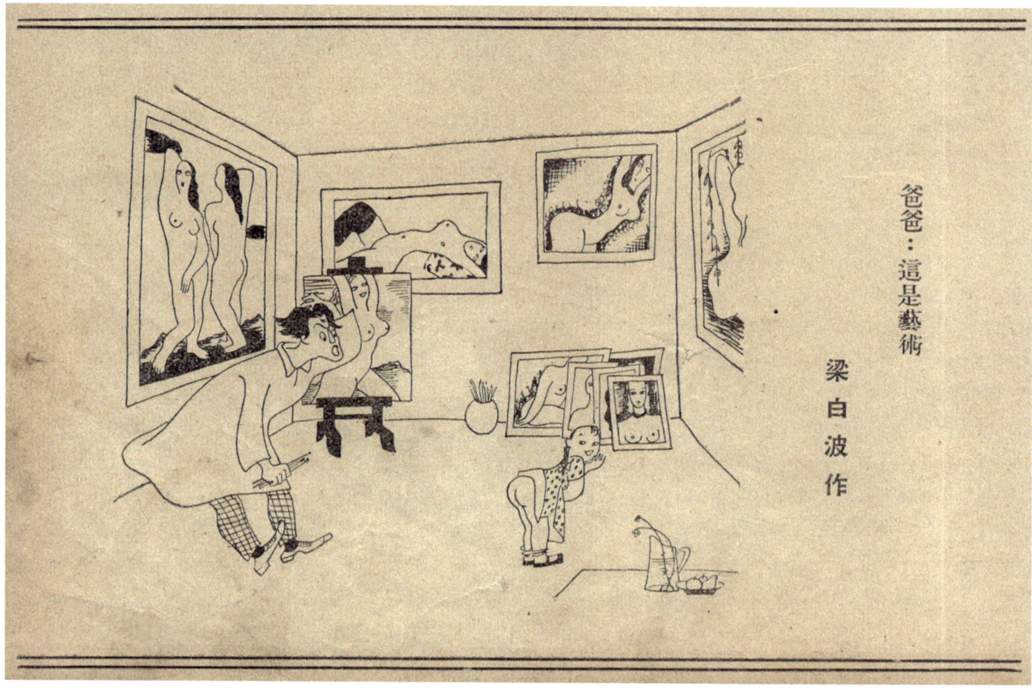

3.9 Liang Baibo, cartoon of a little girl and her artist father. The caption reads, "Daddy, this is art." *Rensheng huabao* [*Life Pictorial*] 2, no. 1 (1935): 17.

nude evaporated from public view nearly overnight.

Pan Yuliang, however, continued painting and publishing her images of nudes—right until her departure from China in 1937. Pan was never to return, but in Paris she continued to paint and draw the female nude for the remainder of her career. Meanwhile, in China, as images of the female nude dwindled, so did the careers of women as artists. With the decline of modernism and the ascendance of social realism came a turn to war cartoons and the use of art as propaganda. Chapter 4 discusses how the few women artists who managed to remain professionally active did so because they switched their attention to the increasingly urgent war effort, largely leaving off gender negotiations in favor of taking action for the national cause. Rather than performing the identity of the Modern Girl or New Woman, which had been the standard persona of a professional female artist, they took up the role of willing martyr for the nation.

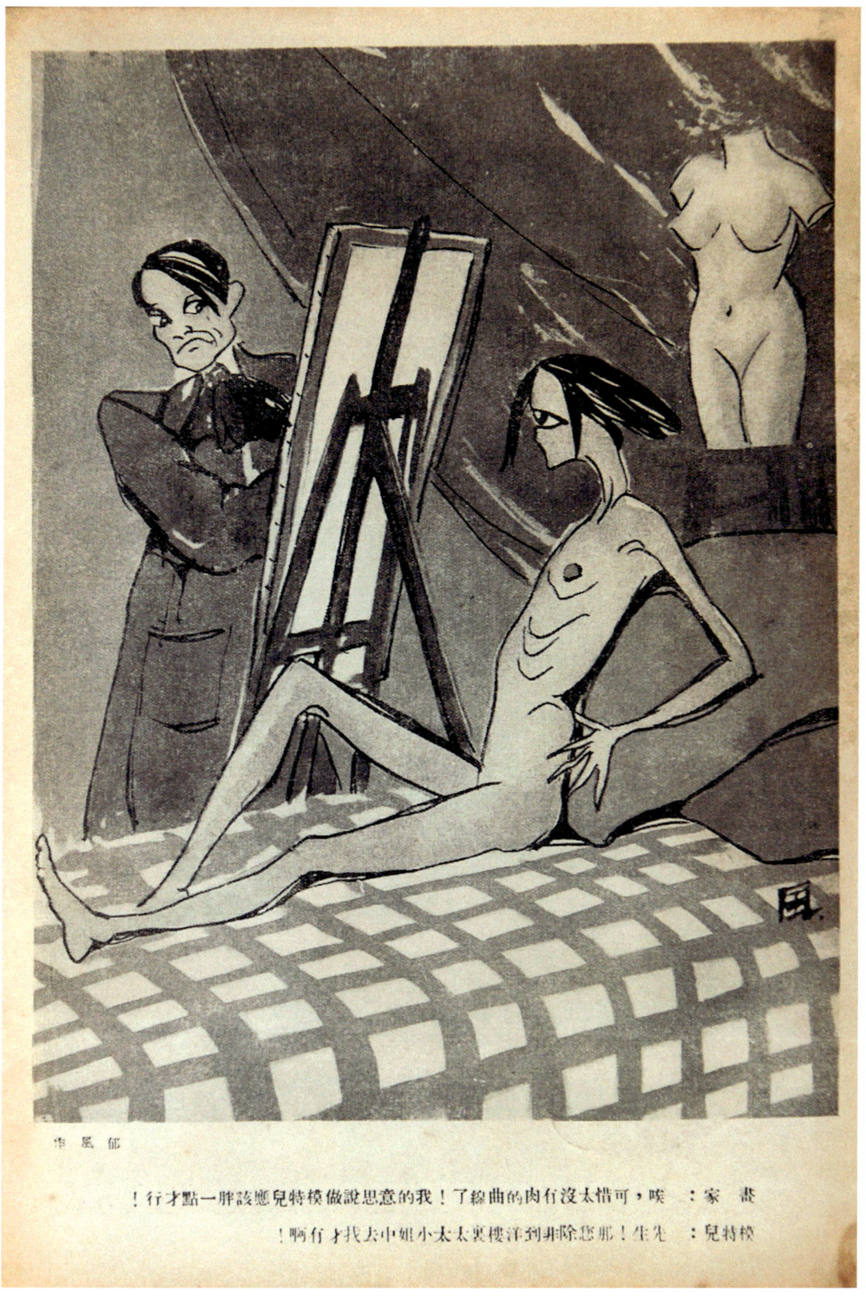

3.10 Yu Feng, cartoon of emaciated model and disapproving artist. *Shidai manhua* 24 (December 20, 1935). Caption reads: "Artist: 'Oh, what a pity there really are no fleshy curves! What I mean to say is, to be a model you should be a bit fatter!' Model: 'Sir! You'll find that only if you go look among the ladies living in mansions!'" Courtesy of the artist's son Huang Dagang.

——在南京

隊長葉淺予繪「擁護領袖」

Yih Chien-Yu, the famous cartoonist of "Mr. Wang's" fame, also the captain of the group, with his drawing.

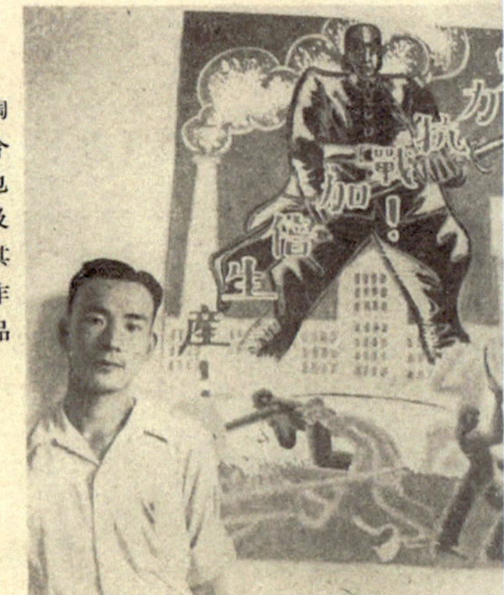

陶今也及其作品

Tao Ching-Yah and his work.

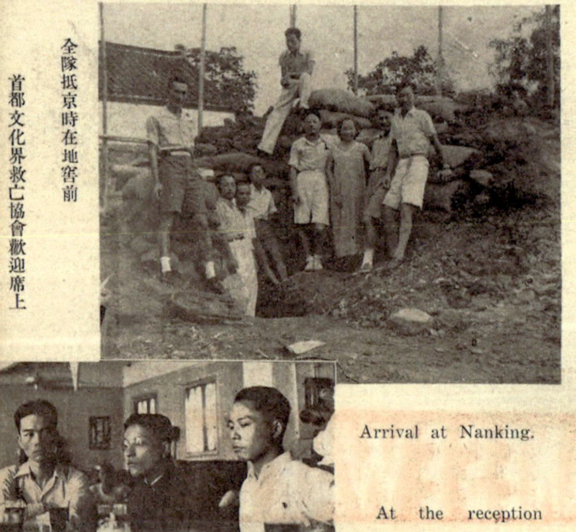

全隊抵京時在地窖前

Arrival at Nanking.

首都文化界救亡協會歡迎席上

At the reception party by the local artists.

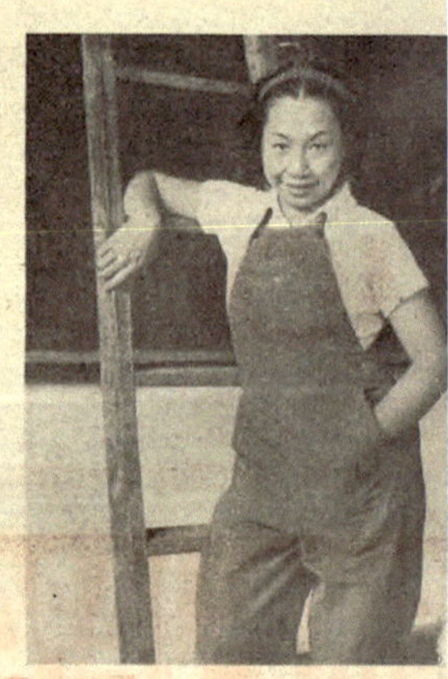

梁白波在小學教室內向學生擬作黑板宣傳

Miss Liang Bai-Poh ready exhibit before school students

4

Embattled Careers

"Oh, can't our female painters descend from the Ivory Tower? How the outside world is shouting, clamoring, struggling, whirling, roaring! Really, isn't this a bit more important than *Peonies, Lake Scenery*, and so on?"[1]

THOUGH THESE LINES from the 1931 article "Meishu jie: Zhongguo xin huajia 美術界：中國新畫家 [Art World: China's New Painters]" conclude an entry dedicated to Guan Zilan, the criticism addresses Chinese women artists at large. Bifurcated in its assessment, the larger essay on the one hand describes the vibrancy of Guan's paintings in glowing terms, noting their elegance and youthful vitality. Guan herself is described as hardworking and her artworks praised for their ability to resonate with the viewer and evoke an emotional response.[2] On the other, the essay also regards work like Guan's as ill-suited to the era, irrelevant for their failure to respond to the tremendous upheaval of the times. Pressing for social realism in art, the author disapproved of the pursuit of art for art's sake given the country's ongoing sociopolitical struggles and impending war with Japan. What good is it to offer even the most praiseworthy rose, the author reasons, in the midst of famine and disaster?

Liang Baibo with the Cartoonists Association for National Salvation (detail of fig. 4.7).

Formalist artworks, of course, were hardly the exclusive purview of female artists. In the same year this article appeared, the mostly male members of the newly organized Storm Society drafted their manifesto based on pure color and shapes. While Guan Zilan may have been a special target of criticism based on stereotypes of female frivolity, the critique taps into the broader call for the reformation of art on the eve of the Second Sino-Japanese War (1937–45) that would spell the end of modernism a few years later. Beyond the pending extinction of modernist art in China—a development that threatened the careers of all artists who approached their work chiefly as a form of creative expression—women artists also faced the evaporation of their access to professional opportunities. While political directives demanded her return to the household and to serve the nation in a unified front of homemakers and caregivers, socioeconomic struggles in a time of national catastrophe pressured her to forego her career in favor of supporting her husband's.

This chapter explores the manifold constraints increasingly exerted on professional Chinese woman artists in the late 1930s, from the push to abandon modernism to the loss of professional opportunities. I begin with an overview of the adversity modernist artists experienced as a community and then document the unrelenting and all-encompassing challenges women in particular faced, using Qiu Ti's experiences as a war refugee as an illustrative example. I then consider the wartime careers of three of her contemporaries, reconstructing the conditions in which they worked and highlighting some of the artworks that they produced. Fang Junbi 方君璧 (1898–1986) took up the role of martyr's widow and supported a Japanese collaborationist regime through art exhibitions for cultural exchange and charity. Liang Baibo 梁白波 and Yu Feng 郁風 (1916–2007), in contrast, traveled to the front lines as anti-Japanese propaganda cartoonists and gender-equality advocates. Each of these three reinvented herself as an activist and, through the production and display of her art, publicly performed selfless dedication to the cause of national salvation. Though the two divergent camps of their political affiliations could not be more opposed, all three artists maintained their careers by the similar means of political activism.

THE BEGINNING OF THE END

Growing nationalism under the threat of war and the art world's turn to greater societal accountability precipitated the demise of modernist art in China. As artists were increasingly expected to produce work that could lead the nation to salvation, domestic interest in international art styles waned dramatically. Kuiyi Shen notes the ailing state of Chinese modernist art in the mid 1930s and explains that:

> . . . modernism with its strong focus on the individual imagination became a luxury to the Chinese people. Whether to the Communists or Nationalists, art that manifested the slightest tendency toward modernism was regarded as displaying a "formalism" that was divorced from the people. It was impossible for these modernists, whose ultimate goal was individuality and pure art, to bear the heavy burden of social responsibility that required using their art as a means to rescue the country.[3]

Simultaneously, the general population experienced rising disenchantment with the perplexities of the modern lifestyle and a pessimistic trend pervaded popular culture.[4] This pessimistic tone permeated the art world and, compounded with the lack of interest in modernist self-expression and ever more limited resources, led to significant changes in the course of oil painting in China. Thus, on the heels of the Japanese invasion in 1937 came a new turn in *xihua* that shared none of the giddy modernist enthusiasm of the 1920s and early 1930s but instead reflected the dismal reality of the downtrodden and displaced masses.[5]

The Storm Society became a casualty of this evolving social climate; its members unable to make ends meet, the group disbanded in 1935. It was not the only avant-garde painting association to experience hardship at this time of increasing conservatism and nationalism. The Chinese Independent Art Association (Zhonghua Duli Meishu Xiehui 中華獨立美術協會), a modernist painting society based in Guangzhou, suffered a similar fate.[6] The association, founded in Tokyo in 1934, was made up of several Cantonese artists studying in Japan and a few Japanese artists. Its members painted in styles as diverse as the Storm Society's and especially favored the styles of surrealism, fauvism, and cubism. Freshly returned from Japan in 1935, the group published a journal titled *Duli meishu* 獨立美術 (Independent Art), the very first issue of which disseminated the group manifesto. In many ways the Chinese Independent Art Association manifesto echoed the sentiment expressed in the Storm Society's manifesto of a few years earlier. Similarly citing inspiration from art movements abroad, the Guangzhou group's manifesto proclaims its dedication to pure art and the freedom of creative expression for a new age in China. That same year, the group staged two exhibitions with the first occurring in Guangzhou in March and the second—which was costaged with the Storm Society's fourth group show—in Shanghai in October.[7] As with the Storm Society, the Chinese Independent Art Association's October 1935 exhibition was to be the group's final show. Their nonobjective art ill-suited for the nationalistic climate and dire social concerns, the group disbanded in 1937.

Likewise, women's careers outside the home increasingly became viewed as reprehensively indulgent. Calls for women to adhere to conservative social models grew more strident as the nationalist government enacted a multifaceted social engineering campaign. In 1934 under Chiang Kai-shek, the Nationalist government in Nanjing initiated the New Life Movement (*xin shenghuo yundong* 新生活運動)—a broad social reform effort based on a mix of Confucian thought, nationalist rhetoric, and authoritarian directives regarding personal hygiene and appearance. The government also proclaimed that same year the Women's National Products Year (*funü guohuo nian* 婦女國貨年), which—as the second in a succession of national products years—was part of a larger antiforeign goods campaign and expressly targeted the consumption habits of China's female population.[8] The government-backed movement strove to push women back into the domestic space, where they were expected to abandon Modern Girl ways and reprise the role of Good Wife and Wise Mother.[9] The divide between gender roles widened, with women channeled into roles facilitating the militarization of society, such as nursing, teaching, and, of course, raising the next generation of good citizens and brave soldiers.

The patriotic domestication of modern women's activities that began in the mid 1930s, however, was not met without resistance. Voicing opposition to the directive, one 1937 issue of *Jiating zazhi* 家庭雜誌 [*Household Magazine*] features three photographs of women seated outdoors, including an image of Zhong Duqing, Guan Zilan's friend (mentioned in chapter 1), taken during her study in France.[10] The accompanying text protests that women, having responded to the earlier call to join the public sphere, would not be so quick or so docile as to meekly return to the home. Noting that "although now there are once again some people who advocate driving them back home," women already held a variety of social roles and careers, and "despite their differing social positions none of them is shy in response any longer."[11] That a periodical devoted to the domestic sphere ran such a protestation gives some indication of the heavy-handedness with which women were pressured to return to traditional roles of servitude and subjugation. The article, which also reasons that change cannot be expected to occur overnight, speaks to how the gendered redivision of social roles in the prelude to war was perceived as abrupt and unjust.

The Second Sino-Japanese War, for its part, spurred great artistic activity and tremendous cultural change. Popular subject matter shifted toward representations of ethnic minorities and rural areas; that is, to the very populations and regions that artists encountered during their time as refugees in China's interior. Two traditional Chinese media—woodblock printmaking and ink painting—experienced revivals, thanks in large part to their affordability and portability. And throughout this period the artistic community engaged in theoretical debate about the purpose of art. Continuing an extended discussion begun in the previous decade, during the war years popular opinion swung dramatically toward the use of art for social good.

Irrespective of the vitality of the artistic world during this period, wartime delivered a major blow to women's careers as professional artists. Following unprecedented occupational gains in the early twentieth century, Chinese women witnessed the hardships of wartime unravel their accomplishments and undermine even the most persistent of career efforts. Impoverished living conditions and the constant threat of air raids reduced many women's activities to supportive roles while male artists monopolized professional resources and recognition. Men claimed first choice among scarce employment opportunities, which might involve long stretches of rugged travel through China's interior. For those women artists who were married and had begun families, such job conditions proved impossible. Many put their personal career aspirations aside and concentrated on the welfare of their families and the day-to-day necessities of refugee life.[12] Such was the case for Chen Zhixiu 陳芝秀 (1908–70), who had studied sculpture in

France but was forced to follow her husband Chang Shuhong's dream career of documenting the Mogao Cave Temples in Dunhuang in 1943. Paris-trained Su Ailan 蘇愛蘭 (1905?–1985) likewise gave up her career in order to nurture Fang Ganmin's. Other women artists simply did not survive; Cai Weilian's promising career was cut short when she died of puerperal fever from lack of medical care following childbirth in 1939.

Qiu Ti's wartime experience typifies the hardship encountered by female modernist artists in wartime China. The avant-garde oil painter and once prominent member of the Shanghai art scene (see chapter 2) struggled to maintain her career following the dissolution of the Storm Society. When Japan declared war in 1937, she and her husband fled inland with their two infant children, and the entire family spent the next decade as refugees. Undertaking a lengthy exodus with multiple relocations, Qiu Ti's migration deep into China's interior and back again involved more than a half-dozen moves. Finally, she and her family settled in Shanghai in 1948.

Qiu Ti's travails as a refugee forced her to sacrifice her own career ambitions in order to support the family's main source of income. She took care of household duties in whatever home her family could find and her husband sought employment through relocated universities and museums.[13] On at least one occasion—when Pang Xunqin left for a three-month research trip to a remote area of Guizhou in the winter of 1939—she endured alone as the sole caretaker of the home and their children. When her husband struggled to finish his book *Gongyi meishu ji* 工藝美術集 *(Collection of Arts and Crafts)*, she again had to give up painting altogether in order to take over all household duties.[14] During this extended period, Qiu Ti only occasionally managed to reassert her professional expertise outside the home. She briefly held a teaching position at Sichuan Chengdu Shengli Yishu Zhuanke Xuexiao 四川成都省立藝術專科學校.[15] Unlike her husband, who put on five independent exhibitions while in Sichuan (or, one almost every year they were there), Qiu Ti only once exhibited her paintings. Hanging her work alongside her husband's at Pang Xunqin's 1941 show, Qiu Ti doubtless came across as little more than the wife of the artist.[16] Thus, while her husband continued his professional career as an artist and teacher, for Qiu Ti basic domestic chores—such as keeping her family clothed, fed, and safe in locations without electricity or running water—became her full-time job. As she nurtured her family through an extended period of extreme hardship, Qiu Ti's career as an oil painter slipped into oblivion. More than aware that all housework and heavy burdens fell mainly to her, she often complained that she had no time to paint or maintain a career.[17] The end of her profession as a modernist painter was not by her own choice.

Like Qiu Ti, the brilliant architectural historian Lin Huiyin (林徽因 1903–55) exerted all her energies on keeping her family fed and clothed during the war years in western China—and watched her own career evaporate while her husband Liang Sicheng found work with the relocated Institute for Research in Chinese Architecture. In the 1930s and 1940s, Lin Huiyin wrote a series of letters to her friends Chinese art historian Wilma Fairbank and her husband sinologist John K. Fairbank describing the misery of refugee life in war-torn, rural Yunnan and Sichuan.[18] For Lin Huiyin, who had received a degree from the University of Pennsylvania in 1927 and, following her return to China, briefly taught in the Architecture Department at Northeastern University (Dongbei Daxue 东北大学), the life she was now forced to live caused her utter frustration. In one letter she explains, "Whenever I am engaged in household chores, I feel what a waste of time it is, thinking that I am neglecting more interesting and more important people whom I do not know."[19] On top of living in constant fear of Japanese air raids and being unable to buy basic provisions due to extreme inflation, in the fall of 1939 Lin Huiyin had to manage the household alone while her husband led a six-month research trip of temple architecture in remote parts of Sichuan. Describing her daily routine, she writes:

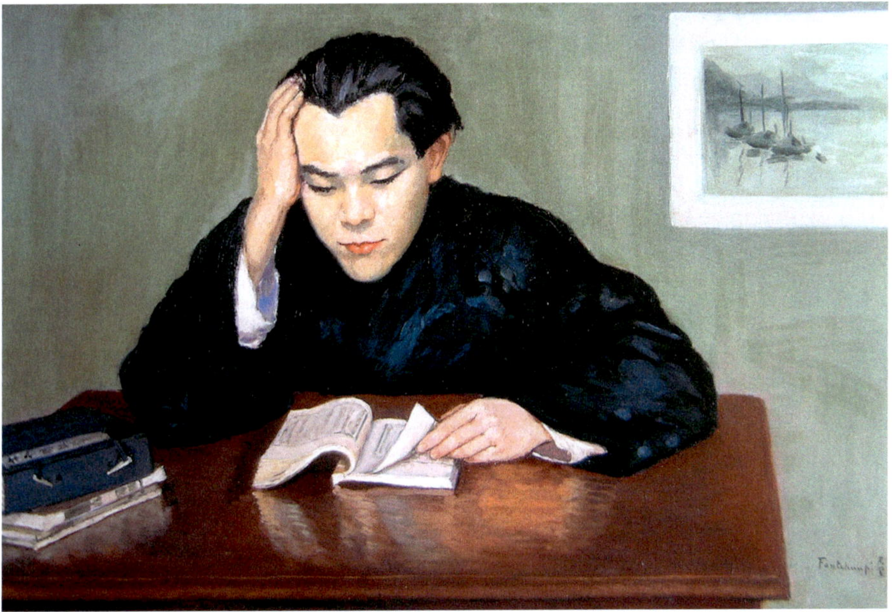

4.1 Fang Junbi, *Portrait of Zeng Zhongming*, 1930. Oil on canvas, 28½ in. × 46½ in. Published as *Studying* (*Dushu*). Courtesy of the artist's son Wen-ti Tsen.

> I get up to scrub and slave, then to buy and cook, then to tidy and wash, then to feel like hell, and have no time to feel at all between the three difficult meals, and then finally to ache and groan again back to bed wondering why I have lived. That is all.[20]

Lin Huiyin's letters give remarkable clarity to not just the miserable living conditions she experienced during the war years, but also what life must have been like for Qiu Ti and so many other women who once had cultivated stylishly modern and independent lifestyles.[21] Recognizing the inequities she faced and attempting to reconcile herself to her fate, in one letter Lin Huiyin reasons, "The worst thing I can do is let myself in for bitterness. I am born a woman and it is wartime."[22] Previously an accomplished poet and writer of fiction, she had lost contact with her friends in literary circles. Overwhelmed with the stress of war and the arduous demands of maintaining some semblance of a home, she frequently fell desperately ill. Not surprisingly, whenever she managed to find the time, Lin Huiyin delighted in the escapism of researching and collaborating with her husband. In a 1943 letter she relates that managing the household was a much bigger burden "than writing a whole chapter on Sung, Liao, and Chin architectural developments or an attempt to reconstruct pictures of the Sung capitals. Both these are jobs I have done with interest and conscientiousness for Sicheng while he was busy over other parts of his writing."[23] In the end, however, her husband alone typically received credit for their joint work.[24]

Although the exigencies of war paralyzed the careers of most women in the visual arts, a few undertook propaganda art projects as a means to remain active in the field. Their activities reveal their individual engagement with the war effort as well as their personal interest in national concerns about the welfare of China and its people. Though these women served opposing sides, they enlisted their artworks for propagandistic purpose and in so doing salvaged their careers. Such is the case with Fang Junbi's oil painting *Studying* (*Dushu* 讀書), which was published with this title in 1930 but was to have special significance to her career over a decade later (fig. 4.1).

THE GOOD WIFE: FANG JUNBI AS PATRIOTIC WIDOW

Fang Junbi's *Studying* would not seem an obvious propaganda piece. At first glance, it bears the hallmarks of the *wenren* 文人 (literati) genre: a gentleman in his study, with a monochromatic landscape beside him, reads a volume of classical prose, the Qing-dynasty compilation *Guwen guanzhi* 古文觀止. And yet upon closer inspection the portrait of the intellectual is not typical at all. The image near him is not a spread-out scroll but a framed black-and-white photograph hanging on the wall. The beveled edges of the desk on which he rests his elbows identify the Western origin of its design. The medium used to depict the sitter is oil on canvas, not traditional ink on paper. And the painting is not one scholar-amateur painter's homage to another of his own kind but a loving portrait of the female painter's husband, Zeng Zhongming 曾仲鳴 (1896–1939). Altogether, the painting presents a synthesis of medium and subject in its combinations of Western and Chinese material culture, as well as conventional literati aspirations with modern cosmopolitanism.[25] This union of familiar Chinese trope and modern signifiers produced a reassuring image in a time of cultural upheaval: here was a man who selectively assimilated modernity into his lifestyle while maintaining a comfortable grasp of his heritage. The painter presented a similar contradiction in the flesh; Fang Junbi possessed an overseas education and a professional career while preserving her wifely dedication to her family.

Fang Junbi painted the portrait in 1930; she had just returned to China and would bear her first child the following year. *Studying* captures a scene of tranquil home life while simultaneously portraying her husband as a man of letters. More than this, however, the painting crystallizes what was to dominate her persona for over a decade: an idealized portrait, not of herself but of her husband. Not coincidentally, her son was to observe decades later, "After 1930, two personae seemed to coexist in her: Fan Tchunpi and Madame [Zeng Zhongming]."[26] Fantchunbi was Fang Junbi's romanized signature for her paintings in oil, and her son's observation implies a conflict between his mother's professional career and the family life she began on her return to China. As we will see, Fang Junbi balanced her career and her responsibilities to her growing family quite successfully—no doubt her personal wealth afforded the hire of domestic assistance. In fact, it was politics and morality campaigns that caused not a split personality so much as a doubled identity, that of the professional artist assuming the concomitant role of chaste widow.

Talented and accomplished, Fang Junbi possessed the credentials and the skills necessary for professional success. She came from a prominent Fuzhou family and at the young age of fourteen joined her older sister to study in Europe, where she was to spend most of the next eighteen years.[27] While in Europe Fang came of age, weathered World War I, and majored in Western painting media and styles at prestigious institutions: entering the Académie Julian in Paris in 1916, the École des Beaux-Arts de Bordeaux in 1917, and the École Nationale Supérieure des Beaux-Arts in Paris in 1920. She began her professional career in Paris, exhibiting two paintings in the Salon de la Société des Artistes Français in 1924: *The Flute Player* and *Portrait of Mlle. H.* (fig. 4.2). Both the artist and her artworks were well received; *The Flute Player* appeared on the cover of the French art magazine, *Les Annales*, and Fang granted multiple interviews. The following year, Fang and her husband returned to China, and she taught oil painting at Guangzhou University and Zhixin College. That same year she met Gao Jianfu, an ink painter of the Lingnan School, and contributed artworks to a charitable arts festival that he had organized. Fang's stay in her homeland was brief, however, and she returned to Paris in 1926. She remained for four more productive years—studying under Paul-Albert Besnard, the principal of the École Nationale Supérieure des Beaux-Arts—and entering four portraits in the 1928 Salon de Tuileries. By the end of her extended stay in Europe, Fang had spent half of her life overseas, where she had received thorough training in Western media and techniques and participated in prestigious exhibitions. These

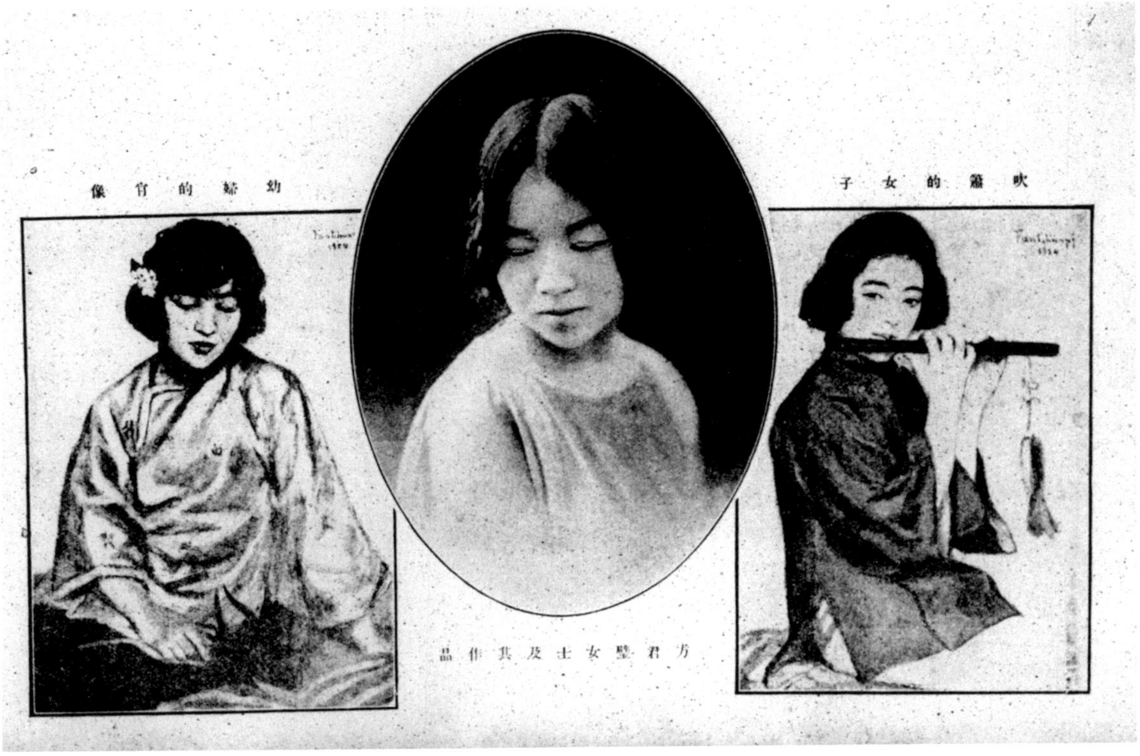

4.2 Fang Junbi's entries in the Salon de la Société des Artistes Français in 1924: *The Flute Player* and *Portrait of Mlle. H.* Published in *The Ladies' Journal* (*Funü zazhi*) 10, no. 9 (1924): 2.

credentials would be cited repeatedly by the Chinese media following her return.

In 1930, the year her son later determined as pivotal, Fang Junbi finally moved back to China. But she did not forsake her artistic practice for a life of domestic duty. Rather, she continued her career even as she raised three young children. In 1932, Fang published an album of her oil paintings, titled *Collection of Fan Tchun Pi's Paintings*, through the Zhonghua Bookstore in Shanghai. Six years later, she published another painting album with a Shanghai publishing house, this time the Commercial Press. The second publication was particularly impressive, as it was printed in color and boasted an introduction written by Cai Yuanpei. In the years between these two albums, Fang also published her artworks in periodicals: her paintings regularly ran in the *China Monthly* (*Zhonghua yuebao* 中華月報), and the July 1934 issue of *Arts & Life* (*Meishu shenghuo* 美術生活) included a full-page, color reproduction of her oil painting of a nude (see fig. 3.2). As these many publications document, Fang Junbi nurtured a high-profile career as a professional artist even after returning to China and starting a family.

During the Sino-Japanese War, however, Fang Junbi's and her husband's political ties dramatically altered both her personal and professional lives. The two had been close friends with husband and wife Wang Jingwei 汪精衛 (1883–1944) and Chen Bijun 陳璧君 (1891–1959) since meeting in Guangzhou in 1912. Wang would become a Japanese collaborator and leader of the Reorganized National Government of China, a puppet state established in Japanese-occupied areas, but in the 1920s and 1930s he was a rising political figure within the Guomindang Nationalist Government. In 1925, the year that Fang Junbi first returned to China, Wang Jingwei rose to the position of chairman of the Nationalist

Government in Guangzhou. Zeng Zhongming from that time assumed the role of Wang's personal secretary and close confidant, and the families of the two men grew increasingly intertwined. When an attempt to assassinate Wang Jingwei in 1939 missed its target, Zeng was killed instead, and Fang Junbi gravely injured in the same spray of gunfire.[28]

Following the death of her husband, Fang Junbi's artistic and political activity intensified. Despite the obvious risks, she remained committed to her friendship with Wang Jingwei and Chen Bijun and to their shared political cause. The year after Wang established the Reorganized National Government of China, Fang launched a series of art exhibitions linked to him and the puppet state. The content and timing of these exhibitions—and their presentation in the occupation news press—unambiguously supported Wang's push for political legitimacy.

Fang staged at least one of these solo exhibitions in Japan in the fall of 1941. Held in mid-October at the Ginza Kōjunsha building in Tokyo, the five-day exhibition contained more than one hundred artworks.[29] A review in the Shanghai weekly *Guomin xinwen zhoukan* 國民新聞周刊 touted it as an event that would advance Sino-Japanese cultural exchange. The article mentions that Fang's son was attending a school in Tokyo and she had timed the exhibition to coordinate with one of her frequent visits to see him. It also describes the content of the exhibition, which was arranged in a large, partitioned exhibition space on the fourth floor of a building located in Japan's most elite commercial district. The artworks included 19 examples of *guohua*, with the remaining 88 paintings categorized as *xihua*. The subjects of the paintings ranged from landscapes to figure paintings, including both nudes and portraits, and the reporter notes that all of the paintings are "remarkably true to life" (*weimiao weixiao* 維妙維肖). The article highlights a few exceptional paintings but pays special consideration to two in particular: a *guohua* artwork titled *Sheng zhai kezi tu* 省齋課子圖 (*Teaching the Son in the Examination Study*), which depicted a young Wang Jingwei receiving his father's instruction and was a memory Wang had requested Fang to paint, and a portrait of Zeng Zhongming, which the reporter selects as the most interesting of the *xihua* works.[30]

The exhibition review pays nearly equal attention to the artist. Fang Junbi, who is immediately described as the wife of Zeng Zhongming in the article's opening sentence, is noted to have worn a gray qipao and black shawl as she greeted guests at the door of the exhibition space. She circulated among them while using both English and Japanese to explain her paintings. The article includes a brief professional biography, which besides praising her as a gentlewoman artist (*guixiu zuojia* 閨秀作家) equal to Marie Laurencin (Luolansang 洛蘭桑), shares that Fang had studied painting in Paris and had her works selected for the Salon des Tuileries (Shalong Daodun 沙龍道頓). The reporter also observes that Fang Junbi is not only famous in China but, because of coverage in Tokyo newspapers, she is similarly well known in Japan. Fang's Tokyo exhibition is said to have aroused considerable excitement in Japanese art circles.

Throughout the article, the particularizing presentation of both the artist and her works lends credence to the Wang Jingwei regime. In its listing of the Japanese individuals who facilitated the exhibition, its observation that the exhibition was well attended, and its assurance that "every single visitor admired Madam Fang's abilities," the article demonstrates Fang's prestige in the occupying nation.[31] Beyond establishing the overseas appreciation of a Chinese artist, Fang's exhibition and its positive reception in Tokyo reassured the reader of Japan's high regard of Wang Jingwei's government. To suit this political agenda, the artworks selected for highest praise were those that imaged the figures most closely associated with the Japanese-backed Reorganized National Government of China. Notably, the imagined portrait of Wang as a filial son, *Sheng zhai kezi tu*, is said to have captivated its Japanese viewers. The news coverage also singles out Fang's portrait of her husband as the most evocative of all her oil paintings and lauds its lifelike appearance. Fang's portrait of her husband, as the reporter shares, evoked the remembrance of Wang's close advisor and his "martyrdom" (*xunguo*

殉國) for "revolution" (*geming* 革命) and the "Peace Movement" (*heping yundong* 和平運動).[32] The article concludes the exhibition, as an instance of "Sino-Japanese cultural exchange" (*Zhongri de wenhua jiaoliu* 中日的文化交流), was "surely not without any benefit," (*ye bu wu biyi ba* 也不無裨益吧), insinuating the strengthening of relations between the two nations to China's own advantage.

Fang Junbi's Tokyo solo show formed part of a touring exhibition with additional venues in Nanjing and Shanghai, each held for the same purpose of bolstering the Wang Jingwei regime.[33] A second article published in *Guomin xinwen zhoukan* describes the three-day Nanjing installation, which began November 30 and was titled the [Nan]Jing Sino-Japanese Cultural Society Exhibition.[34] Once again, Fang—who had arrived in town at the beginning of the month—greeted her guests; she even hosted a private viewing reception the afternoon before the public opening during which she received various dignitaries—both Chinese and Japanese, the article notes—as well as the news reporter. The subsequent newspaper review mentions the inclusion of both old and recent artworks in an exhibition that had grown to encompass more than 130 paintings. Much like the earlier review of the Tokyo exhibition, this article ends with a profile of the artist. She is described as a famous painter in Chinese art circles who has held numerous solo shows in France and China and her teaching position at Guangzhou Zhongshan Daxue is mentioned as well. The exhibition's run in Japan is also detailed and the artist is said to have been lauded by the art community there. Like the review of that exhibition, the review of the Nanjing show similarly identifies her as the wife of Zeng Zhongming at the start of the article's opening sentence; here, however, her husband is more explicitly designated a "Peace Movement martyr" (*heyun xianlie* 和運先烈). The realistic portrait of Zeng Zhongming is exalted once more, described in detail, and yet again proclaimed "remarkably true to life," and the article includes a black-and-white reproduction of the painting. The artwork, it turns out, is none other than Fang Junbi's *Studying*, although the caption now calls it *Portrait of Zhongming* (*Zhongming xiang* 仲鳴像). Though depicting Zeng eight years before his death, within the context of the Japanese and Nanjing exhibitions the painting was now understood to be a commemorative portrait and its subject appropriated and redefined—transforming the sitter from modern-day literatus to enlightened martyr through the repetitious rhetoric of the occupied press.

The following summer, Fang held an exhibition in Guangzhou—her first staged there in over ten years—as part of the Celebrating the Founding of the Guangdong Provincial Government Second Anniversary Cultural Exhibition (*Qingzhu Guangdong sheng zhengfu chengli er zhounian jinnian wenwu zhanlan hui* 慶祝廣東省政府成立二週年紀念文物展覽會), a public event commemorating the Japanese takeover of the city's government. As with the exhibitions of the previous year, the occupied press's coverage of this show sympathizes with the Wang Jingwei government, and this article likewise flatters the administration by celebrating the exhibition and artist—not only observing her credentials, but also particularly noting the number of high-ranking officials in attendance and the widespread appreciation of her artwork.[35] A point of difference, however, is a new emphasis on the artist's individual agency. This article, which is partially an exhibition review and partially an interview of the artist, specifically praises Fang Junbi's commitment to the Peace Movement. The writer mentions Zeng Zhongming but does so to establish a motivation for Fang's self-determined actions.[36] Noting that Fang Junbi had assisted Zeng in his revolutionary contributions (*geming xunlao* 革命勛勞), the article states that she vowed to carry on his mission when he died at the beginning of the Peace Movement. The text, which had already asserted that her lofty character is fully revealed in her artwork, then proceeds to extol Fang's own contributions to the cause. It also provides an explicit purpose for the exhibition when it states that the artist was selling her paintings—which, it is observed, she had never been willing to do before—for the sake of raising charity money for disaster relief. In its detailing of

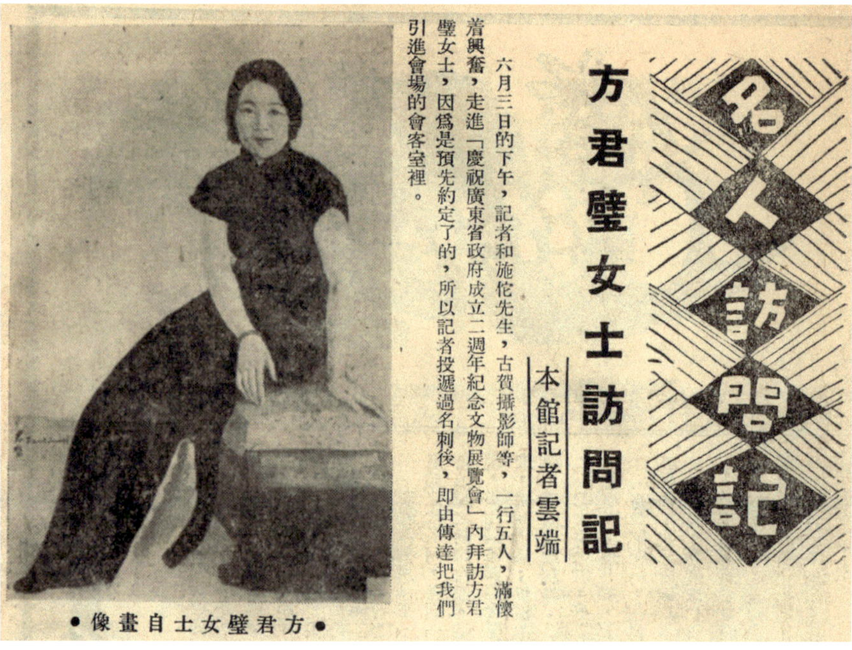

名人訪問記

方君璧女士訪問記

本館記者雲端

六月三日的下午，記者和施佗先生，古賀攝影師等，一行五人，滿懷着興奮，走進「慶祝廣東省政府成立二週年紀念文物展覽會」內拜訪方君璧女士，因爲是預先約定了的，所以記者投遞過名刺後，即由傳達把我們引進會場的會客室裡。

•方君璧女士自畫像•

4.3 Fang Junbi, self-portrait published in *Funü shijie* (*Women's World*) 3, no. 6 (1942): 3.

Fang Junbi's activities and motivations, the article leaves no doubt that her artistic career and political activism were intricately intertwined.

Underscoring the increased emphasis on Fang's own agency, the article's illustration is not an image of her husband, but a black-and-white reproduction of the artist's own self-portrait (fig. 4.3). Her attire fashionable but modest, she wears a fitted, but not overly revealing qipao; its dark fabric conceals her neck and shoulders, its side slit rising just to the height of her bent knees. Fang's pose also follows decorum, she sits with her legs together and to the side, her legs and feet hidden from view, only the toe of one shoe visible beneath the hem of her dress. Fang's body twists to face the viewer directly, her expression open and welcoming, her hair pulled back into a simple style. One arm supports her upright posture, the other crosses in front and conceals her lower body. The artist depicts herself composed and at rest, yet nonetheless alert and ready to spring into action—a model woman of the Reorganized National Government.

As the media coverage of her exhibitions illustrates, following the death of her husband Fang Junbi found her voice in her political activism, and with the explicit intent to elevate the image of the Reorganized National Government, she staged several exhibitions of her artwork. Thus, in the process of lending credibility to Wang Jingwei's government Fang furthered her own professional career. At a time when artists' works were increasingly criticized as frivolous or insufficiently attuned to the suffering of the nation, Fang's artistic practices continued largely unchanged: rather than inspirational scenes of heroism or tragic images of war, her preferred subjects remained pleasant portraits and timeless landscapes. Despite the unchanging nature of Fang's oeuvre, her artworks were appropriated for the national cause and this political use justified the continuation of her own art practice. In this reciprocal relationship with Wang Jingwei's government—her exhibitions validating his regime and these ties to his regime in turn supporting her career—Fang publicly performed the doubled roles of patriotic activist and chaste widow.

Fang Junbi's succession of single-artist exhibitions signal a revived interest in political activism. Fang may have wished to continue her husband's calling after his death, but her own connection to political activism had been longstanding. Her initial awareness of politics likely began in her formative years by watching her activist older siblings: an elder sister had joined a group of anti-Qing empire assassins; an elder brother died as a leader of the 72 Martyrs in Guangzhou in 1911. The following year, the first year of the Republican nation, an adolescent Fang Junbi traveled to Europe with her activist sister, but before leaving, she and her future husband, Zeng, paid their respects to a memorial for the 72 Martyrs, where they first met Wang Jingwei. Years later, on a brief return to China in 1925, and the same year that her husband became secretary to Wang Jingwei, Fang demonstrated her own active interest in politics, this time contributing her artwork to the cause. She exhibited and sold at least one painting at an art festival organized as a fundraiser for the construction of Guangzhou's Sun Yat-sen Memorial Hall.[37] With this history of using her art for political fundraising purposes, Fang publicly declared her dedication to the Peace Movement following her husband's death, as well as her intention to donate profits from the sale of her artworks to a government-backed charity. Thus using her art as a political tool, Fang met with government officials, publicized her activities, and generally groomed herself into a spokesperson for the cause—first exhibiting as a mother and wife, later identifying as a political activist herself.

Ostensibly staged for the good of the nation, Fang Junbi's multiple solo exhibitions also point to the personal affluence and political connections that permitted her a career as a female artist at a time of growing and widespread social conservativism. Chinese women of the late 1930s faced intensifying censure of their lifestyles from all directions. From the mobilization of the Guomindang's New Life Movement beginning in 1934, to Communist pressure for women to abandon self-adornment, to the distribution of visual propaganda in the Provisional Government of the Republic of China (PGROC), politically backed directives expected women to turn away from pleasure and comfort and to embrace moral and ideological rigor instead.[38] The smothering sociopolitical pressure imposed restrictions on women's actions, behavior, and bodies through tactics that, though diverse in origin, were surprisingly uniform in intention and approach. In what Prasenjit Duara characterizes as a "nationalist patriarchy" that stretched across multiple regimes in early twentieth-century China, female virtue became synonymous with the virtue of the nation.[39] Governments portrayed women as the "soul of tradition-within-modernity," thus formulating the ideal of the modern woman with traditional values; women, in turn, legitimized the state as the embodiment of its promise to advance the nation while maintaining the rectitude of traditional morality.[40] Above all else, this state-manufactured ideal conferred greatest value on the traditional feminine virtue of self-sacrifice—both to home and to nation. Jeremy Taylor confirms this authoritarian conscription of women's social identity in his article on the development of gendered archetypes in the PGROC, a puppet regime in occupied north China that was quickly subsumed within the Wang Jingwei government in 1940.[41]

In both of their analyses, Duara and Taylor note the respective regimes' increased emphasis on women's return to domestic roles of wife and mother, but argue that rather than pushing them back into the home states' policies encouraged women to take to the streets as visible political agitators.[42] While it may be accurate to characterize the activities of these women as remaining in the public sphere, their sociopolitical activism should not be confused with access to the professional workplace. As Good Wives and Wise Mothers, women—with the possible exception of those working in care-oriented jobs, such as teaching and nursing—were expected to forego careers in favor of their obligations to the home. Fang's wealth and close relationship with Wang Jingwei, however, allowed her unparalleled opportunities to continue her professional artistic practice while sheltering her from criticism and disdain—so long as she framed her endeavors as patriotic.

News coverage of Fang Junbi, therefore, presents her in ways appropriate to the moral climate. Articles about her exhibitions, besides glorifying

Wang Jingwei and his brush with martyrdom, frame the artist as an exemplary Good Wife and Wise Mother. For example, after stating she had been the wife of Zeng Zhongming, the review of the Tokyo exhibition immediately cites her visit to care for her son during his overseas studies as the reason for her presence in Japan. The review of the Nanjing exhibition similarly opens by labeling her as a widow of Zeng, and the article from Guangzhou frames her activism as undertaken in her husband's honor. Beyond her public performance as chaste widow and loving mother supporting her son's education, Fang's disinterest in financial gain also positions her motives above criticism. With her exhibitions framed as cultural exchanges and goodwill enterprises, Fang is distinguished as an artist who is professional but not commercial. Fang, as the article for the Guangzhou exhibition makes clear, only sells her work for charity.

In this capacity, Fang Junbi deflected sociopolitical pressure to return to the home. Subverting the nationalistic imperative to assume the mantle of Good Wife and Wise Mother, she thereby nurtured her professional career at the height of wartime. Fang's doubled performance as chaste widow of a national martyr and political activist for national cause permitted her to actively maintain her career during the war, but she was not alone. Two other women artists also forwarded their careers in the name of the national good, but they stood on the opposite side of the battlefront.

WOMEN ARTISTS ON THE FRONT LINES: YU FENG AND LIANG BAIBO

In 1938, the same year that Fang Junbi issued a second volume of her paintings, a very different collection of artworks rolled off a press in Guangzhou. *Selection of War of Resistance Masterpieces by the National Cartoonists* (hereafter *War of Resistance Masterpieces*) features over one hundred war cartoons printed in monochromatic ink on yellowing paper.[43] Despite its crude appearance, the publication includes the works of the nation's greatest war cartoonists and may be considered a definitive collection of these artworks.[44] The cartoons, simplistic yet forceful, impart powerful slogans while depicting gruesome casualties of war and touching scenes of camaraderie among resisters. Two women artists contributed to the volume; together, Yu Feng's and Liang Baibo's artworks account for approximately one-tenth of the content.

Younger than Fang Junbi, Yu Feng and Liang Baibo belonged to China's second generation of female artists—Liang having been an infant when Fang first traveled to Europe and Yu not yet born. When Yu and Liang were old enough to pursue artistic training, neither young woman studied abroad; instead, both learned from returned study-abroad graduates in China's now-established art programs. Coming of age amidst the growing threat of Japanese invasion, Yu and Liang both managed to maintain professional careers during the war. Their wartime activities mirroring Fang Junbi's, Yu and Liang likewise exhibited and published their artworks to rally public support for a national cause. Yu's and Liang's sympathies lay with the resistance, however, and they were to create wartime art with a different audience in mind. While Fang Junbi entertained Japanese and Chinese officials at functions supporting the collaborationist government, Yu Feng and Liang Baibo engaged in a guerrilla art movement spearheaded by cartoonists.

Politically conscious from an early age, both Yu Feng and Liang Baibo began publishing satirical cartoons—such as the two mentioned at the end of the previous chapter—early in their careers. The niece of short story writer and poet, Yu Dafu 郁達夫 (1896–1945), Yu Feng studied oil painting first at the Beiping Art School (Beiping Yishu Zhuanke Xuexiao 北平藝術專科學校) and then later under renowned artists Pan Yuliang and Xu Beihong at the National Central University (Guoli Zhongyang Daxue 國立中央大學) in Nanjing. When she returned from her studies to Shanghai in 1935, her uncle introduced her to the art and literature circles and she began publishing her work in leading magazines—including an arresting self-portrait published in *The Young Companion* (fig. 4.4). In it, Yu's

Portrait. By *Miss F. Yue.*

鳳・郁風女士作

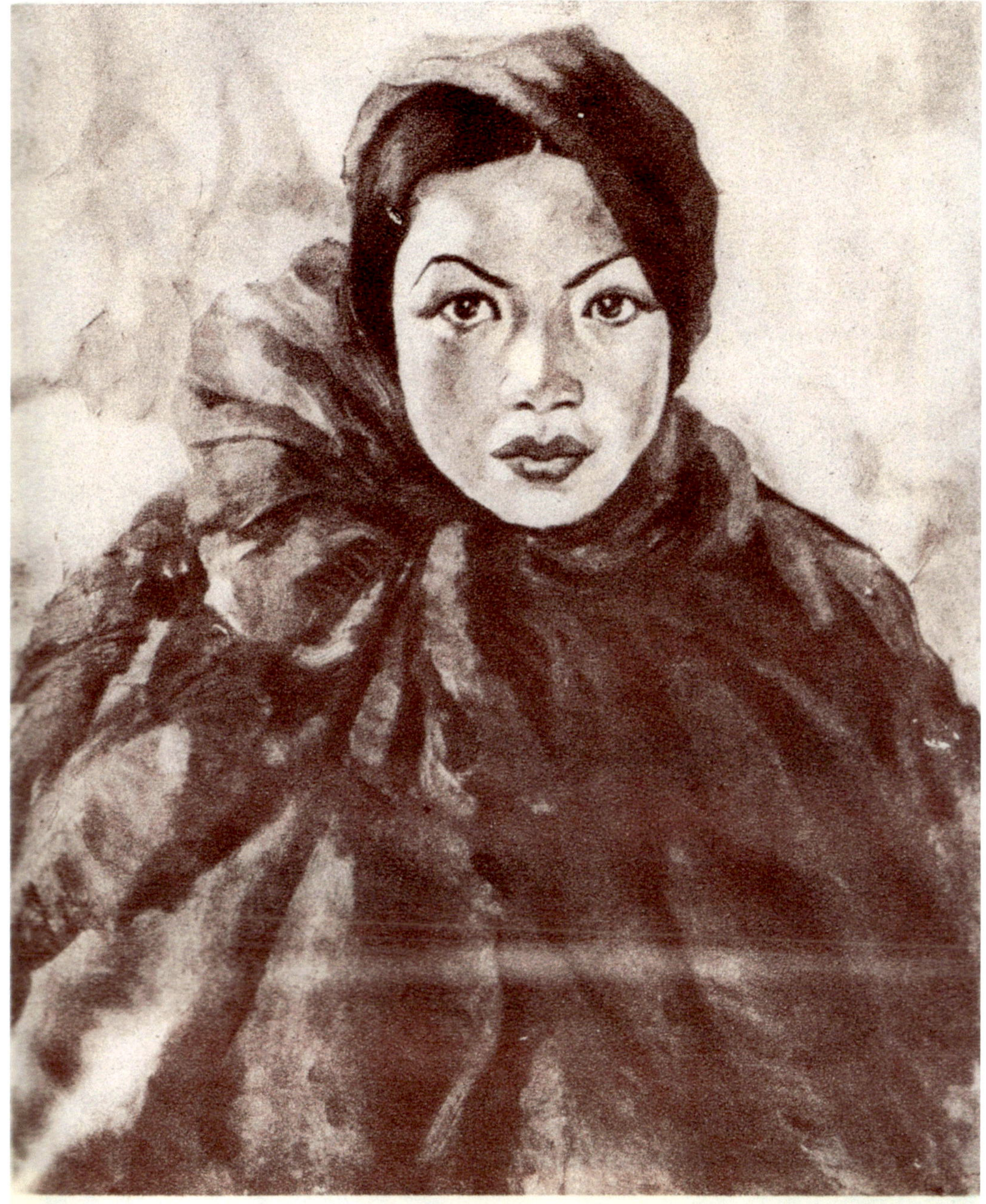

→山水。

羅海空，號落花，粵人，以古文詞詁名噪南服，畫出冷殘居士，山水以墨采靜，花卉以色采靜，均神明煥然，右爲羅之近作。

●

郁風女士，爲文藝家郁達夫先生之姪女公子，作畫瀟洒豪放，筆觸流動，爲現代女畫家之傑出人材，上圖即爲其近作自畫像之一。

●

李仲生氏，我國留日本二科會之新進畫家，以

4.4 Yu Feng, self-portrait published in *The Young Companion*. Courtesy of the artist's son Huang Dagang.

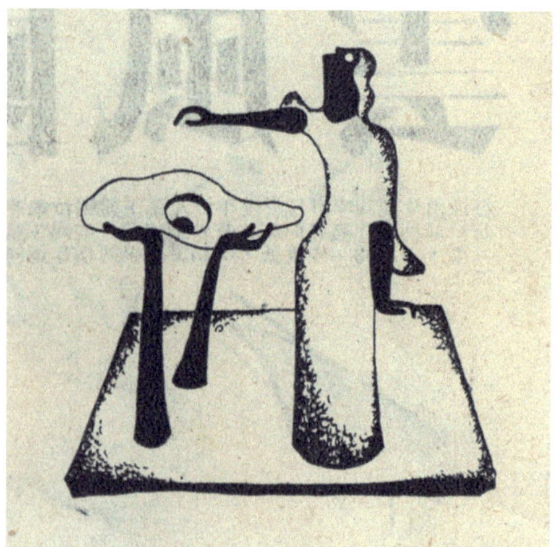

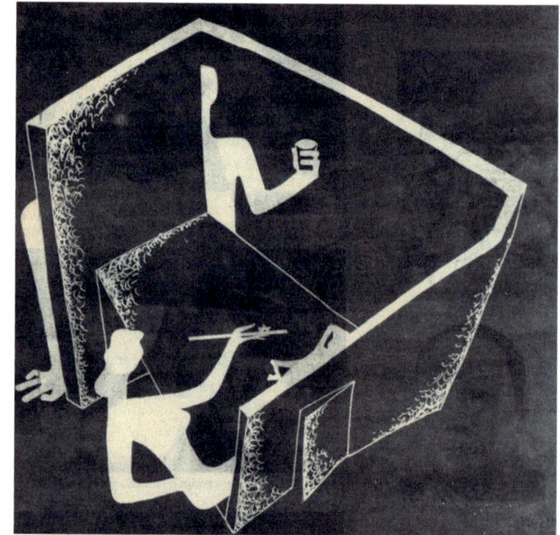

4.5 Liang Baibo's surrealist illustrations for Lin Huiyin's short story, "Hongcai moyan [Inflammation of the Iris]," published in Shidai huabao 8, no. 12 (1935).

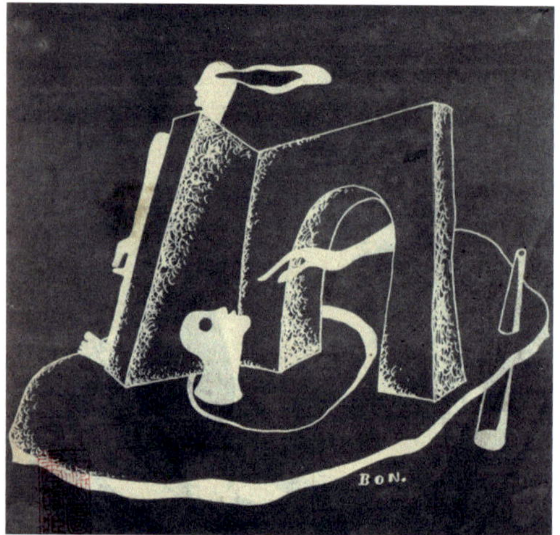

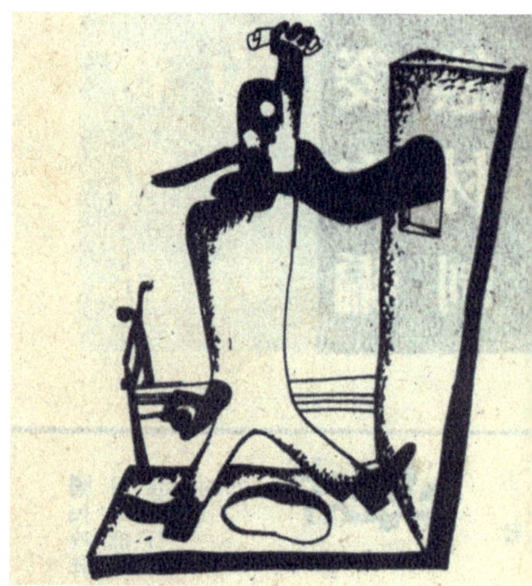

disembodied head emerges from a mountain of drapery, her attractive face framed by a pronounced ruffle on one side and a cocked cap on the other, her sharply arched eyebrows and full lips delineated in trendy makeup. The attendant caption, besides noting her well-known uncle and identifying the image as a recent self-portrait, describes her style as "bold and unrestrained" (*xiaosa haofang* 瀟洒豪放) and designates her an "outstanding talent among modern women painters" (*xiandai nühuajia zhi jiechu rencai* 現代女畫家之傑出人才). The following year, Yu Feng began turning her attention to political activism and founded the Young Women's Club (Qingnian Funü Julebu 青年婦女俱樂部).[45]

A few years older than Yu Feng, Liang Baibo possessed additional professional experience but lacked a famous relative to elevate her public profile.[46] She began her artistic career as an oil painter with academic training from Shanghai Xinhua Art Academy and the West Lake Art Academy in Hangzhou. A member of the Storm Society (see chapter 2), Liang exhibited in at least two of the group's shows, the inaugural exhibition in 1932 and the final exhibition in 1935. In addition to the paintings she exhibited with the Storm Society, Liang's engagement within the art community was diverse and active, producing magazine covers, cartoons, and story illustrations. Along with her popular *Miss Honeybee* cartoon series, Liang contributed covers to *Modern Sketch* (*Shidai manhua* 時代漫畫) and *Xiaoshuo* 小說 (*Short*

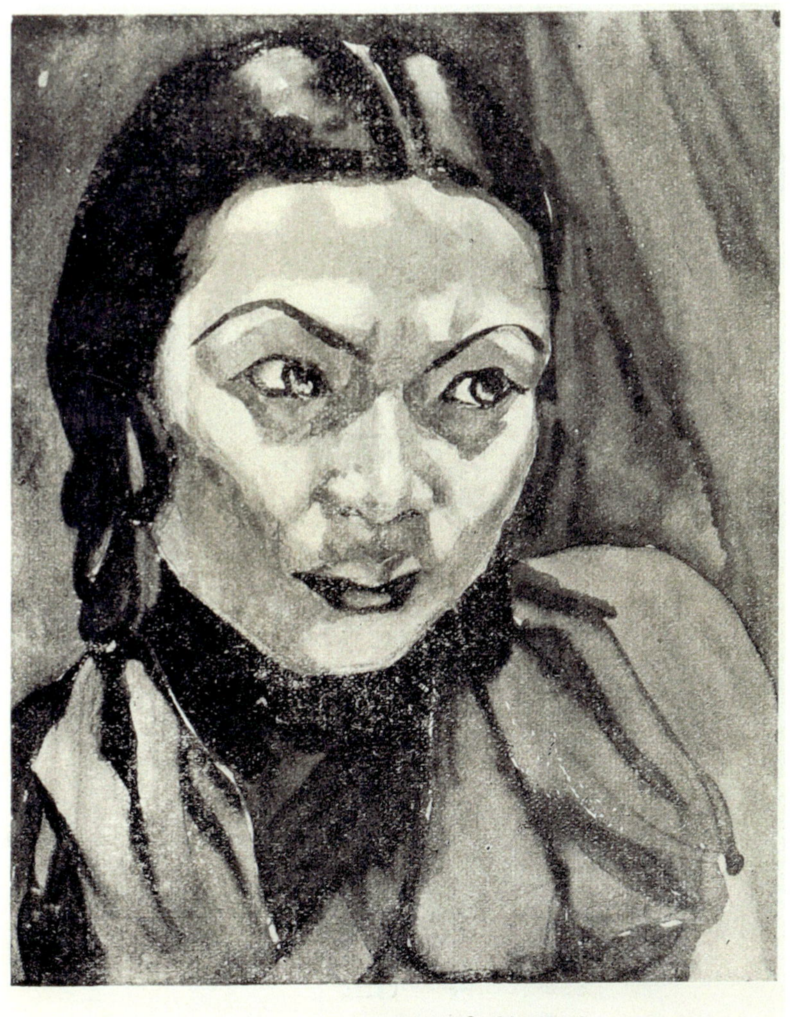

4.6 Yu Feng, *Under the Power of the Times*, exhibited in the Second National Art Exhibition and published in the exhibition catalogue, *A Special Collection of the Second National Exhibition of Chinese Art under the Auspices of the Ministry of Education, Part Three: Modern Chinese Occidental-Painting, Design, and Sculpture*. Shanghai: Commercial Press, 1937.

Story) magazines and produced a range of illustrations to accompany literary publications, including enigmatic images for a children's poetry collection in 1930 and a captivating set of surrealist scenes for a short story in 1935 (fig. 4.5).[47] Since at least 1937, she has been incorrectly credited as Republican China's only female cartoonist.[48] She also held an early interest in politics; besides participating in the leftist Société de Deux Mondes prior to its censure and disbandment in 1931, she had been active in the Communist Youth League (Gongqingtuan 共青團).[49]

The year 1937 marks sudden change for both women, and indeed for the Shanghai art world as a whole. A self-portrait exhibited by Yu Feng that year conveys the changing atmosphere at the cusp of unfolding turmoil. *Under the Power of the Times* (*Shidai de weili xia* 時代的威力下) appeared in the 1937 Second National Art Exhibition, which was held in Nanjing just months before the start of the war (fig. 4.6). Yu's image captures the general sense of ominous foreboding through the tight focus of the composition and dramatic lighting that casts dark shadows under a furrowed brow. Her characteristically arched eyebrows now impart an air of

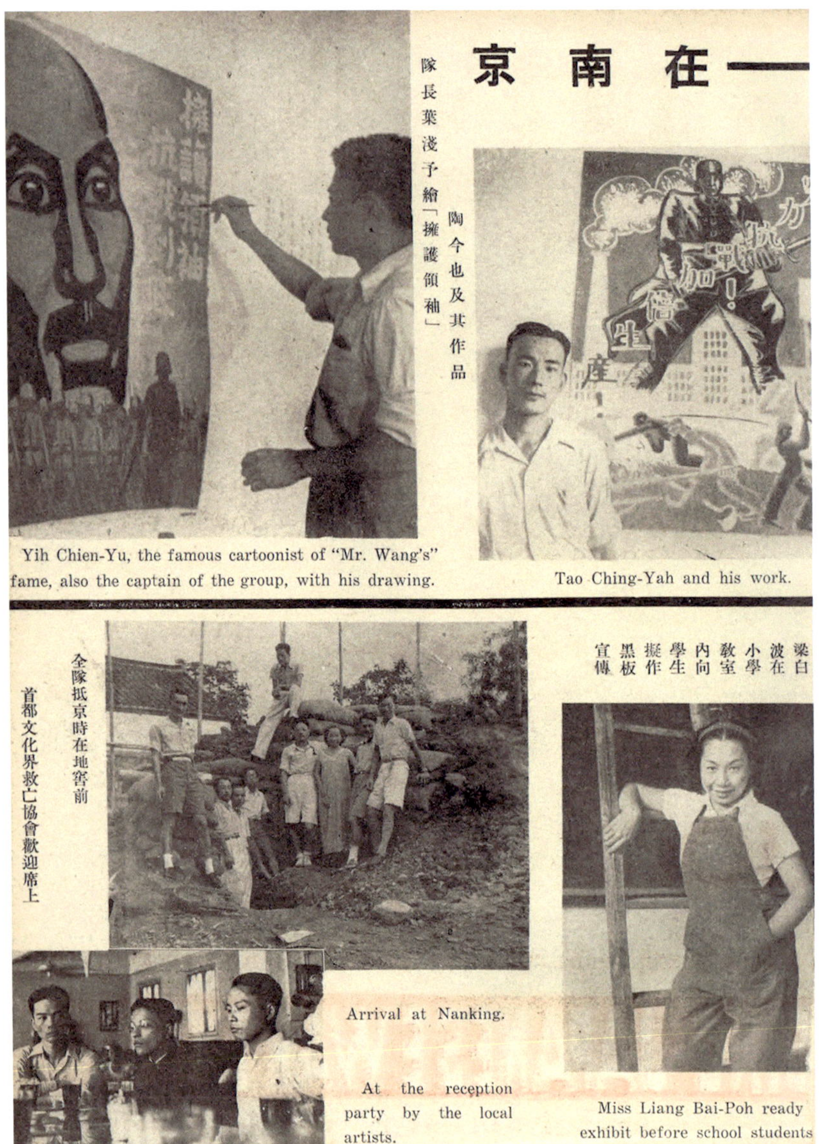
一在南京

陶今也及其作品

隊長葉淺予繪「擁護領袖」

Yih Chien-Yu, the famous cartoonist of "Mr. Wang's" fame, also the captain of the group, with his drawing.

Tao Ching-Yah and his work.

梁白波在小學教室內向學生擬作黑板宣傳

全隊抵京時在地窖前

首都文化界救亡協會歡迎席上

Arrival at Nanking.

At the reception party by the local artists.

Miss Liang Bai-Poh ready exhibit before school students

4.7 "Miss Liang Bai-Poh ready exhibit before school students" from "Cartoonists Take War Area Travel—Nanking First Stop," *Kangri huabao [Anti-Japanese Pictorial]*, 6 (1937): 17.

suspicion as she looks askance at something out of frame. Her body tilts leftward, while her head angles rightward, the diagonals provoking unease and uncertainty in the viewer. Altogether, *Under the Power of the Times* presents a stark contrast to Yu Feng's lighthearted prewar self-portrait of two years prior and marks her abrupt transformation from youthful fashionista to driven resister.

Civic minded and professionally driven, Yu Feng integrated her artistic career with interests in activism and theatrical performance. She participated in the Resistance Movement as a cartoonist and a reporter.[50] With Huang Miaozi, who was later to become her husband, Yu Feng worked for the *Jiuwang ribao* 救亡日報 (*Salvation Daily*), an anti-Japanese newspaper begun in Shanghai. She also met and worked with Tian Han, a leftist playwright who that year wrote and staged a production entitled *Lugou qiao* 盧溝橋 (*Marco Polo Bridge*) about the incident that had led to the official declaration of war earlier that year.[51] When Shanghai fell to the Japanese, Yu Feng fled to Guangzhou, where she continued contributing to the relocated *Salvation Daily* and briefly infiltrated the Guangzhou division of the Guomingdang war effort as a secret agent for the Chinese Communist Party.[52] But the next year Guangzhou also fell, and Yu Feng once again was on the move. In 1939 she appeared in theatrical productions staged on the frontlines in northern Guangdong. Next she went to Hong Kong, where she served as chief editor of *Plowing* (*Gengyun* 耕耘), a magazine she founded with Huang Miaozi in 1940.[53] While in Hong Kong, Yu Feng joined artist associations that collectively produced anti-Japanese images for *Plowing* and public art projects, such as a mural commemorating the sixtieth anniversary of the birth of China's left-leaning literary giant Lu Xun. Thus, in the first few years of the war, at a time when Fang Junbi was increasingly pulled into service for Wang Jingwei's collaborationist government, Yu Feng became wholly committed to using her artistic talents to counter the Japanese.

Meanwhile, Liang Baibo began following a track akin to Yu Feng's. She joined the Cartoonists Association for National Salvation (Manhuajie Jiuwang Xiehui 漫畫界救亡協會)—a propaganda corps devoted to boosting Chinese morale through visual images and public works—and traveled with the group from Shanghai to the northern front in 1937 (fig. 4.7).[54] That same year they returned to the south and worked from Nanjing, only to flee to Wuhan when Nanjing fell. The transient organization—consisting of fifteen core members led by Ye Qianyu—held cartoon exhibitions, printed propaganda posters, painted murals, and published two serials, first a weekly titled *National Salvation Cartoons* (*Jiuwang manhua* 救亡漫畫) and, later, a bimonthly titled *War of Resistance Cartoons* (*Kangzhan manhua* 抗戰漫畫).[55]

Yu Feng and Liang Baibo exemplify the growing patriotic activism practiced by artists following the onset of the Sino-Japanese War. Teams of artists used affordable and portable media to produce posters, murals, and magazines in a guerrilla art movement. Cartoons and woodblock prints were cheap to produce, easy to transport, and thought to be especially effective—the graphic images were appreciated as evocative and a universally comprehensible.[56] The war cartoon, because of its ease of distribution and forceful imagery, was considered an ideal propaganda art form and thus a potent tool for national liberation. In their participation with propaganda art groups, Yu Feng and Liang Baibo contributed toward the salvation of the nation, thus their activities outside the home—recognized as selfless acts of dedication—positioned these women's professional careers in the arts as beyond reproach.

More than justifying their own careers outside the home through patriotic actions, Yu Feng's and Liang Baibo's cartoons beseech other women to do the same. To take *War of Resistance Masterpieces* as an example, while their contributions depict a range of subjects, nearly half portray assertive women in active roles. Liang's images of women concentrate on their wartime professions. Dressed plainly, these young women bear no physical resemblance to the buxom Miss Honeybee of Liang's earlier cartoon serial. The wartime women, however, do share the Modern Girl protagonist's

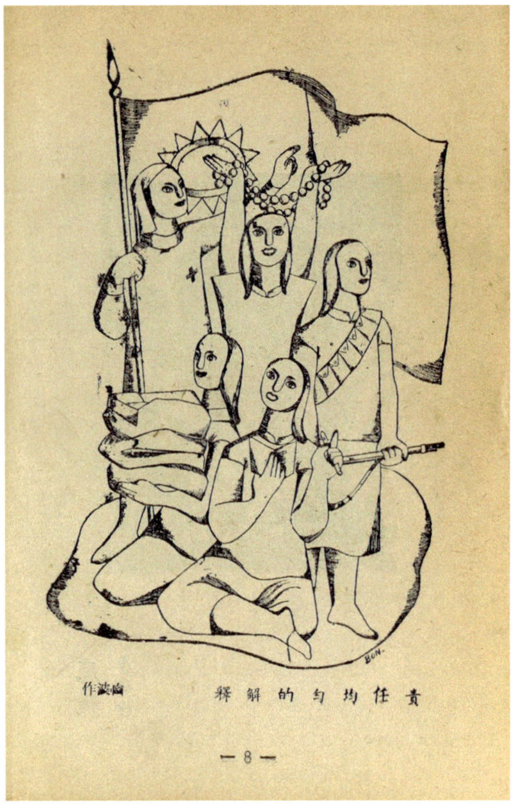

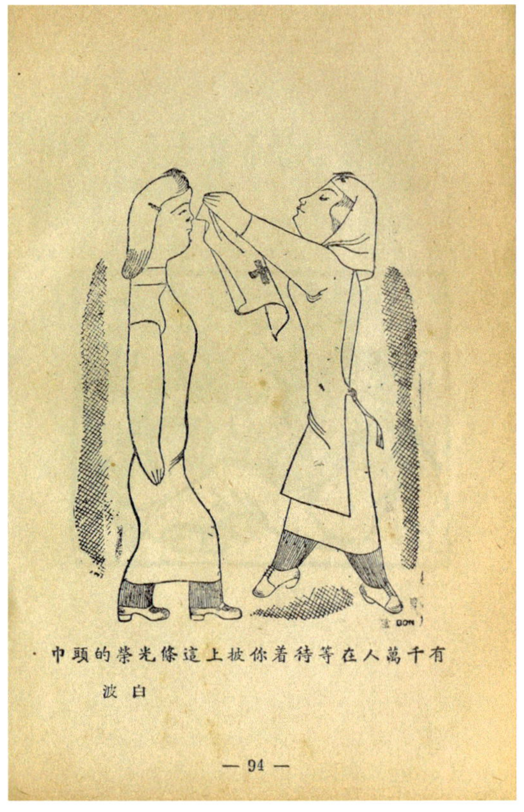

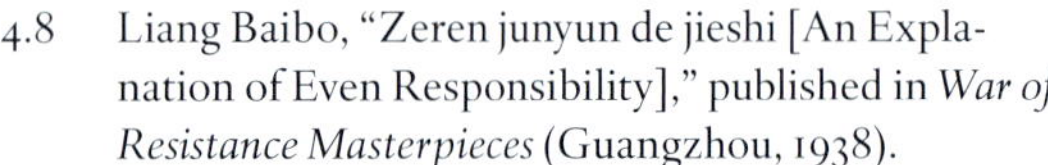

4.8 Liang Baibo, "Zeren junyun de jieshi [An Explanation of Even Responsibility]," published in *War of Resistance Masterpieces* (Guangzhou, 1938).

4.9 Liang Baibo, "You qian wan ren zai dengdai zhe ni pi shang zhe tiao guangrong de toujin [There are ten million people waiting for you to put on this honorable headscarf]," published in *War of Resistance Masterpieces* (Guangzhou, 1938). Photographed by the author, 2019.

confidence and determination. In "An Explanation of Even Responsibility," five women grip implements, such as a book and pen, national flag, and gun, and portray a range of wartime jobs, including those as teacher, nurse, and soldier (fig. 4.8). Smiling as they stand and sit in proximity to each other, these women convey a sentiment of solidarity and support. In another cartoon, Liang focuses on two female nurses: the one on the right is bestowing a professional uniform on the other while saying, "There are countless people waiting for you to put on this honorable headscarf" (fig. 4.9). The exaggerated proportions of the figures and abstract pattern of the hatchwork background evince Liang's modernist beginnings, but this cartoon, as with the others, is meant to deliver an unmistakable message and contains no trace of formalist play. The message, however, is a feminist one and in this way continues Liang's commitment to the presentation of female subjectivity.[57]

Like Liang Baibo, Yu Feng's contributions to the volume present women as equally valuable in the fight against the Japanese. The complex compositions, chiaroscuro, and perspectival depth of the images point to Yu's academic training, but here, too, the images primarily serve as vehicles for the

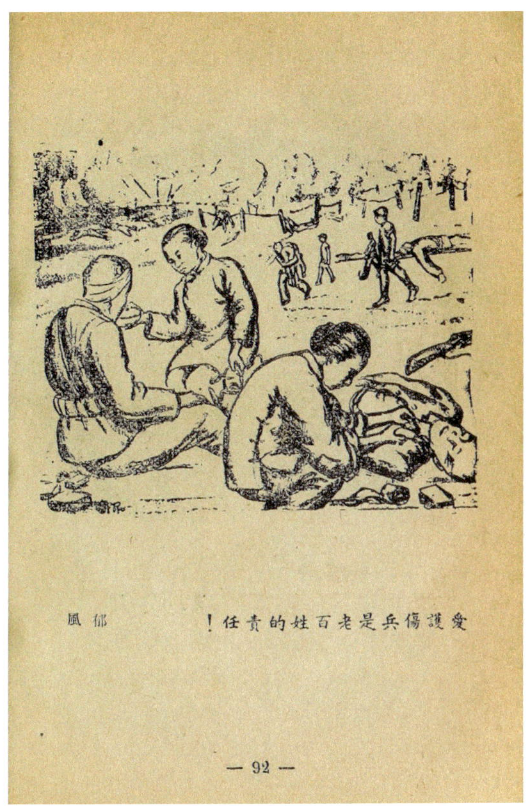

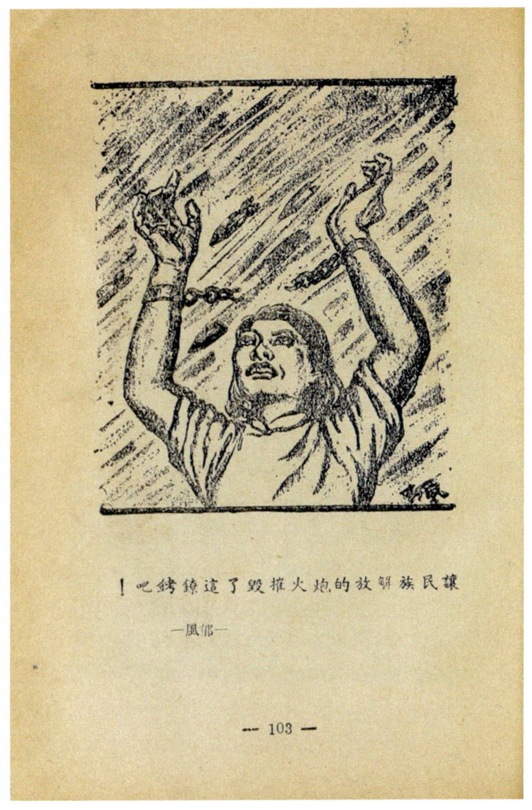

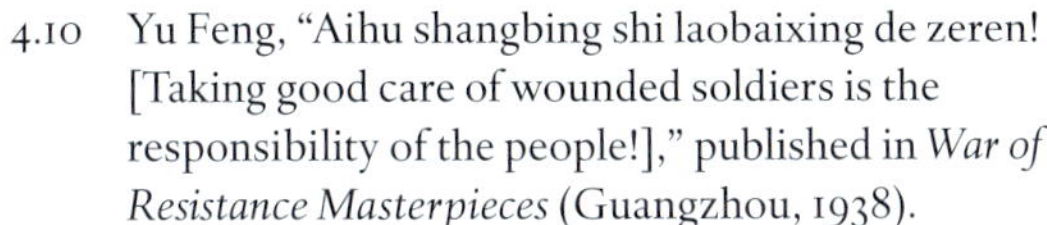
4.10 Yu Feng, “Aihu shangbing shi laobaixing de zeren! [Taking good care of wounded soldiers is the responsibility of the people!],” published in *War of Resistance Masterpieces* (Guangzhou, 1938).

4.11 Yu Feng, “Rang minzu jiefang de paohuo cuihui le zhe liaokao ba! [Let the gunfire of national liberation destroy these shackles!],” published in *War of Resistance Masterpieces* (Guangzhou, 1938).

message of unified resistance. In one cartoon matronly women tend to fallen soldiers while the caption admonishes, “Taking good care of wounded soldiers is the responsibility of the people!” (fig. 4.10). In another, more fanciful cartoon, “Let the gunfire of national liberation destroy these shackles!,” a woman raises her arms over her head and uses incoming shellfire to break the chains that bind her hands (fig. 4.11). Addressing the status of women in China, the cartoon urges women to seize upon the current wartime situation as an opportunity to finally free themselves from oppressive gender roles.

If this cartoon suggests she found her war activism to be liberating, Yu Feng’s participation in a drama troupe provided another unconventional method to advance women’s rights. While still in Shanghai, Yu Feng performed in and promoted the newly written historical drama *Wu Zetian* 武則天. Written by Song Zhidi 宋之的 (1914–56), another leftist playwright, the play was a feminist reenvisioning of the notorious Tang-dynasty empress.[58] Yu Feng shared this new view of Empress Wu and authored an article about the play’s contribution to the women’s rights movement.[59] Published in *Women’s Life* magazine (*Funü shenghuo* 婦女生活), the article speaks of the playwright’s intention to resolve the longstanding "woman question" by examining this strong female leader of the distant past, who he believed had been egregiously misunderstood. As if to underscore the author's support of powerful and independent women, a small illustration above the title depicts a confident young Chinese woman, dressed in uniform and striding forward with determination. It is apparent, then, that Yu Feng envisioned her thespianism in much the same terms as her production of cartoons. Employing popular media for wartime audiences in both cases, acting and cartoons allowed her contributions to the war effort to simultaneously fight for a feminist cause.

Although Yu Feng and Liang Baibo produced war propaganda focused on women's actions and portrayed women as equal contributors to the war effort, they continued to encounter adversity in their own careers. Liang's career especially suffered. The print news published her contributions to the war effort as a member of the group, but just as frequently condemned her romantic relations with the married Ye Qianyu.[60] In 1938 Liang left both Ye and the cartoonist association. Once separated from the group, she not only fell into obscurity, but Ye published her artwork under his name on at least one occasion. The two cartoons—which are captioned as war posters by Ye Qianyu and accompany an article promoting cartoons and graphic art as forms of modern art—clearly evidence Liang Baibo's style in the disproportionately elongated torsos of the figures and foregrounding of female protagonists (fig. 4.12).[61] The captions, "You Take Care of My Children and I'll Take Care of the Soldiers" and "We Will Cook for the Soldiers" echo the sororal comradeship that characterizes several of Liang's contributions to the war cartoon anthology but remains largely absent from the men's. One has to wonder how many other artworks by Liang were similarly misattributed to men.[62]

Beyond the propensity for artworks by women to be claimed as men's, Liang Baibo and Yu Feng also contended with the destructive and demoralizing appropriation of woman's image on a systemic scale. In general, the start of the war marks a pronounced shift in the visibility of women in the arts, both in society and within the popular press; as female arts professionals lost currency in society and began to vanish from the pages of periodicals, so did images of the nude or semiclothed female body as aesthetic object (as observed at the end of chapter 3). In their place, a new type of woman emerged in the public art and cartoons of the propaganda brigade—a myopic and misogynistic vision of the female body as powerless casualty of Japanese aggression. If the abundance of sexualized modern girls and art nudes of early Republican visual culture encouraged an objectifying gaze, the Resistance Movement's depictions of women dwelled primarily on their victimization. Duara has noted that during the war, "the imagery of the raped woman came to represent the defiled purity of the invaded nation" and became a symbol so potent that that the literature was "full of this motif."[63] Louise Edwards's study of the prominence of sexual violence in anti-Japanese war cartoons, however, illuminates the specific discursive function these images served.[64] Demonstrating that depictions of women by propaganda corps artists concentrated on graphic scenes of rape, mutilation, and murder, Edwards argues that the cartoonists largely conceived of the female bodies pictured in their art as "expendable."[65] Whereas the cartoonists' images typically portray Chinese men as capable of fighting against the brutalities of war, cartoons of the raped woman, often with her violator looming over her, "symbolize the ongoing, in-progress humiliation of China by the Japanese," and their dying and disemboweled bodies represent the threatened extinction of the Chinese race.[66] Edwards focuses on the intentions of the male cartoonists responsible for these images rather than on how the images might have been received, but for women viewers such acts of violence repeatedly rendered on female bodies could have inspired little other than terror and dismay. Unsurprisingly, periodicals explicitly produced by and for women, as Edwards notes in passing, do not reproduce these disturbing images of sexual violence against women. In stark contrast to the images produced by male cartoonists, the material published in women's

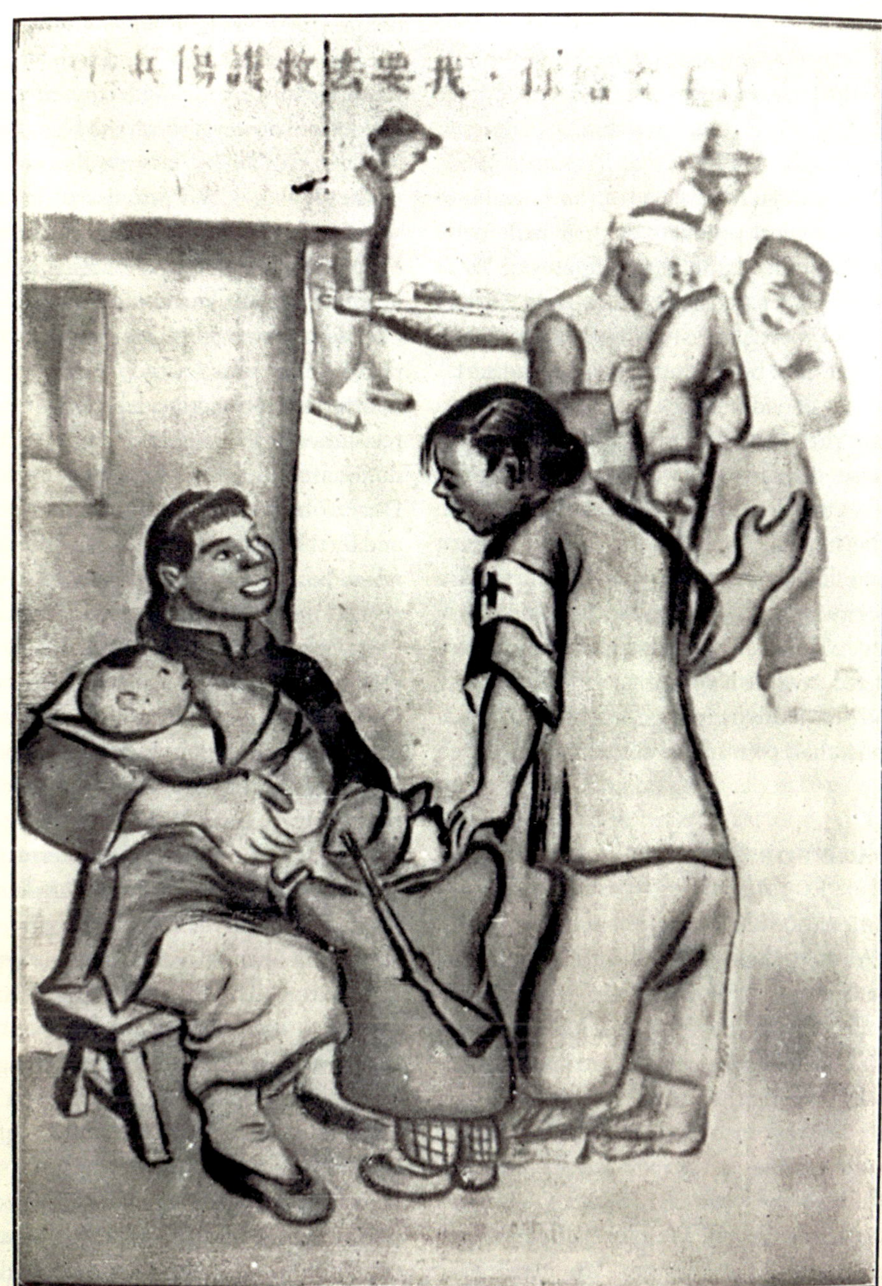

"You Take Care of My Children and I'll Take Care of the Soldiers."
War Poster by Yeh Chien-yu.

4.12 Liang Baibo, "You Take Care of My Children and I'll Take Care of the Soldiers," published in Jack Chen, "Towards a Modern Conception of Art," *T'ien Hsia Monthly* (November 1938).

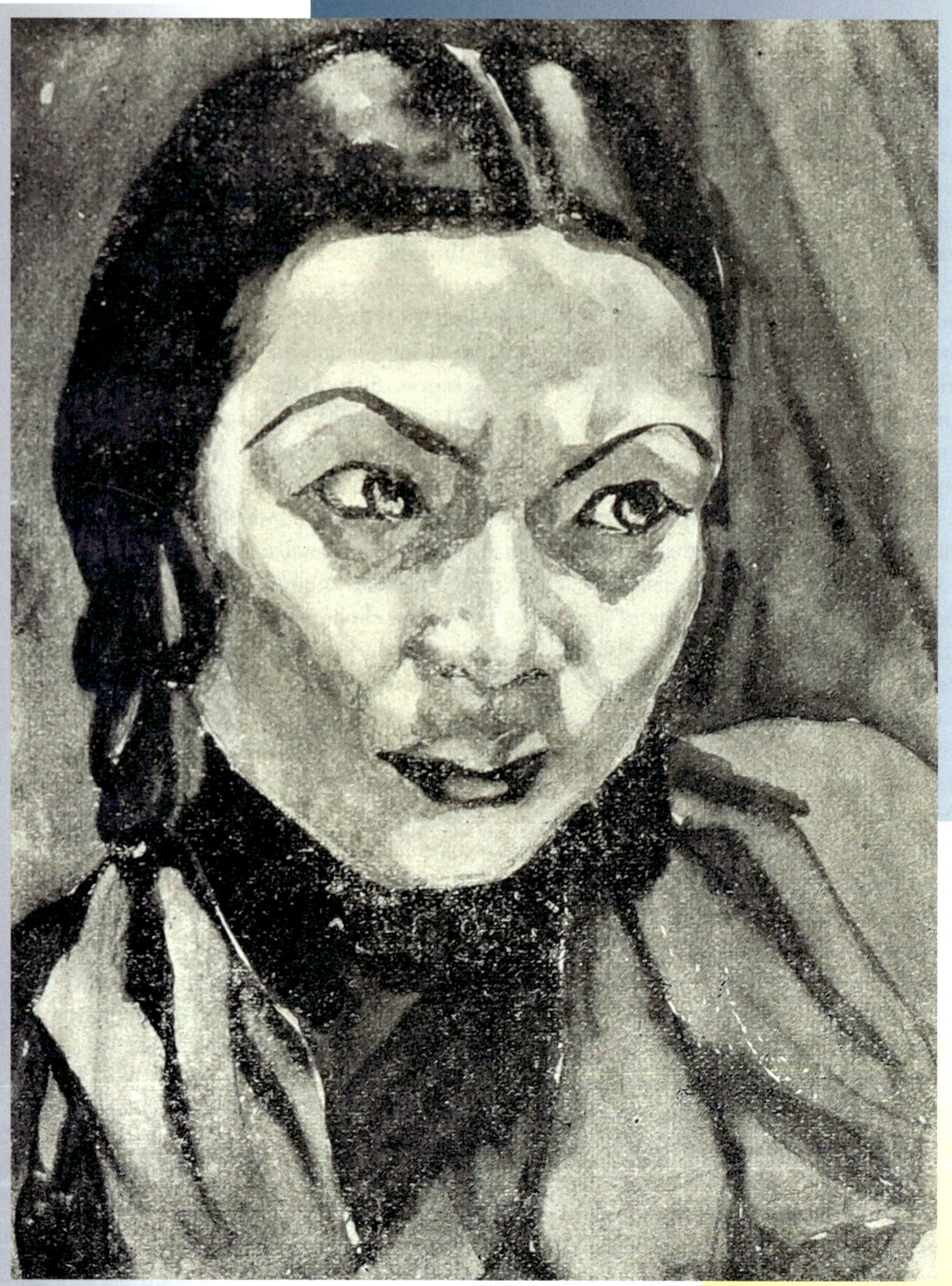

Conclusion

Under the Power of the Times

IN AN ARTICLE published in November of 1935, a month before the fourth Storm Society exhibition opened, Ni Yide had trumpeted:

> Since the general public typically views art as merely 'a means of illustrating certain facts,' it should come as no surprise that the Storm Society is ignored or even sneered at by the public for its pursuit of new techniques. Nevertheless, among Western-style Chinese painters who, as a community, appear to be on their last legs, I am afraid the Storm Society is the only organization that still shows signs of life and struggles onward.[1]

Ni Yide clearly did not foresee that the fourth exhibition would mark the conclusion of the society. Despite the group's influence and the members' own sense of grand mission, the organization came to an abrupt conclusion immediately following the event. Pang Xunqin later described the general dejected mood that permeated the event and the members' decision to disband. He reminisced, "The fourth exhibition was held at the Zhonghua Art School, the same venue as our first exhibition. Very few visitors came on the last two days, which were cloudy. It was in such a quiet and indifferent atmosphere that the society came to the end of its history."[2] Later still, Yang Qiuren reasoned that his colleagues "inevitably did not understand, or perhaps did not understand very clearly, the reality of their time. They were out of touch with reality."[3] While the group succeeded in garnering substantial public recognition through exhibitions and magazine features, it failed to provoke the sweeping and enduring change within the Chinese art world for which it had hoped.

Yu Feng, *Under the Power of the Times* (detail of fig. 4.6).

Recent scholarship nonetheless credits the Storm Society with a powerful impact on the development of modernist art in China and notes that with the demise of the former came the conclusion of the latter. Though the group staged only four exhibitions, the bold ideological vision and daring words of Storm Society members secured their status as the forerunners of modernism within the Shanghai art world. So strongly felt was the absence of the group that art historian Zheng Shengtian observes, "The disappearance of the Storm Society not only stilled the once vibrant artistic community in Shanghai, it also signified that the curtain had finally fallen on this debut performance of modern art in China."[4] When the group disbanded, the field of modernist art was fraught and fractured and was not to be revived for over four decades. The fate of modernist art in turn heralded the end of Chinese women's prominence as modern art professionals. The rhetoric of modernism had encouraged and championed women's participation in professional

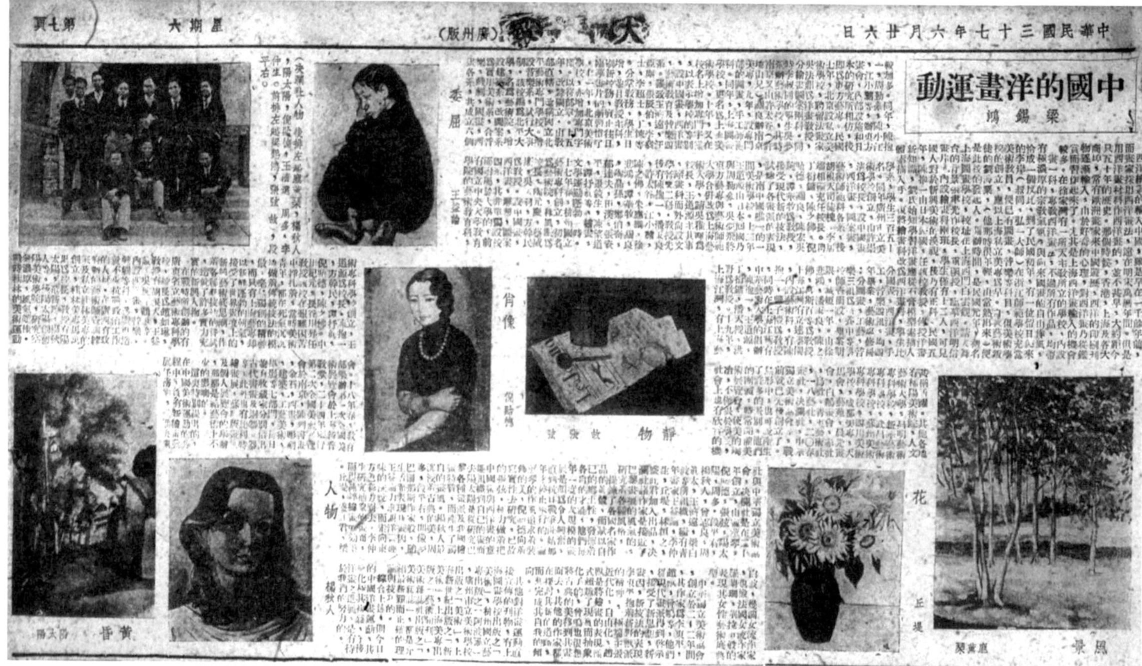

中華民國三十七年六月廿六日

星期六 第七頁

中國的洋畫運動

梁錫鴻

5.1 Liang Xihong's 1948 review of the Chinese modernist art movement. The article reproduces Qiu Ti's painting of sunflowers in a vase (*second image from the right*), which has been generically titled *Hua* [Flowers]. Liang Xihong, "Zhongguo de yanghua yundong [China's Western Painting Movement]," *Da guang bao* (June 26, 1948).

disciplines, particularly that of the arts, but now with diminishing resources for artists and the emergence of a nationalist focus on women's roles within the home, female artists increasingly struggled for professional opportunities. As went the Storm Society, so went modernist art as well as the modern woman artist in China.

Despite growing recognition of modernist art in the early twentieth century and the importance of groups such as the Storm Society, accurately assessing women's contributions to these groups and to the larger modernist art movement has remained a vexing problem. Taking Storm Society member, Qiu Ti, as an example, chapter 2 has shown that scholarship in large part relies on the dubious construal of her painting by Ni Yide, whose flair for the dramatic led him to color his theoretical arguments and writings about her and other society members for sensationalist impact. The memoirs of Qiu Ti's peers likewise do nothing to establish her professional reputation. In his 1948 review of the Chinese modernist art movement, Liang Xihong 梁锡鸿 (1912–82) tacks a brief mention of Qiu Ti to the end of his discussion of key artists. While the styles of male artists warrant individual consideration, the works of Qiu Ti (fig. 5.1) and two other "authors of the weaker sex" (*nüliu zuojia* 女流作家) are simply consolidated under the generic descriptor of "typical women's art" (*nüxing yishu di dianxing* 女性藝術底典型).[5] Perhaps unconsciously revising the past to suit later developments, Storm Society member Yang Qiuren's 1983 article incorrectly states that Qiu Ti began by studying decorative art, and then he dismisses her art with the observation that, "needless to say her work had a decorative taste."[6] Most startling is the absolute silence of Pang Xunqin in regards to his late wife's artistic career. Pang Xunqin's glaring omission of Qiu Ti was perplexing enough to prompt art historian Shui Tianzhong to observe, "In Pang's memoir

Jiushi zheyang zougulai de (the part before 1949) the account of life in the 1930s, actually does not say one word about his relationship with Qiu Ti."[7] How could Qiu Ti's legacy—or that of any woman—hope to withstand the dismissal of her husband and closest colleague, the one for whom she sacrificed her own professional aspirations, through his failure to mention her even once in all of his writings of the Storm Society and the avant-garde art movement?[8]

Michael Sullivan's dismissive appraisal of Qiu Ti in his authoritative *Art and Artists of Twentieth-Century China* also greatly influences our limited understanding today of her contributions to modernist art in China. His only assessment of Qiu Ti in the entirety of the canon-making text is a rather patronizing analysis of a single painting. Of the painting he writes, "Qiu Ti, who had married Pang Xunqin after his return from Paris, was a competent oil painter and a sensitive one, as shown by her portrait of her little daughter, Pang Tao, painted in Chengdu in 1944."[9] Is it merely a coincidence that, rather than select one of her contributions to the Storm Society, Sullivan reinforces Qiu Ti's gender identity by focusing solely on the artist's depiction of her child? Perhaps not, as his underestimation of Qiu Ti's contributions mirrors his treatment of other women artists of her generation. In "Leading Masters between the Wars," another chapter from the same publication, Fang Junbi is the only female artist Sullivan addresses. Predictably, he places her at the very end of the chapter. She is categorized under the subheading "Some Lesser Masters," a designation she shares with Ding Yanyong, who Sullivan describes approvingly as "[l]ively, quirky, humorous" and "too much of an individualist to found a school."[10] Comparing him with the much admired Eccentric painters of China's art history, Sullivan instructs the reader that, "Ding Yanyong stands outside the accepted canons, and so is not to be judged by them."[11] In contrast, Fang Junbi is labeled as "more orthodox," a comment most certainly not intended to be a compliment. Sullivan continues his assessment of her with: "Fang Junbi was a competent oil painter with a romantic streak that only too often, as with her friend Pan Yuliang, strayed into sentimentality. . . . She was one of a number of modern Chinese artists whose adventurous, at times tragic, lives were more interesting than their paintings."[12]

With their work thus branded as inconsequential, modern Chinese women artists did not fare well in Sullivan's canonizing analysis and have only recently begun to have their contributions reassessed. To return to Qiu Ti again as an example, not until nearly thirty years after her death was she finally remembered as a modernist artist of significance. When Shui Tianzhong mentioned Qiu Ti's two contributions to the Second Annual Storm Society Exhibition in his paper at the 1986 Conference on Chinese Oil Painting (*Quanguo youhua taolunhui* 全国油画讨论会), it was the first consideration of her contributions to the Storm Society in well over three decades.[13] Since then, several art historians have referenced Qiu Ti in discussions of the developments of modern art in China. Yet, despite occasional recent inquiries into the life and work of Qiu Ti, the slim 2006 *Schudy* catalogue remains the most extensive published study on this underappreciated artist. Similarly, Qiu Ti has never received a solo exhibition. The exhibition for which the *Schudy* catalogue was published, which was to be Qiu Ti's first solo show, never materialized. Following the exhibition marking the 100-year anniversary of Pang Xunqin's birth, the Nanjing Jiangsu Museum revised its intentions to hold a similar exhibit for Qiu Ti. It was only at the insistence of Pang Tao that her mother's catalogue saw the light of day.[14]

The parallels between Qiu Ti's life—or that of any of her female peers—and the fates of other modern women artists around the world are inescapable. An article by Wendy M. K. Shaw reveals particularly striking similarities with the experiences of Turkish women artists of the early twentieth century.[15] Forty years after Linda Nochlin's seminal article on Western women artists, Shaw, who specializes in the painting of the Ottoman Empire, writes a non-Western response to the same thorny question.[16] Summarizing the direction of her argument, Shaw states that the "retroactive enumeration of female artists from this period repeats the use of women as tropes of modernization rather than critically evaluating their historical opportunities to participate fully as agents in the modern public sphere."[17] The crux of Shaw's article takes a quite different turn, however, when she concludes that not only were there no great Ottoman women artists, there were no great Ottoman artists at all.[18]

Setting aside the question of whether the designation of a nation's "greats"—artists or otherwise—hangs on a universal comparative evaluation or on the significance of the individual to his or her own society, Shaw's analysis of Ottoman women artists is insightful. Shaw views the Ottoman artists' images of women, as well as the women artists themselves, as "signals of modernization." As occurred in China, appreciation of Western art in the Ottoman Empire began in the nineteenth-century when the government encouraged the study of technical drawing for scientific purposes.[19] Looking to the West, modernist artists at the turn of the twentieth century fixated on the female figure and saw the female nude as a means to elevate the art of the nation—creating a perplexing quandary for a conservative Islamic state.[20] Though a minority in their field, women pursued careers as artists and also created paintings featuring styles and genres popular with the avant-garde. Harika Lifij (1890–1991) entered two paintings of nudes in the 1917 Vienna Exhibition and Hale Asaf (1905–38) was one of the first Turkish artists to work in a cubist manner. Many successful women artists of the first generations were either the daughters of reformers, members of the elite, or the wives of influential artists. Neither their privileged circumstances nor the rhetoric of a society proclaiming interest in the emancipation of women, however, prevented these women from eventually making career sacrifices in favor of their domestic obligations. Shaw finds that, "Despite the concurrence of the growth of the arts with increased women's activism and participation in the public sphere during the late-Ottoman period, their artistic practice was largely subsumed within traditional gender roles." Of the few Turkish women who achieved recognition as accomplished artists, their work was often evaluated in terms relative to their gender; Hale Asaf's painting described as feminine in its "delicacy," "purity and calm."[21]

So, too, unfolded the painting careers of the modernist women artists of early twentieth-century China. Much of the recognition and success experienced in their careers related to husbands, lovers, or mentors, who were always the more famous of the two. Rather than rejecting the objectification of women inherent in the production of images of female nudes, they readily engaged in painting the popular subject matter. Much art criticism of their painting then—and to some extent now—focuses on the perceived feminine traits of style.[22] Ultimately, most abandoned their painting careers—catastrophic social upheaval and extended periods of war undermined the tremulous career gains made by this pioneering generation of women artists. As true for Chinese women artists as for their Ottoman counterparts is Shaw's observation: "Even when women took their own pursuits seriously, social practices such as marriage often sidelined their efforts or made them secondary in relation to the professional practices of their husbands."[23] Likewise, the work of the female artists discussed in this book by and large did not result in international prestige, lengthy professional careers, enduring empowerment within their profession, or permanent social gains for women more broadly.

Nevertheless, women artists were significant players in a key chapter of the history of Chinese modernist art and this book has sought to reaffirm their accomplishments. The revolutionizing of artistic practices and modern professionalization of the occupation in early twentieth-century China, as well as the radical redefinition of women's social roles, briefly opened the newly formed career of professional artist to female participants. During this time, women such as Guan Zilan used the popular press to craft public personas for professional exposure and bold self-invention. They thus engaged in the same professional practices as men, even if the press coverage for the women dwelled more so on their gender. Besides self-marketing through printed biographical sketches and exhibition reviews, both men and women participated in professional art societies. Women were contributing members of Chinese modernism's most important art groups, even if they were marginalized by some men then and remain misunderstood by scholars today. Qiu Ti, once publicized as the only female artist given entrance into an exclusive modernist painting society, illustrates the extent to which the complex dynamics of group image and gender politics shaped the development of women's careers. Though two designations traditionally held as indicators of her success—the award and her status as the Storm Society's only female artist—may be suspect, Qiu Ti nonetheless functioned as a core member within the progressive group. Women's artistic practice and modern art theory intersected when female artists pursued the same painting subjects as their male colleagues, including the female nude, but with ideologically different motives. For women artists such as Pan Yuliang, the choice to create artworks featuring the nude was not necessarily radical but suggestive of attunement to standard art practices of the time. Far from indicating a passive adherence to a patriarchal art establishment, Pan's paintings of female nudes demonstrate her equal participation in the art trends followed by her male peers. By the late 1930s, however, political campaigns and wartime hardships forced most women to abandon their careers. Three artists—Fang Junbi, Yu Feng, and Liang Baibo—managed to maintain their careers by turning to activism and reinventing themselves as willing martyrs for the national cause, but they were the exception. Wartime China no longer supported equal opportunities for women but undermined their career gains and quickly forgot their earlier contributions. When Michael Sullivan arrived in Chengdu and began assessing the modern art world in China, this is the new art world he encountered and canonized.

With wartime rhetoric having already applied tremendous social pressure on women as artists and what they would choose to paint, the initial decades of the People's Republic of China (PRC) resolutely closed off modernist art as a mode of expression for everyone. During the mid-twentieth century, the women discussed in this book retained active ties to the visual arts, but most never again secured the level of professional recognition they had attained during the height of Chinese modernism a few decades earlier. Guan Zilan had been in Japan at the start of the Sino-Japanese War; on her return to China in 1938 at the age of thirty-five, she decided it was time to begin a family; she married and gave birth to her first child that year.[24] She continued painting, but political developments dictated her professional activity for the remainder of her life. In 1941 she held an exhibition in occupied Shanghai, but associated news articles highlighted Guan's past accomplishments—in particular, her participation in the Nikakai Exhibition in Tokyo—rather than indicating new professional growth and thus emphasize the artist's ties to Japan (fig. 5.2).[25] In the early 1960s, Guan took a research appointment in the Shanghaishi Wenshi Yanjiuguan, became a member of the Zhongguo Meishujia Xiehui, and periodically with the Shanghai Meishujia Xiehui participated in collective excursions to paint landscapes from life. But with the start of the Cultural Revolution, she gave away her possessions, secretly hid her treasured paintings and materials within a wall, and ceased to paint altogether.

Liang Baibo, following her split with the propaganda cartoon corps, returned to her earlier interests in painting and drawing. In the 1940s, like many artists of the day, she traveled westward and produced artwork inspired by new cultural encounters. During her journey to China's northwestern Xinjiang province, she created scores of watercolor paintings.[26] As is the case for most Chinese women artists, though, little of Liang's work from this period survives. A few published images and a relatively unstudied album of her paintings and drawings gives some small insight into her artistic inclinations.[27] The contents indicate her shared interest in the period's ethnographic turn, as she focuses on portraying the customs and attire of the minority groups of China's rural regions (fig. 5.3). Before the founding of the PRC, Liang fled her homeland and relocated to Taiwan with her husband and young

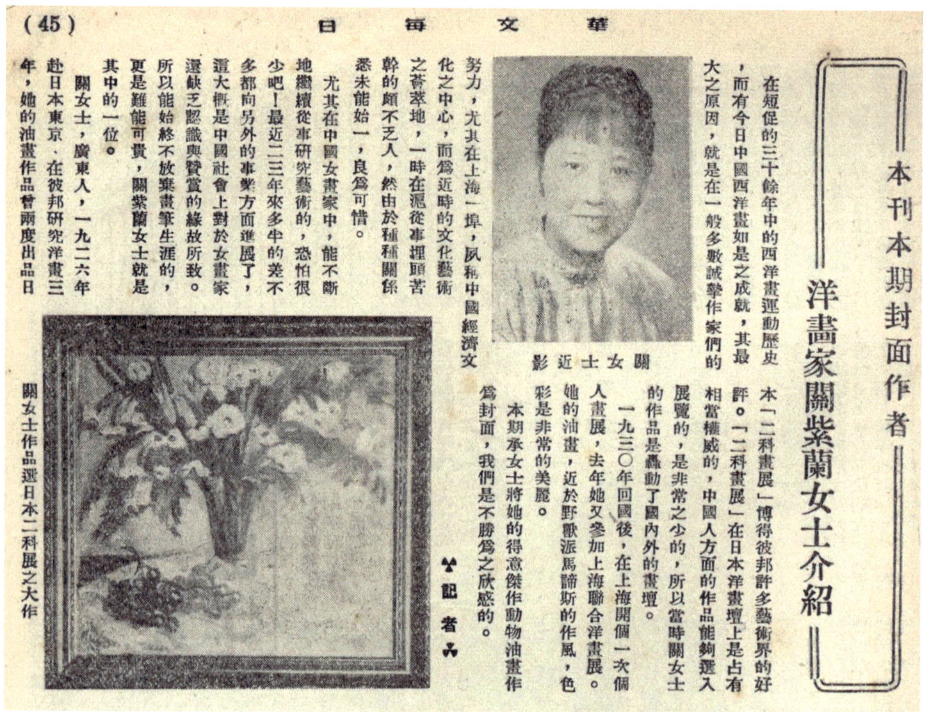

華文每日 (45)

本刊本期封面作者
洋畫家關紫蘭女士介紹

在短促的三十餘年中的西洋畫運動歷史，而有今日中國西洋畫如是之成就，其最大之原因，就是在一般多數誠摯作家們的努力，尤其在上海一埠，夙稱中國經濟文化之中心，而爲近時的文化藝術之薈萃地，一時在滬從事埋頭苦幹的頗不乏人，然由於種種關係悉未能始一，良爲可惜。

尤其在中國女畫家中，能不斷地繼續從事研究藝術的，恐怕很少吧！最近二三年來多半的差不多都向另外的事業方面進展了，這大概是中國社會上對於女畫家還缺乏認識與贊賞的緣故所致。所以能始終不放棄畫筆生涯的，更是難能可貴，關紫蘭女士就是其中的一位。

關女士，廣東人，一九二六年赴日本東京．在彼邦研究洋畫三年，她的油畫作品曾兩度出品日本「二科畫展」博得彼邦許多藝術界的好評。「二科畫展」在日本洋畫壇上是占有相當權威的，中國人方面的作品能夠選入展覽的，是非常之少的，所以當時關女士的作品是轟動了國內外的畫壇。

一九三〇年回國後，在上海開個一次個人畫展，去年她又參加上海聯合洋畫展。她的油畫，近於野獸派馬諦斯的作風，色彩是非常的美麗。

本期承女士將她的得意傑作動物油畫作爲封面，我們是不勝爲之欣感的。

☆記者☆

關女士近影

關女士作品選日本二科展之大作

5.2 A 1943 article about Guan Zilan that illustrates *Narcissus* (*Shuixianhua*), her entry into the Nikakai Art Exhibition a decade and a half earlier. "Benkan benqi fengmian zuojia—yanghuajia Guan Zilan [Our Cover Artist for This Issue: Introducing Western-Style Painter Guan Zilan]," *Huawen meiri* [*Chinese Daily*] 9, no. 11 (1943): 45.

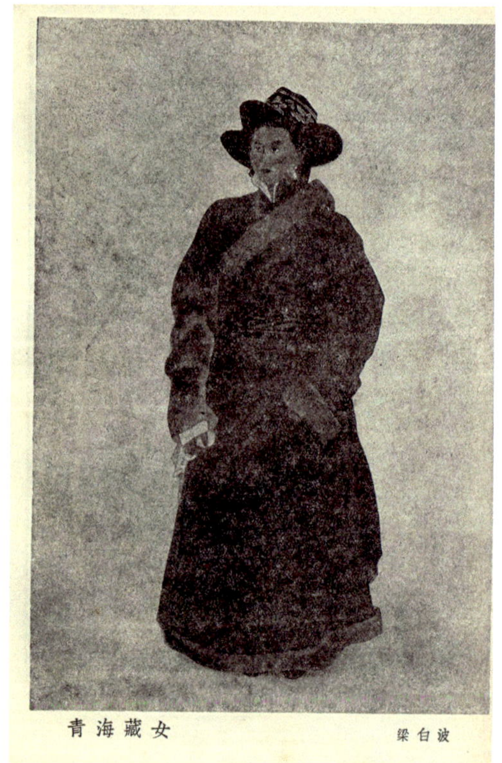

5.3 Liang Baibo, *Qinghai Cangnü* (*Tibetan Woman from Qinghai*). Published in *Wenchao yuekan* (*Culture Current Monthly*) in 1947.

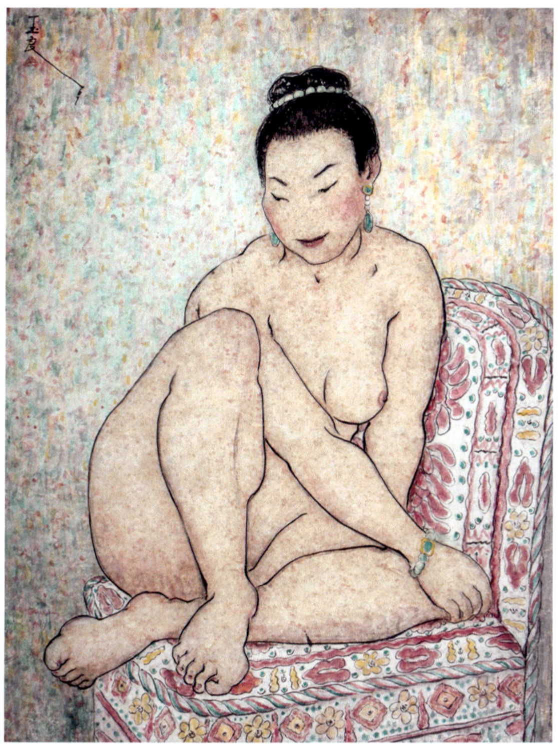

5.4 Pan Yuliang, *Woman Seated on a Sofa* (*Zuo zai shafa shang de nü ren*), 1967, ink and color on paper. Courtesy of the Anhui Museum.

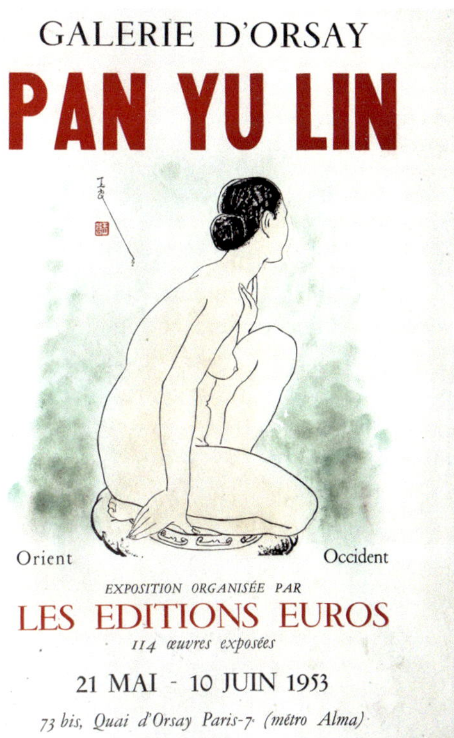

5.5 Exhibition poster for Pan Yuliang's solo exhibition at Galerie d'Orsay in 1953. Courtesy of the Anhui Museum.

child. There, her life becomes even more obscured and she likely committed suicide in the late 1960s following a mental breakdown.[28]

Some of the other women artists might be considered modestly successful later in life, if the definition of professional success is modified. Pan Yuliang and Fang Junbi maintained lifelong commitments to producing and exhibiting art; however, both managed to do so only as self-exiles in Europe. As such, these two demonstrate the struggles Chinese women artists encountered outside of China; abroad they became doubly marginalized, not just as women artists, but also as ethnic minorities. Pan Yuliang, who had left China in 1937 to spend the remaining four decades of her life in Paris, may have fixated on her peripheral status within the Parisian art community to produce images that suggest a self-Orientalizing eye (fig. 5.4).[29] Having long favored the female nude as the subject of her work (chapter 3), she continued this artistic interest and over the remainder of her life painted scores of such images featuring Asian women.[30] While the intention behind the artist's preoccupation with the image of the non-Western female nude remains enigmatic, it would seem in part that for Pan the nude female body served as a vehicle to span the divide between East and West, as a poster for her 1953 solo exhibition physically illustrates (fig. 5.5).[31] While living in Paris, she participated in group exhibitions, held solo shows around the world, and won prestigious awards from French institutions for her work. Yet, never having attained commercial success, she died poor, and her work only recently has received critical acclaim within her homeland.[32]

Fang Junbi, was to move abroad two decades after Pan Yuliang's departure from China. Having manipulated the political rhetoric of the Reorganized National Government of China to her professional advantage, Fang remained dedicated to the cause even after Japan's defeat. When Wang Jingwei's widow, Chen Bijun, was sentenced to life imprisonment in 1946, Fang fought relentlessly for her friend's clemency. She later held an exhibition in Shanghai in 1948, for which she billed herself as the wife of Zeng Zhongming—perhaps a defiant expression of her continued sympathy for the Wang Jingwei government and her husband's role in it but perhaps also an attempt to publicly deny slanderous rumors claiming her to have been Wang's mistress.[33] Following the political turnover in 1949, Fang's personal wealth allowed her to gather her artworks and flee overseas.[34] There she resumed her activities as an artist and, without the sociopolitical pressures to prioritize home and nation that she had experienced in China, she traveled and exhibited her artwork internationally. Since collaborating with Gao Jianfu of the Lingnan School in the 1930s, Fang had added painting in ink on paper to her repertoire, and late in life the traditional medium held even greater appeal for her. In 1972, during the final years of the Cultural Revolution, she visited China for over a year, and there painted a quaint rural landscape, its naïve style and aerial view clearly inspired by Chinese Communist collectivist and folk paintings (fig. 5.6).[35] She was to visit and temporarily live in China two more times, residing in between these trips first in Boston and then in Geneva, while continuing to exhibit her work and bequeathing parts of her collection to the Boston Museum of Fine Arts and to her homeland. Despite her unceasing professional activity, Fang remains relatively unknown today.

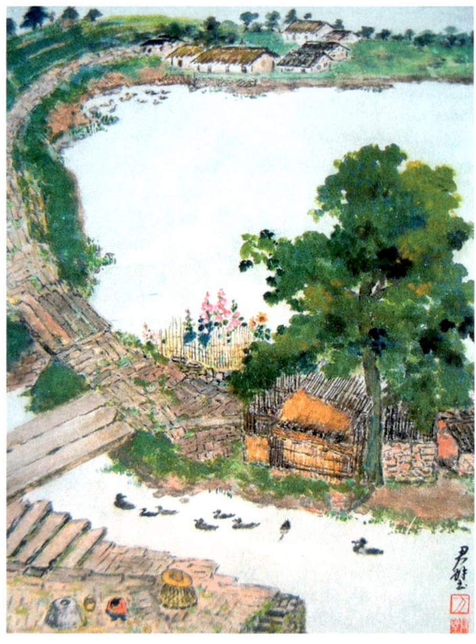

5.6 Fang Junbi, *A Little Village near Fuzhou*, 1973. Ink and color on paper, 23 in. × 17 in. Courtesy of the artist's son Wen-ti Tsen.

Qiu Ti and Yu Feng mark the extent of the professional reinvention demanded of those modernist women artists who remained in China, and in the 1950s both were to turn their attention to politically condoned artistic practices such as collectivism. Qiu Ti retained a passionate commitment to the visual arts throughout her years as a refugee wandering with young children in tow. She had never ceased to paint in oil, and with the relative stability of the early 1950s she even produced ten large-scale paintings of rural life in Zhejiang—acclamatory images of the proletariat already approved as a politically appropriate subject at the start of the PRC.[36] In 1953, however, she turned to a new profession as a designer at the Research Institute of Art and Design and, in what were to be her final years, brought a second artistic career to fruition. Under state support, Yu Feng directed a Dress Reform Campaign that consisted of a team of women artists and designers dedicated to guiding the development of Chinese women's clothing (fig. 5.7).[37] Qiu Ti served as a member of this team and contributed folk-dance costume designs based on the clothing of China's ethnic minorities (fig. 5.8). The policies of the PRC pushed women into gender-segregated fields and the degree of social progress for women made under the new political regime is questionable.[38] Nonetheless, during the four years Qiu Ti worked as a fashion designer, she received official recognition for her talent, and for a time her peers once again validated the importance of her artistic contri-

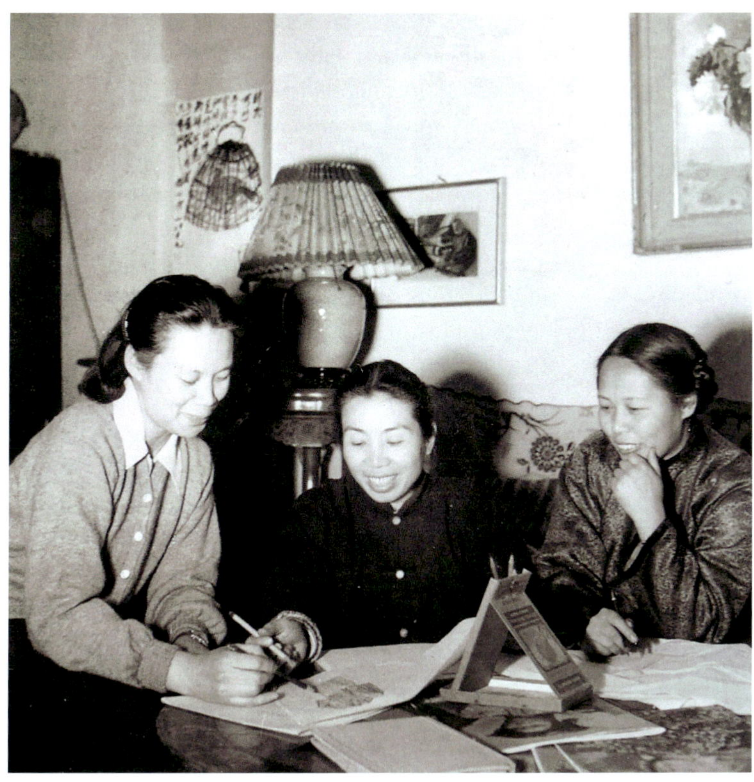

5.7 Xiao Shufang (1911–2005), Yu Feng, and Qiu Ti sketching garment designs for the Dress Reform Campaign. Courtesy of the Schudy [Qiu Ti] Archives at The Li Ching Cultural and Educational Foundation.

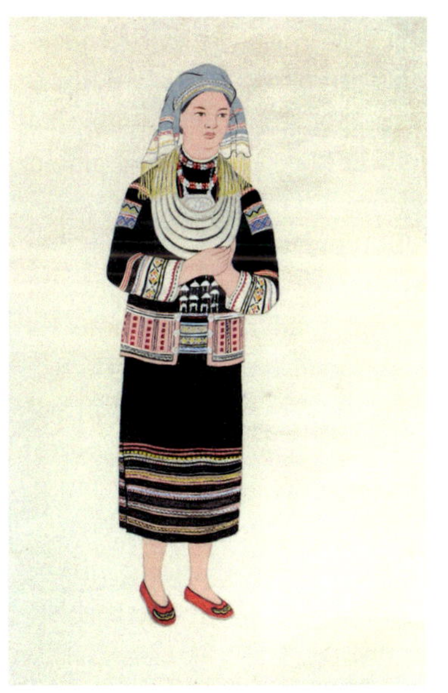

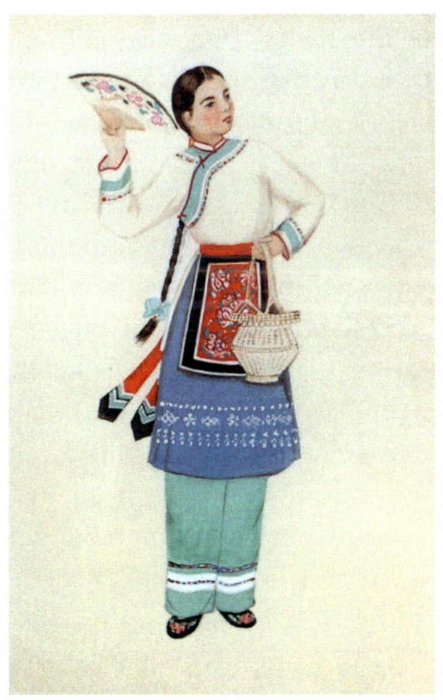

5.8 Qiu Ti, Folk-dancing costume designs, 1953–57. Courtesy of the Schudy [Qiu Ti] Archives at The Li Ching Cultural and Educational Foundation.

butions.[39] Had she lived longer, perhaps Qiu Ti would have returned to oil painting on a professional level. As it was, life had become exceptionally precarious for the former modernist artists of China. Her husband was branded a Rightist in 1957, and Qiu Ti, who was suffering from a heart condition at that time, was denied medical attention that might have saved her life.

Of the half dozen women discussed at length in this book, Yu Feng alone remained professionally active within China well into her old age. After fleeing to the southwestern areas of Chengdu and Chongqing with Huang Miaozi as wartime refugees in 1941, she explored the mountainous landscape of Sichuan and painted the rugged natural settings and the ethnic groups she encountered.[40] She also continued to foster ties with the refugee art community. In Chongqing, she and Huang reconnected with bohemian friends from Shanghai and together the ragtag group of artists, writers, and thespians formed a bohemian collective they named "The Layabouts Lodge" (Erliu tang 二流堂).[41] In 1944 she joined the Art Institute headed by Xu Beihong in Chongqing, and in 1945 she participated in the Joint Exhibition of Modern Painting in Chongqing.[42] After the defeat of Japan, Yu Feng returned to Shanghai for a while, where she became part of the Shanghai Artists' Association's (Shanghai Meishu Zuojia Xiehui 上海美術作家協會) first exhibition.[43] Following the end of the Civil War, she and Huang Miaozi relocated to Beijing and Yu Feng spent the next few decades associated with the Central Academy of Art.[44] In the mid 1950s, she also turned to fashion design, and as the director of the Dress Reform Campaign spearheaded an effort to beautify Chinese women's attire through the integration of indigenous folk designs.[45] Though an ardent Communist activist, Yu Feng fell victim to the purges of the Cultural Revolution and was imprisoned for seven years. Taking up painting again a few years after her release in 1975, however, Yu Feng exhibited her *Life Awakening in Springtime* (*Chunfeng chui you sheng* 春风吹又生) at the 1982 French Salon Exhibition and won the gold prize, securing international recognition (fig. 5.9).[46] Indeed, redemption for most of the modernists, including the men, came only in their twilight years, if not posthumously.

It is possible that had more women been blessed with long careers within China, such as was true for Yu Feng, female artists would be better remembered today for their roles in the development of modernist art in China, but based on the examples of other women around the world, such a scenario seems unlikely. A global recovery effort is currently underway, as art historians and curators excavate the roles of centuries' worth of forgotten women artists.[47] In a raft of scholarly literature, major museum exhibitions, and art auctions, modern women artists are finally receiving their due. The many women of abstract expressionism, Bauhaus, Viennese modernism, Dada, as well as radical standouts such as Hilma af Klint and Yayoi Kasuma, have all benefitted from unprecedented attention.[48] But these individual cases jointly confirm a cross-cultural standard of critical dismissal and professional neglect of women artists despite their lifetimes of dedication and ingenuity. In "Women Artists of Cercle et Carré: Abstraction, Gender and Modernity," for instance, M. Lluïsa Faxedas explicates the reductionist philosophy underpinning a seemingly inclusive abstract art society in 1929–30 Paris.[49] Though women members were abundant and prominent, the group rooted its founding ideology in gender essentialism, which the female artists readily embraced themselves though it did little to heighten their esteem in the eyes of their peers. This philosophy of dualism scripted gendered roles onto the universe—with the maternal female force seen as inferior to the rational thought of the male principle—and meant that women found places within the group as creative agents but received little accommodation as contributors to the group's theoretical discourse. Decades later, with their contributions already forgotten and their careers less suc-

5.9 Yu Feng, *Life Awakening in Springtime* (*Chunfeng chui you sheng*), 1981. Ink and color on paper, 66 cm × 51 cm. Exhibited at the 1982 French Salon Exhibition. Courtesy of the artist's son Huang Dagang.

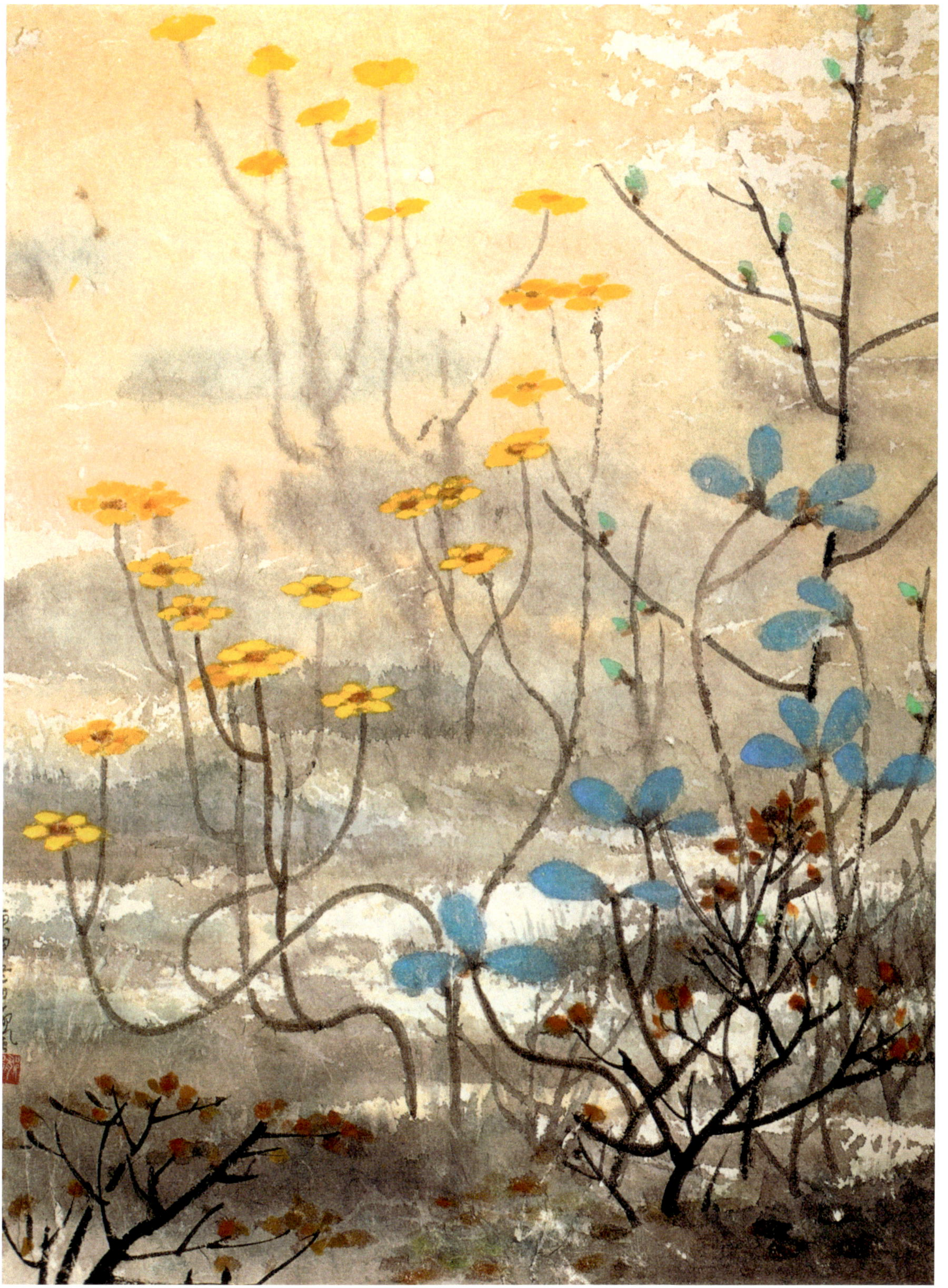

cessful than that of the male group members, one female member, Franciska Clausen, recalled that she and the other women participating in the group had not been "taken seriously."[50] The accumulation of myriad similar accounts make the subtle yet unrelenting corrosion of women's positions within the art historical canon all the more apparent.

While the insidious devaluation of women artists' careers is nothing new, recent responses to women's experiences in the workforce might indicate a measure of progress. Consider, for example, the recent reprint of *Life with Picasso*, in which Françoise Gilot documents the marginalization of her own professional ambitions for the duration of the decade that she lived with the abusively manipulative and controlling male artist.[51] Picasso's misogynistic and misanthropic ways were no secret, but in the wake of the Me Too movement his derision is only now being recognized for its detrimental effect on her career, even though Gilot first published her account in 1964.[52] So, too, the Centre Pompidou's exhibition of the artwork of Picasso's earlier lover, Dora Maar—which will travel to London's Tate Modern and Los Angeles' Getty Center and is her most expansive retrospective to date—stems from this reassessment of the persistent and pernicious dissolution of women's professional worth.[53] With men's bad behavior frequently rewarded and women's careers subjected to an endless onslaught of professional slights and personal attacks, the posthumous reappraisals of female artists' contributions may signal change, but for these women that might be said to offer too little, too late.

This book, then, has also explicated the pitfalls women's careers suffered during the unfolding of modern art in China. The art community recognized Guan Zilan's and her sisters' professionalism, even as it nonetheless pigeonholed them as female artists. Collectively with their male colleagues, women like Qiu Ti stood as pioneers of a modern conceptionalization of art professionals and as forebears of modernist art, but they often have been individually and incorrectly labeled as exceptions, that is, as the only or the first woman to have accomplished one feat or another. Despite working alongside men to produce equal work and finding ways to remain professionally active even as war brought modernist art to a close, their contributions to the development of modernist art practices have been ghettoized or erased entirely from the canon.

It may be that the women artists of modern China ultimately endured a fate similar to that of their sisters elsewhere in the world, but for roughly a decade—from the mid 1920s to the mid 1930s—they also briefly enjoyed an unparalleled access to the professional field. Although never truly egalitarian, the modern Chinese art community—particularly the sector dedicated to *xihua*—presented women artists opportunities seldom seen in Western art history prior to the second wave of the feminist movement. These opportunities sprang from the theoretical discourse of Chinese modernism and nationalism, which pitted the modern woman against Confucian tradition and promised the reform and revitalization of the entire nation through her emancipation, education, and professionalization. Women artists who received coeducational training, traveled internationally, and participated in the newly institutionalized practice of the public art exhibition thereby demonstrated the forward momentum of national progress. It is this association, and its abrupt and dramatic rejection of traditional values and institutions, that gave women the means to become vital contributors to a brief florescence of modernist art in early twentieth-century China. Sensing their unprecedented, if ultimately fleeting, opportunity, these women reached for careers in the arts with the optimistic belief that they had discovered a golden key to unlock not just their own empowered futures but a nation reborn.

Endnotes

Introduction

1 "You tian le ji wei nüyishujia 又添了幾位女藝術家 [A Few More Female Artists]," *Shenbao* 申報 *[Shun Pao]* 20385 (December 21, 1929): 17.

2 In comparison with its Western counterpart, modern art in China has received little scholarly attention. Prior to the twenty-first century, the majority of art historians routinely dismissed modern Chinese art as derivative and uninspired.

3 Elaine O'Brien, ed., *Modern Art in Africa, Asia, and Latin America: An Introduction to Global Modernisms* (Malden, MA: Wiley-Blackwell, 2013), 6. The depressing second sentence clearly references Linda Nochlin's seminal "Why Have There Been No Great Women Artists?," which accounts for the overall absence of women artists in art history textbooks by detailing the ways in which women never received the training necessary to compete with men. Linda Nochlin, "Why Have There Been No Great Women Artists?," *ARTnews* (January 1971): 22–39, 67–71.

4 This book concentrates on the roles of women active in modernist art circles. By modernist, I am referring to artists who primarily looked to the Western artistic tradition, particularly the media of oil painting, sculpture, watercolor, sketch, and cartoons. By rejecting indigenous media and styles, these artists chose to assert their modernity via a conspicuous break with Chinese tradition. While the realistic and postimpressionistic styles popular among China's male and female modernist artists might not strike today's art historians as particularly innovative in comparison to contemporary art movements in the West, for the artists themselves, as well as the larger Chinese society, their very choice to create *xihua* (what may be translated as "Western-style painting," but more than anything else indicates the use of nonindigenous art materials and techniques) signified modernist inclinations.

5 Marsha Weidner, "Women in the History of Chinese Painting," in *Views from Jade Terrace: Chinese Women Artists 1300–1912*, ed. Marsha Weidner (Indianapolis: Indianapolis Museum of Art, 1988), 13. See also, Ellen Johnston Laing, "Women Painters in Traditional China," in *Flowering in the Shadows: Women in the History of Chinese and Japanese Painting*, edited by Marsha Weidner, 81–101 (Honolulu: University of Hawaii Press, 1990).

6 The Yuan-dynasty calligrapher and ink bamboo expert Guan Daosheng stands as the one exception, and even her fame is overshadowed by the success of her husband Zhao Mengfu. Weidner, 13.

7 Weidner, 25.

8 Weidner, 15.

9 Weidner, 26.

10 Republican-period biographies for male artists are equally derivative.

11 Here I follow Wang Zheng's translation of *funü wenti* as "the woman problem" instead of "the woman question." Whereas *funü wenti* was the Chinese translation of the longstanding English phrase "the woman question," with her use of "problem" instead of "question," Wang is able to "emphasize that linguistic importation often alters the connotation of a phrase. *Funü wenti,* as it was used at the turn of the century, suggests not only an awareness that problematized the women's situation formerly regarded as normal but also a presumption that women hindered the nation's ascendance to 'modernity.'" Wang Zheng, *Women in the Chinese Enlightenment: Oral and Textual Histories* (Berkeley: University of California Press, 1999), 3, n. 5.

12 Dorothy Ko and Wang Zheng, eds., *Translating Feminisms in China: A Special Issue of Gender & History* (Oxford: Malden Blackwell Publishing, 2007), 2–7.

13 Ling-ling Lien, "Searching for the 'New Womanhood': Career Women in Shanghai, 1912–1945" (PhD diss., University of California, 2001), 4. Wang Zheng, *Women in the Chinese Enlightenment*, 14–15.

14 Jacqueline Nivard, "Women and Women's Press: The Case of the Ladies' Journal (Funü Zazhi) 1915–1931," *Republican China* 10, no. 1 (1984): 37–55.

15 Nivard, 44–48. Nivard's survey of the Republican period's most successful women's journal *Funü zazhi* provides a detailed look at the men behind the publication of material on women's rights and the inaccessibility of journalism as a career choice for women. Ma Yuxin examines opposing feminist discourses of male and female journalists and concludes that, "a new autonomous women's feminism was born from within or discursively from without male feminist discourse in the late 1920s by writers such as Chen Xuezhao, and soon grew to eclipse male feminist discourse as the dominant feminism in China in the 1930s." Ma Yuxin, "Male Feminism and Women's Subjectivities: Zhang Xichen, Chen Xuezhao, and The New Woman," *Twentieth-Century China* 29, no. 1 (November 2003): 23.

16 Bryna Goodman, "The Vocational Woman and the Elusiveness of 'Personhood' in Early Republican China," in *Gender in Motion: Divisions of Labor and Cultural Change in Late Imperial and Modern China*, ed. Bryna Goodman and Wendy Larsen (New York: Rowman & Littlefield Publishers, 2005).

17 Qiu Jin, "An Address to My Two Hundred Million Women Compatriots in China [Trans.]," in *The Search for Modern China: A Documentary Collection*, ed. Janet Y. Chen et al. (Vancouver: Langara College, 2017), 185–87.

18 Wang Zheng, *Women in the Chinese Enlightenment*, 62; Goodman, "The Vocational Woman," 269.

19 Goodman, "The Vocational Woman," 276–78.

20 Lien, "Searching for the 'New Womanhood,'" 64–65.

21 Lien, 65–66.

22 There is a significant amount of research on the Modern Girl and her many iterations across the globe. See, for example, Tani E. Barlow, "Buying In: Advertising and the Sexy Modern Girl Icon in Shanghai in the 1920s and 1930s," in *The Modern Girl Around the World: Consumption, Modernity, and Globalization*, edited by The Modern Girl Around the World Research Group, 288–316. (Durham: Duke University Press, 2008). A new monograph dedicated to the topic will be published later this year: Sumei Wang, *The East Asian Modern Girl: Women, Media, and Colonial Modernity in the Interwar Years* (Leiden: Brill, 2020). Regarding the popular usage of the term, Sarah E. Stevens's surveys provide detailed analyses of the opposing archetypes—the nation-building New Woman and the dangerous Modern Girl. See Sarah E. Stevens, "Figuring Modernity: The New Woman and the Modern Girl in Republican China," *NWSA Journal* 15, no. 3 (2003): 82–103. Tze-lan D. Sang acknowledges Stevens's study in a footnote within her own informed analysis of the Modern Girl persona but argues that a precise distinction between the Modern Girl and the New Woman cannot be made. See Tze-lan Deborah Sang, "Failed Modern Girls," in *Performing Nation: Gender Politics in Literature, Theater, and the Visual Arts of China and Japan, 1880–1940*, ed. Doris Croissant, Catherine Vance Yeh, and Joshua S. Mostow (Leiden: Brill, 2008). Shu-mei Shih ponders the market's impact on the varying depictions of the New Woman and the Modern Girl in occupied Shanghai's commercial advertisements. Shu-Mei Shih, "Shanghai Women of 1939: Visuality and the Limits of Feminine Modernity," in *Visual Culture in Shanghai, 1850s–1930s*, edited by Jason C. Kuo, 205–40 (Washington, DC: New Academia Publishing, 2007). I find that, while there was slippage in the use of these two terms, magazines generally embraced the New Woman as a positive concept in the 1920s and later largely regarded the Modern Girl as the object of disdain in the 1930s.

23 Wang Zheng, *Women in the Chinese Enlightenment*, 263.

24 Lien, "Searching for the 'New Womanhood,'" 67–68.

25 The name of the magazine, *Linglong*, is an onomatopoeia for the tinkling sound of jade ornaments and could be used to describe a delicately made object or a clever person. Li Ying, "Zuo yi wei xiandai nüzi 做一位現代女子 [Being a Modern Woman]," trans. C.V. Starr East Asian Library, *Linglong tuhua zazhi* 玲瓏圖畫雜誌 *[Lin Loon Ladies' Magazine]* 4, no. 10 (April 4, 1934): 583–84. University of Columbia's C.V. Starr East Asian Library maintains a high-quality webpage devoted to this journal that includes archived digital images of every page from all issues in the library's collection at https://exhibitions.library.columbia.edu/exhibits/show/linglong.

26 Li Ying, 583. A translation of this article may be found on the C.V. Starr Library's *Linglong* webpage at https://exhibitions.library.columbia.edu/exhibits/show/linglong/about_linglong/woman/contemporary.

27 Both of these terms are written in English.

28 Bo Wang, "'Breaking the Age of Flower Vases:' Lu Yin's Feminist Rhetoric," *Rhetoric Review* 28, no. 3 (2009): 253–54.

29 Wang, 256.

30 Lu Yin, "Huaping shidai 花瓶時代 [The Age of Flower Vases]," *Shishi xinbao* 時事新報, *Qingguang* 青光 supplement (August 11, 1933). Reprinted in *Lu Yin daibiaozuo* 庐隐代表作 (Beijing: Huaxia chuban she, 1998): 373–74.

31 Lu Yin, 374.

32 Wang, "'Breaking the Age of Flower Vases,'" 259.

33 To cite a few examples, scores of issues of *Xinren zhoukan* (*New People's Weekly*) from 1935 include a page devoted to photographs of charming modern ladies, the thrice-weekly Tianjin publication *The Pei-Yang Pictorial News* (*Beiyang huabao*) reserved the center of each front page for a portrait photograph of a prominent young woman. For one example, see *Xinren zhoukan* 1.27 (March 18, 1935). A cover girl welcomes the readers to each issue of *The Young Companion*, and several issues of the magazine contain a "Women's Page" consisting of flattering photographs of select, socially prominent women. One example of a "Women's Page" can be found in *Liangyou huabao* 良友畫報 *[The Young Companion]* 62 (October 1931): 36–37. The Chinese title, "Guixiu fangying 閨秀芳影 [Pleasant Visages of Gentlewomen]," is certainly more descriptive than its English counterpart.

34 The sexualized presentation of the women in the pages of the popular magazines is all the more telling when precursors to these images are taken into consideration. Leo Ou-fan Lee suggests that the use of alluring cover girls for Republican-period publications, such as *Liangyou huabao* 良友畫報 *[The Young Companion]*, continued practices of the late Qing courtesan journals; cover shots of the New Woman of the modern era merely replacing the Qing-dynasty images of the courtesans. Whereas the Qing publications underscored the market value of the women, the later publica-

tions "had to reinvest the female body with an entirely new meaning and ethical value." Leo Ou-fan Lee, *Shanghai Modern: The Flowering of a New Urban Culture in China, 1930–1945* (Cambridge: Harvard University Press, 1999), 65, 73.

35 Hu Ying, "Naming the First New Woman," *NAN NÜ* 3, no. 2 (2001): 230.

36 For many reformers, the term Talented Woman had come to signify a woman of some literary skill who lived under and perpetuated an oppressive system that only allowed her limited access to knowledge. Recent scholarship demonstrates that the rise of the New Woman archetype symbolized the triumph of modern social progress over China's history of feudal backwardness. For the rhetoric of the modern liberated woman to succeed, it had to discredit the notion of the Talented Woman, whose existence as an earlier model of educated woman in China's history proved problematic. Hu Ying, 199–206. Paul Bailey also discusses early twentieth-century attitudes toward the *cainü* and the New Woman, as well as analyzes pervasive social anxiety over the perceived character flaws of women. Paul Bailey, "Women Behaving Badly: Crime, Transgressive Behavior and Gender in Early Twentieth-Century China," *NAN NÜ* 8, no. 1 (2006): 156–97. Joan Judge describes the vilification of *cainü* for the purpose of spurring reform in the late Qing dynasty. Joan Judge, "Blended Wish Images: Chinese and Western Exemplary Women at the Turn of the Twentieth Century," *NAN NÜ* 6, no. 1 (2004): 102–35.

37 Just as reportage on women labeled as *nühuajia* circulated in print media in great frequency throughout the Republican period, so too a sister social category—*nüzuojia* 女作家 (woman writer)—gained popular attention. Megan Ferry's recent book focuses on *nüzuojia* and argues that in its use of the term "print media classified and normalized female authors as belonging to a specified sphere of modernity," and could thereby exercise control over "women authors' intellectual contribution to cultural modernity." Megan M. Ferry, *Chinese Women Writers and Modern Print Culture* (Amherst, NY: Cambria Press, 2018), 33. Much the same could be said of *nühuajia* and their treatment in the Republican press, of course, but because most artworks have been lost and less is known of the visual arts from this period, this book concentrates more on reconstructing their forgotten contributions.

38 Maysching Margaret Kao, "China's Response to the West in Art: 1898–1937" (PhD diss., Stanford University, 1972). Andrews and Shen use the year 1930 as point of division around which their discussion of *guohua* painting is split, pointing to the significance of the period of the late 1920s through the early 1930s in all fields of Chinese art. Julia F. Andrews and Kuiyi Shen, eds., *Between the Thunder and the Rain: Chinese Paintings from the Opium War Through the Cultural Revolution, 1840–1979* (San Francisco: Asian Art Museum, 2000).

39 Andrews and Shen, *Between the Thunder and the Rain*, 141.

40 Kao, "China's Response," 151. Kuiyi Shen discusses several of the painters that sought to reform traditional painting with the selective application of Western techniques and styles in his essay. Kuiyi Shen, "Traditional Painting in a Transnational Era, 1900–1950," in *A Century in Crisis: Modernity and Tradition in the Art of Twentieth-Century China*, ed. Julia F. Andrews and Kuiyi Shen (New York: Guggenheim Museum, 1998), 86–88.

41 Xu Beihong initiated a high-profile debate over the relevance of modernist art when in reaction to the 1929 First National Art Exhibition he published "Huo 惑 [Perplexed]" in the exhibition newsletter, in which he bitterly criticizes many of the modernist painters in Europe. A public dialogue involving poet Xu Zhimo, painter Li Yishi, and Xu Beihong ensued. Zheng Shengtian, "Waves Lashed the Bund from the West: Shanghai's Art Scene in the 1930s," in *Shanghai Modern, 1919–1945*, ed. Jo-Anne Birnie Danzker Danzker, Ken Lum, and Zheng Shengtian (Ostfildern-Ruit: Hatje Cantz Verlag, 2004), 187–92.

42 Julia F. Andrews, "A Shelter from the Storm: Chinese Painting in a Cataclysmic Age, 1930–1979," in *Between the Thunder and the Rain: Chinese Paintings from the Opium War Through the Cultural Revolution, 1840–1979*, ed. Kuiyi Shen and Julia F. Andrews (San Francisco: Asian Art Museum, 2000), 182–83. Andrews observes that the Western leanings of the art schools in Shanghai favored oil painters and notes that the art market was critical of the *guohua* painters. Conversely, teaching appointments served as the main source of income for the modernist painters, as they made few successful sales of their work. Ralph Croizier, "Post-Impressionists in Pre-War Shanghai: The Juelanshe (Storm Society) and the Fate of Modernism in Republican China," in *Modernity in Asian Art*, ed. John Clark (New South Wales: Wild Peony, 1993), 142.

43 Lisa Claypool, "Ways of Seeing the Nation: Chinese Painting in the National Essence Journal (1905 – 1911) and Exhibition Culture," *Positions: East Asia Cultures Critique* 19, no. 1 (March 20, 2011): 57, 65–71, https://doi.org/10.1215/10679847-2010-024.

44 Claypool dates the institutionalization of the exhibition within China to the Qing-sponsored Nanyang Exposition in 1910. Claypool, 69.

45 Claypool, "Ways of Seeing the Nation."

46 "Autumn—The Season of Arts: Exhibition of works by the faculty of S. H. Academy," *Liangyou huabao* 良友畫報 *[The Young Companion]* 71 (1932). The Chinese-

language title reads, "Qiu zhi huazhan: Xinhua yizhuan jiaoshou zhanlanhui yu Pang Xunqin geren zhanlanhui 秋之畫展：新華藝專教授展覽會與龐薰琴個人展覽會 [Autumn's Painting Exhibitions: Xinhua Art Academy Professors' Exhibition and Pang Xunqin's Solo Exhibition]." Perhaps in the timing of their exhibitions the Chinese artists had decided to follow the relatively recent Parisian tradition of the seasonal exhibition first established by the inaugural Salon d'Automne (Autumn Salon) in 1903.

47 Though open to the public, in reality the exhibitions for modernist artists, such as the members of the Storm Society, drew a majority of attendees from the rarefied ranks of the intellectual and artistic communities. Croizier examines how the crux of the modernists' inability to secure widespread and enduring support lay in its basic ideology, which was "subjective, individualistic, innovative, and, by implication if not intent, elitist. The emphasis on the individual's inner vision and constantly changing creativity meant that it could brook no rules or regulations, no source of external authority." Croizier, "Post-Impressionists," 147.

48 Guohua painting societies with manifestos included the Chinese Epigraphy, Calligraphy, and Painting Study Society (Zhongguo Jinshi Shuhua Yiguan Xuehui 中國金石書畫藝觀學會) and the Chinese Painting Society (Zhongguo Huahui 中國畫會). Julia F. Andrews and Kuiyi Shen, "The Traditionalist Response to Modernity: The Chinese Painting Society of Shanghai," in *Visual Culture in Shanghai, 1850s–1930s,* edited by Jason C. Kuo, 79–93 (Washington, DC: New Academia Publishing, 2007). Idealistic proclamations became so prevalent that the art community experienced something of a manifesto fatigue, as evident from a group statement presented on the back cover of the journal *Bai E* 白鵝 [*White Goose*]. The journal was published by a painting association of the same name established by Chen Qiucao, Fang Xuegu, and Pan Sitong in 1924. Labeling all manifestos as impotent lies, the group refused to characterize their text as a manifesto per se and instead focused on the future content of the magazine. Their intent was not to provide any particular ideological bent or spur social progress but, rather, to cater to the editors' personal interests, which might range from art and fiction to news and satirical cartoons. Moreover, the organization reserved the right to pause publication of the journal when lacking inspiration. "Bai' E de kaishi 白鵝的起始 [The Beginnings of White Goose]," *Bai E yishu banyue kan* 白鵝藝術半月刊, June 15, 1930, back cover. The organization designated itself the Bai E Huihua Yanjiusuo in 1928 and opened the Bai E Huihua Buxi Xuexiao, a painting continuation school. On March 15, 1930, the association began publication of a bimonthly journal, which concluded in June of the same year after a total of five issues. The school burnt down August 13, 1937, during the Japanese invasion.

49 *Apollo* was an art journal edited by Lin Wenzheng 林文錚 (1903–89) and published by the National Hangzhou Art College.

50 Translation from Jo-Anne Birnie Danzker Danzker, Ken Lum, and Zheng Shengtian, eds., "Manifesto of the Art Movement Society (1929)," in *Shanghai Modern, 1919–1945* (Ostfildern-Ruit: Hatje Cantz Verlag, 2004), 373. The catalogue provides an English translation of the entire National Art Movement Society Manifesto.

51 Translation from Danzker, Lum, and Zheng Shengtian, "Manifesto of the Art Movement Society (1929)."

52 Author's translation. A copy of the original text is reprinted in simplified Chinese in Zhao Li 赵力 and Yu Ding 余丁, eds., *Zhongguo youhua wenxian* 中国油画文献 *[Literature on Chinese Oil Painting]* (Changsha: Hunan Meishu Chubanshe, 2002), 572.

53 For the Republican-period press, female *xihua* painters appear to have literally embodied modernity. Contemporary periodicals generally posit *xihua* (which began to be widely taught in China after the start of the twentieth century) as the opposite of traditional painting and thus modern by default. Moreover, the female artists who made their appearances in introductory profiles fashioned conspicuously modern appearances, availed themselves of higher education, and pursued modern careers within the incipient *xihua* art world. In all of these aspects, the contemporary press consistently portrayed female *xihua* artists as both modern women and as modern artists.

54 Jin Qijing 金啟靜, "Nüxing yu meishu 女性與美術 [Women and Art]," *Funü zazhi* 婦女雜誌 *[Ladies' Journal]* 15, no. 7 (July 1929).

55 Jin Qijing. Author's translation.

56 Tamar Garb's brilliant analysis of the Union des Femmes Peintres et Sculpteurs benefits from an enviously rich supply of published and archived primary writings by and about these women artists. Despite this comparatively abundant resource material, the women artists of the Union, like their younger sisters in China, are routinely overlooked today. Tamar Garb, *Sisters of the Brush: Women's Artistic Culture in Late Nineteenth-Century Paris* (New Haven: Yale University Press, 1994).

57 As translated in Garb, 160.

58 Garb, 1.

59 Garb, 68–69.

60 For monographs dedicated to the particularities and distinctions of feminist thought in China, see Tani E. Barlow, *The Question of Women in Chinese Feminism* (Durham: Duke University Press, 2004); Louise Edwards, *Gender, Politics, and Democracy: Women's Suffrage in China* (Stanford: Stanford University Press, 2008).

61 Joan Judge, *Republican Lens: Gender Visuality, and Experience in the Early Chinese Periodical Press* (Oakland, CA: University of California Press, 2015), 6.

62 This is a question with no easy answers and served as the subject of a symposium at the Seattle Art Museum and a subsequent book. Josh Yiu and Seattle Asian Art Museum, eds., *Writing Modern Chinese Art: Historiographic Explorations* (Seattle, WA: Seattle Art Museum, 2009).

63 See, for example, Julia F. Andrews and Kuiyi Shen, "Traditionalism as a Modern Stance: The Chinese Women's Calligraphy and Painting Society," *Modern Chinese Literature and Culture* 11, no. 1 (Spring 1999): 1–30; Claypool, "Ways of Seeing the Nation."

Chapter 1

1 Hujiang Sheying Lou 滬江攝影樓 [Wou Kong Photo Studio], "Guan Zilan Nüshi shan danqing po fu shengming 關紫蘭女士擅丹青頗負盛名 [Famous Painter Miss Guan Zilan]," *Zhongguo Sheying Xuehui huabao* 中國攝影學會畫報 *[Pictorial Weekly]* 5, no. 242 (1930): cover.

2 Jane Zheng, "The Shanghai Fine Arts College: Art Education and Modern Women Artists in the 1920s and 1930s," *Modern Chinese Literature and Culture* 19, no. 1 (Spring 2007): 192–235; Lesley W. Ma, "Blossoming Beyond the Pages: Female Painterly Modernities in Liangyou," in *Liangyou: Kaleidoscopic Modernity and the Shanghai Global Metropolis, 1926–1945*, ed. Paul Pickowicz, Kuiyi Shen, and Yingjin Zhang (Boston: Brill, 2013), 203–25.

3 Ma, "Blossoming Beyond the Pages," 216. Ma primarily focuses on female *guohua* painters and rightly observes that periodicals seldom presented these women working in traditional materials as innovative or progressive. For example, it would seem that Ma is thinking only of *guohua* painting when she writes that the *Liangyou* painting series "never featured a woman artist." In fact, the *xihua* portion of the series included Pan Yuliang. Ma's article also discusses in some depth the activities of the *guohua* association the Chinese Women's Calligraphy and Painting Society. Ma, 209.

4 Several essays published in a recent monograph devoted to Guan Zilan serve as the primary source for biographic information on this artist. CANS Yishu Xinwen Bianji Tuandui CANS藝術新聞編輯團隊 [CANS Art News Editorial Team], ed., *Guan Zilan (1903–1985)* 關紫蘭 *(1903-1985)* (Taipei: Huayi Wenhua, 2012). Another source of general information about Guan Zilan, in which her elderly daughter is interviewed, comes from a video compilation on Chinese artists. See Shanghai Wenguang Xinwen Chuanmei Jituan 上海文广新闻传媒集团 [Shanghai Media Group] et al., *Minghua mingjia mi'an* 名画名家谜案 *[Mysteries of Famous Paintings and Famous Artists]*, vol. 4, *"Faxian" Guan Zilan* 发现关紫兰 ['Discovering' Guan Zilan] (Beijing: Zhongguo Guoji Dianshi Zonggongsi, 2009).

5 Kris Imants Ercums, "Exhibiting Modernity: National Art Exhibitions in China during the Early Republican Period, 1911–1937" (PhD diss., University of Chicago, 2014), 67.

6 Phyllis Hwee Leng Teo, "Alternative Agency in Representation by Contemporary Chinese Women Artists," *Asian Culture and History* 2, no. 1 (January 2010): 66.

7 Jane Zheng, "A Local Response to the National Ideal: Aesthetic Education in the Shanghai Art School (1913–1937)," *Art Criticism* 22, no. 1 (2007): 51, n. 45.

8 Although recent scholarship assumes Guan Zilan spent three years studying in Japan, her biography in *Truth Beauty Good*—which was likely printed around the beginning of the year—places her in Shanghai by 1929. Zhang Ruogu 張若谷, ed., "Nüzuojia hao: Zhen mei shan zazhi yi zhou nian jinian haowai 女作家號: 真美善雜誌一周年紀 念號外 [Women Writers Issue: Truth, Beauty, Good Magazine's First-Year Anniversary Special Issue]," in *Zhen mei shan zazhi* 真美善雜誌 *[Truth, Beauty, Good Magazine]*, Shanghai: Zhen Mei Shan Shudian, 1929.

9 "Zhonghua Yishu Daxue meishu zhanlanhui zhi yibufen zuopin ji zuozhe 中華藝術大學美術展覽會之一部分作品及作者 [A Few Artworks and Artists from the Chinese University of the Arts' Fine Art Exhibition]," *Liangyou huabao* 良友畫報 *[The Young Companion]* 17 (August 1927): 20. *Liangyou*, self-titled *The Young Companion* in English, is easily the Republican-period's most renowned periodical. An extraordinarily long-running (1926–41) comprehensive pictorial magazine founded by Wu Liande, it was published in Shanghai once a month.

10 Cui Wenying's portrait photograph—in which she wears a more conservative hairstyle, sits in profile, and demurely looks away from the camera—provides a stark contrast to Guan's.

11 "Yanghuajia Guan Zilan nüshi 洋畫家關紫蘭女士 [Western Painter Miss Guan Zilan]," *Tuhua shibao* 圖畫時報 *[The Eastern Times Photo Supplement]*, no. 375 (1927): 3. I have no precise date of publication for this piece, but calculating backward from a later dated issue I estimate it to have been published sometime in late July or early August.

12 Li Yuyi 李禹一, Jin Qijing 金啟靜, and Jiang Zhaohe 蔣兆和, eds., "*Jiaoyu bu quanguo meishu zhanlanhui teji hao* 教育部全國美術展覽會特輯號 [Special Issue on the National Art Exhibition of the Ministry of Education]," *Funü zazhi* 婦女雜誌 *[Ladies' Journal]* 15, no. 7 (July 1929).

13 Jonathan Hay, "Painters and Publishing in Late Nineteenth Century," in *Art at the Close of China's*

Empire, ed. Ju-hsi Chou (Tempe, AZ: Arizona State University, 1998), 134–88. Jane Zheng extends Hay's term to the Republican art world in her investigation of the ties between the Shanghai Academy of Art and the publishing industry. Jane Zheng, "The Shanghai Art School and the Modern Mechanism of Artistic Celebrity (1913–1937)," *Art Criticism* 22, no. 1 (2007): 7–28. A focus of my own current research is an in-depth analysis of the larger phenomenon of published artist profiles with particular attention to the *Truth, Beauty, Good* and *The Ladies' Journal* special issues.

14 "Miss Kuan Chi-lan in Japan," *Tuhua shibao* 圖畫時報 *[The Eastern Times Photo Supplement]*, no. 383 (1927): 1.

15 "Miss Kuan Chi-lan, a Chinese painter, tendered a reception to Japanese painters," *Tuhua shibao* 圖畫時報 *[The Eastern Times Photo Supplement]*, no. 388 (1927): 2.

16 "Rowing in a lake near Kobe: Miss Kuan Tsu-lan, a famous Chinese painter, is first from right. Mr. C. T. Pao, our correspondent in Japan, is fourth from right," *Tuhua shibao* 圖畫時報 *[The Eastern Times Photo Supplement]*, no. 393 (September 11, 1927): cover.

17 For information about the *guixiu's* travel restrictions at the turn of the century, see Ellen Widmer, "Gentility in Transition: Travels, Novels, and the New Guixiu," in *The Quest for Gentility in China: Negotiations beyond Gender and Class* (New York: Routledge, 2007), 21–44.

18 "Guan Zilan nüshi zai Riben zhanlan zuopin 關紫蘭女士在日展覽作品 [Artworks from Miss Guan Zilan's exhibition in Japan]," *Chenbao xingqi huabao* 晨報星期畫報 *[The Morning Post Sunday Picture Section]* 2, no. 100 (1927): 2.

19 Xue Fen 雪芬, "Guan Zilan gezhan de guangan 關紫蘭個展的觀感 [View of Guan Zilan's Solo Exhibition]," *Shenbao* 申報 *[Shun Pao]*, no. 4 (August 29, 1927). Information about this article comes from CANS Yishu Xinwen Bianji Tuandui, *Guan Zilan (1903–1985)*, 21. I have not seen the original.

20 "Guan Zilan nüshi he tade hua 關紫蘭女士和她的畫 [Guan Zilan and Her Paintings]," *Jindai funü* 今代婦女 *[The Modern Lady]*, no. 5 (1928): 14.

21 The four paintings are: *Narcissus* (*Shuixianhua*), *Beautiful Country House* (*Xiangjian mei wu*), *West Lake* (*Xi Hu*), and *Idly Sitting at with Family* (*Jiazhong jian zuo*).

22 "Miss Kwan Tsu-lan, whose works recently exhibited in Japan," *Liangyou huabao* 良友畫報 *[The Young Companion]*, no. 30 (September 1928): 4.

23 The chronology at the back of the Zilan (1903–85) exhibition catalogue notes that from 1930 to 1935 Guan held positions at the Shanghai Xiyang Meishu Yuan 上海晞陽美術院 and the Shanghai Yishu Zhuanke Xuexiao 上海藝術專科學校. CANS Yishu Xinwen Bianji Tuandui, *Guan Zilan (1903–1985)*, 162.

24 See the Introduction for a discussion of the Modern Girl in China.

25 "Qing zhuang jiu shi 輕妝就試 [Trying on a Bit of Makeup]," *Shidai huabao* 時代畫報 *[Modern Miscellany]* 1, no. 7 (1 August 1930): 25. *Shidai huabao*, a comprehensive pictorial, chose *Modern Miscellany* as its English title. Also published in Shanghai, it ran from 1929 to 1937 and was edited primarily by Zhang Guangyu, Ye Lingfeng, and Zhang Zhenyu. Ye Qianyu and Liang Desuo also contributed as editors in later issues. Although initially a monthly publication, *Modern Miscellany* switched to semimonthly printings by the fourth issue.

26 See *Liangyou huabao* 良友畫報 *[The Young Companion]*, no. 45 (1930): cover.

27 Instead of crediting the Wou Kong Photo Studio as the creator of the photograph, a small note in the corner of the page cites *Pictorial Weekly* the as the source for all four photographs in the piece. In this case it may be possible that the editor of *Modern Miscellany* acted without the women's consent, but most likely the women themselves supplied the original photographs to *Pictorial Weekly*. It is hard to imagine that Guan Zilan, a repeat customer of the studio, would not have known and condoned the press's access to the images.

28 The English name for the Wou Kong Photo Studio may be found in the corner of a number of Guan Zilan's portrait photographs. The studio specialized in the production of glamour shot photographs for Shanghai's socialites and movie stars. Dozens of photographs credited to the business appear in issues of *Linglong* women's magazine and span the periodical's entire run (1931–37). These images may be found with a search for Hujiang Sheying Lou on the immensely useful *Chinese Women's Magazines* website. Universität Heidelberg, Chinese Women's Magazines in the Late Qing and Early Republican Period, 2015, https://kjc-sv034.kjc.uni-heidelberg.de/frauenzeitschriften/index.php.

29 Although I was not granted permission to publish them in this book, the sketches may be viewed in CANS Yishu Xinwen Bianji Tuandui, *Guan Zilan (1903–1985)*: 118–30.

30 See examples in CANS Yishu Xinwen Bianji Tuandui, *Guan Zilan (1903–1985)*, 123, 129 fig. 86. Chen Baoyi likewise sketched at least one image of a Western Modern Girl, with treatment nearly identical to Guan Zilan's. See his sketch in CANS Yishu Xinwen Bianji Tuandui, 156. But no matter how sensitively attuned, Chen's sketch is that of an outsider, as he could never assume the role of Modern Girl himself.

31 This photograph is reproduced in CANS Yishu Xinwen Bianji Tuandui, *Guan Zilan (1903–1985)*, 64.

32 Kuiyi Shen, "A Modern Showcase: *Shidai (Modern Miscellany)* in 1930s Shanghai," *Yishuxue Yanjiu* 12 (September 2013): 129–70.

33 "Some Masterworks of Miss C. L. Kuan," *Shidai huabao* 時代畫報 *[Modern Miscellany]* 1, no. 6 (1930): 8. Author's translation.
34 Shanghai Wenguang Xinwen Chuanmei Jituan et al., *Minghua mingjia mi'an*.
35 Joan Judge, *Republican Lens: Gender Visuality, and Experience in the Early Chinese Periodical Press* (Oakland, CA: University of California Press, 2015), 4.
36 Ma, "Blossoming Beyond the Pages," 223.
37 Dorothy Ko, *Cinderella's Sisters: A Revisionist History of Footbinding* (Berkeley, CA: University of California Press, 2005), 228.
38 For discussion of the struggles faced by female contemporary artists in China specifically, see Britta Erickson, "The Rise of a Feminist Spirit," *Art AsiaPacific*, no. 31 (2001): 64–71; Patricia Karetzky, "Four Artists from Beijing: Li Hong, Feng Jyali, Cai Jin, Xing Fei," *Woman's Art Journal* 23, no. 2 (Autumn 2002–Winter 2003):28–32; Xu Hong, "Dialogue: The Awakening of Women's Consciousness," trans. Claire Roberts, *Art AsiaPacific* 2, no. 2 (1995): 44–51; Peggy Wang, "Subversion, Culture Shock, and 'Women's Art': An Interview with Lin Tianmiao," *N. Paradoxa* 29 (January 2012): 22–31; Amanda Wangwright, "Double Vision: The Culture China Overseas Chinese Women's Invitational Exhibition [Review]," *SECAC Review* 16, no. 5 (December 2015): 661–64.
39 Linda Nochlin and Maura Reilly, *Women Artists: The Linda Nochlin Reader*, 2015, 64–67.
40 Judith Butler, "Performative Acts and Gender Constitution: An Essay in Phenomenology and Feminist Theory," *Theatre Journal* 40, no. 4 (December 1988): 531.

Chapter 2

1 Citing the Shanghainese pronunciation of "堤," Qiu Ti's daughter Pang Tao romanizes her mother's name as Ti instead of Di. I follow Pang Tao's romanization.
2 Despite standing as Qiu Ti's most publicized work, many questions surround *Flower*. The date Qiu Ti painted *Flower* is uncertain, although its showing at the Second Annual Storm Society Exhibition in October of 1933 provides a terminus ante quem. In all probability *Flower* was painted in oil on a canvas of modest size, as are all other extant examples of Qiu Ti's work. Some sense of the painting's size might be discerned from the photograph of Qiu Ti in *Modern Miscellany's* feature of the Second Annual Storm Society Exhibition. The painting behind Qiu Ti is almost certainly *Flower* and based on the fact that the upper and lower corners of the painting in the background extend outside the frame of the photograph, it may be surmised that the canvas is at minimum a couple of feet in height. "Exposition of Storm Society Paintings," *Shidai huabao* 時代畫報 *[Modern Miscellany]* 5, no. 1 (November 1933): unnumbered page. The Chinese-language title reads, "Juelanshe di er hui zhanlanhui chupin 決瀾社第二回展覽會出品 [Artworks from the Second Storm Society Exhibition]." As will be discussed later in this chapter, an announcement in the Shanghai pictorial *Modern Miscellany* reproduces the painting and gives a short written description of the circumstances surrounding the award. "Juelanshe jiang 決瀾社獎 [The Storm Society Award]," *Shidai huabao* 時代畫報 *[Modern Miscellany]* 5, no. 4 (16 December 1933). A second and more widely cited source of information about *Flower* is an essay written and published in 1935 by Storm Society cofounder and promoter Ni Yide, which will be discussed in detail below. Ni Yide 倪貽德, "Yiyuan jiaoyou ji: Juelanshe de yi qun 藝苑交遊記: 決瀾社的一群 [Notes on Friendly Connections in the Art Community: The Storm Society's Group]," *Qingnian jie* 青年界 *[Youth World]* 8, no. 3 (October 1935): 65–70.
3 While a few studies offer fairly in-depth analyses of the Storm Society, such as Ralph Croizier's 1993 article, a chapter in the 2004 exhibition catalogue *Shanghai Modern, 1919–1945*, and Li Chao's 2008 book, little in these works pertains directly to Qiu Ti. Scholarship focusing more directly on Qiu Ti mainly comprises biographical accounts and overviews of her entire oeuvre. An essay by Xu Hong, "Early 20th-Century Women Painters in Shanghai," references Qiu Ti in a brief biography, but there is no discussion of her paintings. Two exhibition catalogues, *Three Generations of Chinese Modernism* and *Schudy*, provide rare studies focused specifically on Qiu Ti but both encompass the artist's entire life and are confined by a biographical methodology. These two broad surveys of Qiu Ti's oeuvre do not offer thorough analysis of individual paintings or provide focused investigation of cultural issues, nor do they answer many questions concerning her relationship with the group. Ultimately, these studies dramatize Qiu Ti's life story at the expense of a deeper understanding of her goals as an artist. Ralph Croizier, "Post-Impressionists in Pre-War Shanghai: The Juelanshe (Storm Society) and the Fate of Modernism in Republican China," in *Modernity in Asian Art*, ed. John Clark (New South Wales: Wild Peony, 1993); Zheng Shengtian, "Waves Lashed the Bund from the West"; Li Chao 李超, *Kuangbiao jiqing—Juelanshe ji xiandai zhuyi yishu xiansheng* 狂飙激情--决澜社及现代主义艺术先声 *[Hurricane Passion: Juelanshe and the Modernist Art Prelude]* (Shanghai: Shanghai Jinxiu Wenzhang Chubanshe, 2008); Xu Hong, "Early 20th-Century Women Painters in Shanghai," in *Shanghai Modern, 1919–1945*; *Three Generations of Chinese Modernism: Qiu Ti, Pang Tao, Lin Yan* (Vancouver: Art Beatus Gallery, 1998); Pang Tao, ed., *Schudy* (Qiu Ti) 丘堤 (Nanjing: Jiangsu Jiaoyu Chubanshe, 2006).

4 Qiu Ti kept even the most fundamental information, such as her real age and the identity of her parents, hidden from most of the world, including her children. Ni Jun, "Schudy: Her Art and Life," in *Schudy* (Qiu Ti) 丘堤, ed. Pang Tao (Nanjing: Jiangsu Jiaoyu Chubanshe, 2006), 83; Amanda S. Wright, "Qiu Ti's Contributions to Juelanshe and the Intersection of Modernist Ideology, Public Receptivity, and Personal Identity for a Woman Oil Painter in Early Twentieth-Century China" (PhD diss., University of Kansas, 2011), 18.

5 Qiu Ti attended Xiapu County No. 1 Primary School (Xiapu xianli di yi gaodeng xuexiao) in 1911 and transferred to Xiapu County Girls' Middle School (Xiapu xian nüzi gaodeng xiaoxue zhongxue bu) in 1915. Ni Jun, "Schudy: Her Art and Life," 83. Qiu Ti's biographer, Ni Jun, states that at this time Qiu Ti read *Xin qingnian* [*New Youth*] magazine and became familiar with the ideals espoused by Chen Duxiu and Hu Shizhi.

6 It is difficult to precisely identify when the group of young women were first referred to as the Four Talented Women of East Fujian, however, the relative anonymity of Qiu Ti following her death suggests that the term originated during her lifetime and most likely during her years of schooling at Fuzhou Women's Normal School. While Qiu Ti dedicated herself to oil painting, her closest friend and primary school classmate, You Shou (1906–94), grew up to become an archeologist and an accomplished calligrapher; Cao Yingzhuang specialized in poetry; Pan Yuke excelled in *guohua*. Perhaps the most radical of the four young women, Pan Yuke dressed in men's attire from childhood onward and, after refusing an arranged marriage at age sixteen, remained single her entire life.

7 During her study at Shangai Academy of Art the faculty included one Japanese oil painting instructor, Tsujimoto Hiroshi, as well as eventual Storm Society cofounder Ni Yide. Ni Yide had graduated from Shangai Academy of Art in 1922 and was employed as an oil painting instructor after graduation. In the fall of 1927 he went to Japan to study at Kawabata Painting School but left Japan in protest of the Japanese attack in Shandong (Jinan Incident, late April through early May 1928). It is possible that Qiu Ti took courses from Ni Yide during her initial study at the Shangai Academy of Art.

8 Details about Qiu Ti's time in Japan remain unclear. No Japanese record of Qiu Ti's enrollment in any school there has yet been found despite a search conducted by Japanese art historian and Republican-period painting specialist Tsuruta Takeyoshi. Ni Jun, "Schudy: Her Art and Life," 85. The only extant documentation concerning Qiu Ti's studies in Japan comes from a personal data form Qiu Ti submitted to the Democratic Women's Federation years later. Many thanks to Professor Li Chao of Shanghai University who, having uncovered this important document in the Shanghai Municipal Archive, kindly shared a copy with me.

9 At first, Qiu Ti lived in an apartment with her old friend Pan Yuke, who was now a researcher in the academy's *guohua* department. Records of their appointments can be found in Izumi-shi Kubosō Kinen Bijutsukan, Kuboso Kinen Bunka Zaidan, and Toyo Bijutsu Kenkyujo, *Kiyō: Minkoku-ki bijutsu gakkō kagyō dogakuroku, bijutsu daitai kaiinroku shūsei* 紀要：民國期美術學校畢業同學錄·美術団體會員錄集成 *[Bulletin: Integrated Records of Republican-period Art School Graduates, Art Group Members]*, vol. 2•3•4 (Izumi-shi: Izumi-shi Kubosō Kinen Bijutsukan, 1991). At that time, the position of researcher at a college was roughly equivalent to that of today's graduate student.

10 Pang Xunqin returned to Shanghai from Paris in 1930, probably not long after Qiu Ti had returned from Japan. The two met at his solo exhibition (September 15th–25th, 1932) and the First Annual Storm Society Exhibition took place the following month (October 9th–16th, 1932). Julia F. Andrews and Kuiyi Shen, "Schudy, the Storm Society, and China's Early Modernist Movement," in *Schudy* (Qiu Ti) 丘堤, ed. Pang Tao (Nanjing: Jiangsu Jiaoyu Chubanshe, 2006), 73.

11 Croizier, "Post-Impressionists," 142.

12 An issue of *The Young Companion* gives "The Storm & Stress Society" as an English translation for the group. "Art Exhibition of the Storm & Stress Society," *Liangyou huabao* 良友畫報 *[The Young Companion]* 82 (November 1933): 30. Ken Lum observes that the group's name corresponds with that of a contemporary avant-garde art periodical *Der Sturm* (1910 to 1932), which "also promoted modern and revolutionary art (in the sense of promoting radical social and political change), emphasizing the aspect of personal expression." Ken Lum, "Aesthetic Education in Republican China: A Convergence of Ideals," in *Shanghai Modern, 1919–1945*, ed. Jo-Anne Birnie Danzker Danzker, Ken Lum, and Zheng Shengtian (Ostfildern-Ruit: Hatje Cantz Verlag, 2004), 223.

13 The coverage presented in the periodicals of the time is especially valuable today as it is often the only extant evidence of many of the paintings in the exhibitions.

14 Croizier, "Post-Impressionists," 139.

15 *L'Art* was a journal that the Muse Society (Mo She), an artist society largely associated with the Shanghai Academy of Art, produced; it was published every ten days. Zhu Boxiong 朱伯雄 and Chen Ruilin 陈瑞林, *Zhongguo xihua wushinian, 1898–1949* 中国西画五十年, *1898–1949 [Fifty years of Western painting in China, 1898–1949]* (Beijing: People's Art Publishing House, 1989), 301.

16 "Juelanshe xuanyan 决澜社宣言 [The Storm Society Manifesto]," *Yishu xunkan* 藝術旬刊 *[L'Art]* 1, no. 5 (October 1932): 8. For a translation, see Jo-Anne Birnie Danzker Danzker, Ken Lum, and Zheng Shengtian, eds., "The Storm Society Manifesto (October 1932)," in *Shanghai Modern, 1919–1945* (Ostfildern-Ruit: Hatje Cantz Verlag, 2004), 234.

17 Writing about *guohua* in 1928, Ni Yide ends his article by admonishing young *guohua* artists to give up the themes and sentiments of the past and instead use fresh sentiments and skills to depict new worlds in their art. Ni Yide 倪貽德, "Xin de guohua 新的國畫 [New Guohua]," in *Yishu mantan* 藝術漫談 (Shanghai: Guanghua Shuju, 1928).

18 Danzker, Lum, and Zheng Shengtian, "The Storm Society Manifesto (October 1932)."

19 Croizier, "Post-Impressionists," 140.

20 Ken Lum identifies Ni Yide as "one of the key artist-intellectuals of China's first modernist movement." Lum, "Aesthetic Education in Republican China: A Convergence of Ideals," 223.

21 Ni Yide, "A Galaxy of the Storm Society (1 October 1935)," in *Shanghai Modern, 1919–1945*, ed. Jo-Anne Birnie Danzker Danzker, Ken Lum, and Zheng Shengtian (Ostfildern-Ruit: Hatje Cantz Verlag, 2004), 238.

22 Kuiyi Shen, "The Lure of the West: Modern Chinese Oil Painting," in *A Century in Crisis: Modernity and Tradition in the Art of Twentieth-Century China*, ed. Julia Frances Andrews and Kuiyi Shen (New York: Guggenheim Museum, 1998), 176.

23 Yang Taiyang 陽太陽, "The Storm Society (Interview)," in *Shanghai Modern, 1919–1945*, ed. Jo-Anne Birnie Danzker Danzker, Ken Lum, and Zheng Shengtian (Ostfildern-Ruit: Hatje Cantz Verlag, 2004), 242.

24 Shen, "The Lure of the West," 176.

25 The perceived political message provoked death threats from exhibition attendees. Shen, 176.

26 The Storm Society perhaps was not quite as controversial as its members wished it to appear. The subject of plentiful media coverage in magazines and newspapers, the members of the group resemble cultural attachés more than rebels of the art scene, as they saw themselves. Moreover, many Storm Society members and other modernists survived by teaching in art departments at national universities and private art schools, where they received institutional support and trained the next generation of artists.

27 Kuiyi Shen characterizes his style as falling between two waves of artistic influence from Japan—one in the mid-1920s and the other occurring later in the 1930s. Shen, 176. Ni Yide's paintings were not particularly bold in terms of style nor radical in choice of subjects, which primarily consisted of landscapes, still-lifes, portraits, and female nudes—this last genre being quite popular at the time, as I argue in chapter 3.

28 A number of uncertainties cloud Qiu Ti's biography: she deliberately concealed her age; the exact date of her entry into the Shangai Academy of Art is unknown; and she refused to tell her children about her time in Japan. It may be that Qiu Ti deliberately obscured certain details in her personal history to avoid the potentially embarrassing admission that Pang was not her first husband. Decades after Qiu Ti's death, revelations from friends led to the startling discovery that Qiu Ti had been married prior to her meeting with Pang Xunqin. By avoiding discussion of her time in Japan, Qiu Ti might have been concealing personal details and a timeline of events that threatened to reveal her prior marriage. Wright, "Qiu Ti's Contributions to Juelanshe," 19–20.

29 "Exposition of Storm Society Paintings."

30 "Yishujia Pang Xunqin shi 藝術家龐薰琴氏 [Artist Mr. Pang Xunqin]," *Liangyou huabao* 良友畫報 *[The Young Companion]*, no. 90 (July 1934): 14. The pictorial appears to have produced a typo in its incorrect use of 琴 for Pang Xunqin's name.

31 "Qiu Ti nüshi 丘堤女士 [Miss Qiu Ti]," *Dazhong huabao* 大眾畫報 *[The Cosmopolitan]*, no. 13 (November 1934): 33. *The Cosmopolitan*, a comprehensive monthly pictorial magazine founded and edited by Liang Desuo, was published in Shanghai from November 1933 to May 1935.

32 In assessment of Qiu Ti's painting skills, the pictorial observes, "Her works are refreshingly elegant and graceful, just as she is." (*Qi zuopin qingli xiuyi, yi ruqi ren.* 其作品清麗秀逸,一如其人。) "Qiu Ti nüshi 丘堤女士 [Miss Qiu Ti]."

33 "Juelanshe jiang."

34 In fact, the coleus may have been a plant that Qiu Ti knew well and it is possible that while she lived in Shanghai the plant held sentimental significance for her as a reminder of her childhood home. Qiu Ti's daughter Pang Tao notes that the plant in *Flower* grew in Qiu Ti's hometown. See Pang Tao, "Early Works of Qiu Ti and Pang Xunqin," *Meishu Yanjiu* 美术研究 *[Art Research]* 104 (2001). She reiterated this view during an interview I conducted when I remarked on a lush coleus plant prominently displayed in her Beijing residence. Pang Tao, interview by author, Beijing, China, March 20, 2009. *Flora of China* lists the coleus as native to the southern provinces of Fujian, Guangdong, and Guangxi. Today the coleus is cultivated in all of China's provinces and is quite popular worldwide. See "Coleus Scutellarioides (Wucaisu 五彩苏)," *Flora of China Www. Efloras.Org* 17 (n.d.): 293.

35 This essay was the final installment of a three-part article. Ni Yide, "Yiyuan jiaoyou ji."

36 Ni Yide, 1935.

37 An alternate translation of this passage may be found in the important German exhibition catalogue, *Shanghai*

Modern, 1919–1945, with one significant point of difference. The catalogue's translation interprets Ni's phrase "*bei yi ge wushi de pipingzhe zhizhai* 被一個無識的批評者指摘" as "while some people criticized her," whereas I am more precisely translating it as a single critic. Ni Yide, "A Galaxy of the Storm Society" (1 October 1935).

38 Croizier, "Post-Impressionists," 146.

39 Croizier, 146.

40 Shen, "The Lure of the West," 176.

41 The most comprehensive volume on modern Chinese women artists to date, *Shiluo de lishi: Zhongguo nüxing huihua shi* [*Lost History: The History of Chinese Women's Painting*], provides a biographic entry for Qiu Ti, a substantial portion of which discusses *Flower*. The authors, Tao Yongbai and Li Shi, base their entire assessment of the painting on Ni Yide's interpretation, both paraphrasing and quoting from the 1935 essay. The only point of divergence from his words comes when the authors, presumably elaborating upon Ni Yide's mention of the critical reaction of a single critic (*bei yi ge wushi de pipingzhe zhizhai*), infer that *Flower* "drew objections from not a few people" (*yinqi le bushao ren de yiyi* 引起了不少人的异议). Tao Yongbai 陶咏白 and Li Shi 李湜, *Shiluo de lishi: Zhongguo nüxing huihua shi* 失落的历史: 中国女性绘画史 *[Lost History: The History of Chinese Women's Painting]* (Changsha: Hunan Meishu Chubanshe, 2000), 215. In a 2001 review of her parents' early artistic works, Pang Tao candidly mentions that the subject of *Flower* is a variety that grows in the southern part of her mother's home province, but she also says that some people asserted that leaves should be green and flowers should be red and thus the painting "led to a controversy" (*yinqi le yi fan zhenglun*). Though she does not specifically refer to Ni Yide's essay, her analysis closely follows his words. Pang Tao, "Early Works of Qiu Ti and Pang Xunqin," 28–29. In "Schudy, the Storm Society, and China's Early Modernist Movement," Shen and Julia Andrews provide no source for their observation that, though *Flower* was generally accepted, at the same time the painting also provoked the consternation of conservative members of the contemporary art world for "presumably reversing the natural order of things" with its "daring color and non-representational quality." Andrews and Shen, "Schudy, the Storm Society, and China's Early Modernist Movement," 73. The only study to directly question whether *Flower* was truly controversial is Huajing Xiu's dissertation on the Shanghai art world during the Republican period. Though Xiu's assessment does not identify the species of the plant nor the fact that Qiu Ti's home province was its native habitat, she nonetheless acknowledges that the painting is a relatively faithful portrayal of a plant found in nature. Without citing Ni Yide's 1935 article, Xiu maintains that Qiu Ti must have received the Storm Society award for its artistic merits alone rather than for any provocative conceptual content that has been attributed to it. Confident that the painting portrays a real plant, Xiu faults Croizier for fabricating a controversy based on Qiu Ti's use of color. But as this chapter demonstrates, Croizier is far from alone in believing that the painting generated a hot debate. Huajing Xiu (Maske), "Shanghai–Paris: Chinese Painters in France and China, 1919–1937" (PhD diss., University of Oxford, 2000), 242.

42 For images of the artworks displayed in Ni Yide's solo exhibition, see "Ni Yide Zhejiang Hangzhou ren 倪貽德浙江杭州人 [Ni Yide from Hangzhou, Zhejiang]," *Meishu shenghuo* 美術生活 *[Arts & Life]*, no. 7 (October 1934): 12.

43 "Flowers by F. M. Lin: *The Young Companion*'s Series of Contemporary Paintings by Chinese Artists. Section II Occidental: 4," *Liangyou huabao* 良友畫報 *[The Young Companion]*, no. 87 (1934): 18.

44 "Art Exhibition of the Storm & Stress Society."

45 A color photograph in *Modern Miscellany* features a coleus variety planted in terracotta planters lined up in a row, suggesting that the plant was not completely unknown to the Shanghai magazine's audience. Wang Yilun 王益論, "Sheying 攝影 [Photography]," *Shidai huabao* 時代畫報 *[Modern Miscellany]* 5, no. 8 (16 February 1934).

46 *Shenbao* 申報 *[Shun Pao]*, September 4, 1933, 19. Here I follow Shen's and Andrews's translation of *Shijie Xueyuan* as "World Society." Andrews and Shen, "Schudy, the Storm Society, and China's Early Modernist Movement," 73.

47 Pang Xunqin 龐薰琹, *Jiushi zheyang zou guolai de* 就是这样走过来的 *[It Happened Just Like This]* (Beijing: Shenghe, Dushu, Xinzhi Sanlian Shudian, 1988), 178.

48 Pang Xunqin, 178. Wang Jiyuan's connections to the World Society allowed the exhibit to be held there for free. Pang Xunqin describes the exhibition visitors comprising only art students from the Shangai Academy of Art and Xin Hua Art Academy as well as close friends within the art community.

49 Since no list of exhibited paintings survives, the images published in these two features provide invaluable records of the content of the show. "Art Exhibition of the Storm & Stress Society"; "Exposition of Storm Society Paintings."

50 Qiu Ti first met Pang Xunqin a few weeks before the inaugural Storm Society Exhibition and did not exhibit with the group herself until the following year.

51 A biography of Pang Xunqin written by his second wife Yuan Yunyi provides additional information about the award. By this account, Wang Jiyuan used his connec-

tions to the World Society to invite its head, the Republican Central Committee member Li Shizeng, to formally present the Storm Society Award to Qiu Ti. According to Yuan Yunyi, the award he presented consisted of 50 yuan. This amount, it should be noted, is half of that advertised in *Shenbao* and, according to Yuan, it had all been collected at Pang Xunqin's expense. Yuan Yunyi 袁韵宜, *Pang Xunqin zhuan* 庞薰琹传 *[Biography of Pang Xunqin]* (Beijing: Beijing Gongyi Meishu Chubanshe, 1995), 79.

52 This may also be why the profile piece on Qiu Ti in *The Cosmopolitan*, as well as a wedding announcement in *Xiaoshuo yuebao*, state that the couple married in 1934. The couple might not have wanted to alert the readers to the fact that they were already married the previous year. "Yishu huabao: guben duizhao 藝術畫報：古本對照 [Literature and Art Pictorial: Comparison with the Ancient Books]," *Xiaoshuo yuebao* 小說月報 *[Fiction Monthly]*, July 1934.

53 Jane Zheng notes that Zhang Xuan wrote in Xie Ling's yearbook, "Are you also going to graduate? In my eyes, you still look like a primary school student. Both your painting and your behavior are rather naïve. I hope you will study even harder after graduation. Do not be satisfied with graduation!" (Translation by Zheng.) Zheng cites this note as evidence of Xie Ling's disinterest in a professional application of her artistic training. Jane Zheng, "The Shanghai Fine Arts College: Art Education and Modern Women Artists in the 1920s and 1930s," *Modern Chinese Literature and Culture* 19, no. 1 (Spring 2007): 219–20. Zheng also argues that female graduates of the Shanghai Academy of Art may be categorized into three tracks: art educators, professional artists, and "modern Shanghai ladies" (namely, social butterflies). She acknowledges that the three postgraduate paths were not mutually exclusive, and, indeed, most of the academically trained female artists of the Republican period can be assigned to all three categories by varying degrees. For example, Guan Zilan, who never attended the Shanghai Academy of Art, easily straddles any perceived gap between these three social roles. Zheng, 201.

54 In contrast to his discussions of the male group members, he begins his paragraph on Qiu Ti with the words, "If our memory serves well, we may still remember . . . ," suggesting that his readers might not recall her. Yet he makes no effort to bring them up to date. He does not mention her current professional activity or any other artworks of hers at all. He ignores the possibility that, as the subject a substantial amount of publicity over the previous two years—including at least two marriage announcements and two introductory profiles with accompanying artwork reproductions—Qiu Ti may have been more recognizable to readers than several of the other group members.

55 See "Juelanshe di san jie huazhan 决瀾社第三屆畫展 [The Third (*Sic*) Storm Society Exhibition]," *Liangyou Huabao* 良友畫報 *[The Young Companion]*, no. 111 (November 1935); "Juelanshe di si jie zhanlanhui 决瀾社第四屆展覽會 [The Fourth Storm Society Exhibition]," *Shidai huabao* 時代畫報 *[Modern Miscellany]* 8, no. 10 (October 1935); "Third Exhibition of The 'Torrents Society,'" *Meishu shenghuo* 美術生活 *[Arts & Life]*, no. 21 (December 1935); "Juelan huazhan 決瀾畫展 [Storm Society Painting Exhibition]," *Xinren zhoukan* 新人周刊 *[New People's Weekly]* 2, no. 10 (November 2, 1935). Ni Yide timed his essay to coincide with the final exhibition, but the accompanying images do not appear to be drawn from the artworks hung in that exhibition. For example, he includes the tabletop still-life by Zhuo Duo that was found in the Second Exhibition.

56 News coverage of the final Storm Society Exhibition documents that Qiu Ti displayed at least two of her paintings, both still-lifes.

57 Although the discovery of an album of her paintings and drawings a decade ago encouraged a bit more attention, Liang Baibo largely remains a neglected artist. The album was purchased in New York City and brought back to China by the new owner, where the discovery was subsequently heralded in the press. See Xu Wenhua 徐文华 and Li Chao 李超, "Niu Yue: Zhongjian Liang Baibo de yishu shengming 纽约:重见梁白波的艺术生命 [New York: An Important Look at the Artistic Life of Liang Baibo]," *Xinmin wanbao* 新民晚报 *[New People's Evening News]*, August 29, 2009, sec. B.

58 Liang Baibo relocated to Taiwan after the Nationalists lost the civil war in 1949. Little is known of her life following her move and it is generally believed that she died of schizophrenia sometime in the late 1960s. As schizophrenia is a nonfatal mental disorder, it is likely that as little is known about Liang Baibo's death as is known of her life. To date, the best source of information on Liang Baibo is an exceptionally well-researched Master's thesis, which interviews the artist's son to determine the late 1960s as the probable date of her death. Zhang Qiongwen 張瓊文, "Minguo nühuajia Liang Baibo huihua zhong de nüxing zhanxian 民國女畫家梁白波繪畫中的女性展現 [Female Representation in the Paintings of Republican Period Woman Artist Liang Baibo]" (Master's thesis, National Taiwan Normal University, 2016). For more information on Liang Baibo, see my discussion in chapter 4.

59 Andrews and Shen, "Schudy, the Storm Society, and China's Early Modernist Movement," 69. Taimeng huahui was banned for its reactionary views in January 1931.

60 Pang Xunqin lists twelve artists involved at the inception of the Storm Society. "Excluding the author,

those at the January 6, 1932, meeting were: Liang Baibo, Duan Pingyou, Chen Chengbo, Yang Taiyang, Yang Qiuren, Zeng Zhiliang, Zhou Mi, Deng Yunti, Zhou Duo, Wang Jiyuan, Ni Yide. Altogether there were 12 in attendance." Pang Xunqin 龐薰琹, "Juelanshe xiaoshi 决澜社小史 [The Brief History of the Storm Society]," *Yishu xunkan* 藝術旬刊 *[L'Art]* 1, no. 5 (October 11, 1932): 9. The list does not include Qiu Ti as she likely joined the group around the end of its first year.

61 "Juelan huazhan." The linear qualities of Liang Baibo's painting suggest the hand of an illustrator. Liang Baibo's friend Huang Miaozi (b. 1913), a calligrapher and art critic, has briefly discussed her painting style and interactions with other Storm Society members. See Huang Miaozi 黄苗子, "Fengyu luohua—yi huajia Liang Baibo 风雨落花—忆画家梁白波 [Wind and Rain Scatter Petals: Recalling the Painter Liang Baibo]," in *Fengyu luohua* 風雨落花 (Beijing: Zuojia Chubanshe, 2005), 8.

62 Liang briefly taught art at a middle school for the children of overseas Chinese in the Philippines and returned to Shanghai in 1935. Perhaps this leave of absence explains why Ni Yide did not deem her a member despite her ongoing involvement. Tao Yongbai and Li Shi, *Shiluo de lishi*, 217.

63 The list of founding members was published in the second year of the group's existence in its inaugural—and simultaneously terminal—issue of *Dawn Light* (*Chenguang* 晨光) 1 (June 1921): 1. See Kris Imants Ercums, "Exhibiting Modernity: National Art Exhibitions in China during the Early Republican Period, 1911–1937" (PhD diss., University of Chicago, 2014), 120–21.

64 Ercums, 123.

65 The First Yifeng Society Exhibition was held in Shanghai, June 3–10, 1934. Its grand scale—nearly 900 artworks in a variety of media, including *guohua*, *xihua*, calligraphy, and sculpture—reflects the organizers' desire to foster a national dialogue of artistic exchange across the larger artistic community. Ercums, 199–202.

66 For a succinct overview of Pan Yuliang's prolific career, see The Li Ching Cultural & Educational Foundation, "Chronology," Pan Yuliang, n.d., http://www.artofpanyuliang.org/chronology.php.

67 For overviews of female artists' professional activity, see Xu Hong, "Early 20th-Century Women Painters in Shanghai"; Zheng, "The Shanghai Fine Arts College: Art Education and Modern Women Artists in the 1920s and 1930s."

68 Jane Zheng gives 1903–67 for Tang Yunyu's birth and death dates, but Tani Barlow provides 1906–92 for her dates. Zheng, "The Shanghai Fine Arts College: Art Education and Modern Women Artists in the 1920s and 1930s," 206; Tani E. Barlow, "Commercial Cartoon Genre and the Cliché Mise-En-Scene of the Gazing Girl," in *A Companion to Chinese Art* (Chichester, West Sussex: Wiley-Blackwell, 2016), 437. As members of the Yiyuan Painting Research Society, Pan Yuliang and Tang Yunyu both contributed works to the West Lake Exhibition in June 1929. The Li-ching Cultural & Educational Foundation, "Chronology." The pictorial *Shanghai Sketch* (*Shanghai manhua*) documents her entry to the Ninth Pegasus Society Exhibition in June 1928. For information on this society and its exhibition, see Ercums, "Exhibiting Modernity: National Art Exhibitions in China during the Early Republican Period, 1911–1937," chap. 3.

69 The *Truth, Beauty, Good* special issue notes that Tang was a member of the Eastern Art Research Society and was currently teaching at the Shanghai Art Research Society. Zhang Ruogu 張若谷, ed., "Nüzuojia hao: Zhen mei shan zazhi yi zhou nian jinian haowai 女作家號: 真美善雜誌一周年紀 念號外 [Women Writers Issue: Truth, Beauty, Good Magazine's First-Year Anniversary Special Issue]," in *Zhen mei shan zazhi* 真美善雜誌 *[Truth, Beauty, Good Magazine]* (Shanghai: Zhen Mei Shan Shudian, 1929). Zheng, "The Shanghai Fine Arts College: Art Education and Modern Women Artists in the 1920s and 1930s," 207.

70 For a sense of Ni Yide's essentializing of the opposite gender, see the discussion of his essays on the female nude painting genre and the role of the life model in chapter 3.

Chapter 3

1 For a comparison, Norman Bryson discusses a photograph of male Japanese art student Kume Keiichirō posing with his male classmates and nude female model in Paris in the 1880s. Bryson argues that the practice strengthened bonds of masculine camaraderie and the Japanese student's participation helped to equalize his standing among his peers. Norman Bryson, "Westernizing Bodies: Women, Art, and Power in Meiji Yoga," in *Gender and Power in the Japanese Visual Field*, ed. Joshua S. Mostow, Norman Bryson, and Maribeth Graybill (Honolulu: University of Hawaii Press, 2003), 111–12.

2 In recent years this photograph has fascinated the Chinese academic community and general populace alike and has appeared in a number of publications, most notably as the subject of a 2005 CCTV documentary titled *Zhaopian beihou de gushi* [*The Story behind the Photograph*]. In this documentary, contemporary painter Liu Dahong traces the image to a 1935 Shanghai Academy of Art yearbook and a number of the students in the photograph are identified and interviewed. Zhongyang Dianshitai Wenhua Zhuantibu et al., *Zhaopian beihou de gushi* 照片背后的故事 *[The Story behind the Photograph]*, DVD, *Tansuo faxian* 探索

发现 [Explore, Discover] (China: Zhongguo Guoji Dianshi Zonggongsi, 2005).

3 For examples of scholarship on the female nude in Western art, see Lynda Nead, *Female Nude: Art, Obscenity and Sexuality* (London: Routledge, 1992); Gillian Perry, *Women Artists and the Parisian Avant-Garde: Modernism and "Feminine" Art, 1900 to the Late 1920s* (Manchester: Manchester University Press, 1995); Paula Birnbaum, *Women Artists in Interwar France: Framing Femininities* (Farnham: Ashgate, 2011).

4 Amanda Wangwright, "The Sick Man of Asia and the Anatomically Perfect Woman: Remodeling China's (Body) Image through the Visual Arts," in *Visualizing the Body in Art, Anatomy, and Medicine since 1800: Models and Modeling*, Science and the Arts since 1750 (Routledge, 2019).

5 At first, finding life models proved difficult and all Shanghai Academy of Art models were men until 1920, when the school finally secured its first female model. For more information on art education and the nude art debate, see Julia F. Andrews, "Luotihua lunzheng ji xiandai Zhongguo meishushi de jiangou 裸体画论争及现代中国美术史的建构 [The Nude Painting Debate and the Construction of Modern Chinese Art History]," in *Haipai huihua yanjiu wenji* 海派绘画研究文集 *[Studies on Shanghai School Painting]* (Shanghai: Shanghai Shuhua Chubanshe, 2001), 125–29; Julia F. Andrews, "Art and the Cosmopolitan Culture of 1920s Shanghai: Liu Haisu and the Nude Model Controversy," *Chungguksa yon'gu*, no. 35 (April 2005): 323–72. Andrew's and Shen's recent textbook provides a lucid summary of her important findings. Julia F. Andrews and Kuiyi Shen, *The Art of Modern China* (Berkeley: University of California Press, 2012), 67. See also Wu Fangcheng 吳方正, "Luode liyou - ershi shiji chuqi Zhongguo renti xiesheng wenti de taolun 裸的理由——二十世紀初期中國人體寫生問題的討論 [The Reason for the Nude: Questions Concerning Nude Figure Drawing in China at the Beginning of the Twentieth Century," *Xin shixue* 新史學 *[New Studies in History]* 25, no. 2 (June 2004): 55–110; Chen Zui 陈醉, "Zhongguo luoti yishu fazhan licheng 中国裸体艺术发展历程 [Chinese Nude Art History]," *Wenyi yanjiu* 文艺研究 *[Literature and Art Research]*, no. 1 (2006): 130–36.

6 Andrews, "Art and the Cosmopolitan Culture of 1920s Shanghai," 368–70.

7 Ni Yide, "Lun luoti yishu 論裸體藝術 [Considering Nude Art]," *Shishi xinbao* 時事新報 *[The China Times]*, December 14, 1924, Shanghai: A Daily Supplement of China Times (312) edition, sec. Yishu [Art] no. 82. It was later republished in 1928. Ni Yide, "Lun luoti yishu 論裸體藝術 [Considering Nude Art, reprint]," in *Yishu mantan* 藝術漫談 *[Art Chat]* (Shanghai: Guanghua Shuju, 1928). An alternate version appeared in the Beijing periodical *Chenbao fukan* in 1925. Ni Yide, "Luoti yishu zhi zhenyi 裸體藝術之真義 [The True Meaning of Nude Art]," *Chenbao fukan* 晨報副刊 *[Morning News Supplemental]*, September 17, 1925, 1274 edition. More recently, the article was published in an anthology of important primary texts on modern Chinese art theory. Ni Yide, "Lun luoti yishu 論裸體藝術 [Considering Nude Art]," in *Ershi shiji zhongguo meishu wenxuan (I)* 二十世纪中国美术文选（上卷）*[20th Century Chinese Art Literary Selections]* (Shanghai: Shanghai Shuhua Chubanshe, 1999), 123–29.

8 This exhibition appears to be the event that sparked the larger debate involving Liu Haisu and the Shanghai Academy of Art the following year. For more information, see Andrews, "Art and the Cosmopolitan Culture of 1920s Shanghai," 343; Wu Fangcheng, "Luode liyou," 87–89.

9 Liu Haisu later joined the fray in 1925 with his newspaper publication on September 8 and a radio address on September 23. Between his two well-known public appeals, Ni Yide published another version of his own article on September 17, 1925. Three years later, presumably following the reversal of the ban on nude models in the classroom, the victorious Ni Yide reprinted his original article in a 1928 collection of his essays.

10 Ni Yide, "Lun luoti yishu."

11 Ni Yide, "Lun luoti yishu." Ni offers Renoir as an example of an artist successful in responding to people's delight in softness.

12 Ni Yide, "Lun luoti yishu."

13 A sense of the public's view may be gleaned from a comparison of Ni Yide's essay and the letters of those who oppose nude models. See Andrews, "Art and the Cosmopolitan Culture of 1920s Shanghai," 345–49.

14 Clearly in his estimate, Ni Yide is talking only of female models and is not including the male models employed for years prior to 1920.

15 During Qiu Ti's study at Shangai Academy of Art, the faculty included Ni Yide, who had graduated from Shangai Academy of Art in 1922 and was employed as an oil painting instructor after graduation. In the fall of 1927 he went to Japan to study at Kawabata Painting School, but left Japan in protest of the Japanese attack in Shandong (Jinan Incident, late April through early May 1928). It is possible that Qiu Ti took courses from Ni Yide during her initial study at the Shangai Academy of Art.

16 While he advocates the admiration of female model's noble contribution, in reality he undermines the model's act by stating that it was not usually performed willingly in pursuit of an artistic ideal but rather reluctantly out of economic necessity.

17 Not surprisingly, many treatments of the subject came from the Shanghai Academy of Art and the Storm Society. Academy director Liu Haisu, the outspoken

defender of the institutionalized study of nude figure painting, shared his paintings of nudes with the Shanghai public in a 1932 solo exhibition upon his return from a European trip. See Amanda S. Wright, "Qiu Ti's Contributions to Juelanshe and the Intersection of Modernist Ideology, Public Receptivity, and Personal Identity for a Woman Oil Painter in Early Twentieth-Century China" (PhD diss., University of Kansas, 2011), 84. Other contributors to the movement around this time included Academy instructor Guan Liang (1900–1986) and graduates Fang Ganmin (1906–84), Yang Taiyang, and Yang Qiuren. Guan published his *Nude* in the widely distributed pictorial *Young Companion* (*Liangyou huabao* 良友畫報) in 1934. Fang, who had studied at the École Nationale Supérieure des Beaux Arts in Paris, publicized his *White Doves* (*Baige* 白鴿), in which geometric shapes of softly graduated pastels define the reclining form of a female nude. The two Yangs exhibited their paintings of nudes with the 20 Spring Painting Society (Erling Chun Huahui 二零春畫會) in 1932. Both Yangs studied at the Shanghai Academy of Art in 1928 and later studied under Chen Baoyi. Michael Sullivan, *Modern Chinese Artists: A Biographical Dictionary* (Berkeley: University of California Press, 2006), 196–97. In addition to 20 Spring Painting Society, the two also organized Art Society of the Eleven (Yiyi Yishe 一一藝社), before joining the Storm Society in 1931, the same year as their graduation from the Academy. Lü Peng, *A History of Art in 20th-Century China* (Milano: Charta, 2010), 309. The two Yangs were members of the Storm Society and paintings of nudes figured prominently in the association's annual exhibitions of 1932, 1933, and 1934. The first Storm Society exhibition, held in 1932, contained paintings of nudes by Yang Taiyang, Pang Xunqin, and Wang Jiyuan (1893–1975). Of the entries in the first exhibition, Li Chao lists Wang Jiyuan and Yang Taiyang's nudes but also includes a nude by Pang Xunqin. He cites an unspecified historical document as his source. Li Chao 李超, *Kuangbiao jiqing—Juelanshe ji xiandai zhuyi yishu xiansheng* 狂飙激情--决澜社及现代主义艺术先声 *[Hurricane Passion: The Storm Society and the Modernist Art Prelude]* (Shanghai: Shanghai Jinxiu Wenzhang Chubanshe, 2008), 7. In the same year, Pang displayed two more paintings of female nudes in an independent exhibition and published a third. Wright, "Qiu Ti's Contributions to Juelanshe," 85. Pang Xunqin's paintings of nudes mostly consist of linear abstractions. Pang Xunqin's *Wicker Chair*, in particular, resembles the oeuvre of Chinese-Parisian artist, Chang Yu (Fr. Sanyu, 1901–66), who produced no small number of images of female nudes. In addition to Qiu Ti's painting of nudes in a landscape, a painting of a reclining nude by Ni Yide appeared in the second exhibition. The painting can be spotted hanging on the wall behind Ni Yide in a photograph taken at the exhibition. The Third Annual Storm Society Exhibition (1934) presented multiple depictions of female nudes, including works by the two Yangs and Duan Pingyou.

18 David Clarke, "Iconicity and Indexicality: The Body in Chinese Art," *Semiotica* 155, no. 1/4 (2005): 235. The examples Clarke uses to illustrate in his analysis—*Daydreaming* by Yang Jianhou, *Study* by Zhou Xijie, and *Woman by the Riverside* by Hu Yiwen—share the characteristics he describes. But these three examples, as well as five others that he cites but does not reprint, all come from a two-year span of a single magazine, *Yifeng* (April 1933—May 1935). Thus, it would be reasonable to wonder if the consistencies Clarke observes simply reflect the personal preferences of the magazine's editor. When these images are analyzed alongside the additional examples mentioned in my discussion, however, a safer estimation of painting trends in 1930s Shanghai emerges and confirms Clarke's observations.

19 Clarke, 234.

20 Clarke, 237.

21 Chun Tai 春臺, "Huajia Fang Junbi nüshi 畫家方君璧女士 [The Painter Miss Fang Junbi]," *Jingbao fukan* 京報副刊 *[Jingbao Supplemental]*, no. 435 (March 11, 1926): 1–2.

22 "Renti, Fang Junbi zuo 人體，方君璧作 [Figure by Fang Junbi]," *Meishu shenghuo* 美術生活 *[Arts & Life]*, no. 4 (July 1934): 5.

23 Review of Guan Zilan's exhibition. "Some Masterworks of Miss C. L. Kuan," *Shidai huabao* 時代畫報 *[Modern Miscellany]* 1, no. 6 (1930): 8.

24 Weng Yuanchun, "*Renti*," *Wenhua*, vol. 1 (August 1929): 31; Wang Jingyuan, "*Nüxiang*," *The Ladies' Journal* 婦女雜誌 (*Funü zazhi*) 15, no. 7 (July 1929): 64.

25 The following sources provide detailed information about Pan Yuliang's life and career. Eric Lefebvre, ed., *Song of Spring* 春之歌*: Pan Yu-Lin in Paris* 潘玉良在巴黎 (Hong Kong: Yazhou Xiehui Xianggang Zhongxin, 2018), https://hkupress.hku.hk/pro/1761.php; Doris Ha Lin Sung, "Redefining Female Talent: Chinese Women Artists in the National and Global Art Worlds, 1900s–1970s" (PhD diss., York University, 2016); The Li-ching Cultural & Educational Foundation, PAN YU LIN 潘玉良, accessed June 29, 2019, http://www.panyulin.org/index.php.

26 Pan attended the École Nationale Supérieure des Beaux-Arts de Lyon, the École Nationale Supérieure des Beaux-Arts de Paris, and the Accademia de Belle Arti di Roma.

27 Most of these reproductions may are accessible online via a website dedicated to Pan Yuliang, The Li-ching Cultural & Educational Foundation, "Documents," Pan Yuliang, n.d., https://www.panyulin.org/documents.

php?lang=en. Pan published at least a dozen paintings and drawings of female nudes, and many of these were printed in multiple periodicals.

28 There are examples of male nudes—such as Xu Beihong's well-known *The Fool Who Moved the Mountain* (1940) and Qian Ding's (1896–1989) bizarre *Portrait of Xu Langxi* (*Xu Langxi xiaoxiang* 徐朗西肖像)—but these are exceptions in a genre dominated by images of female nudes.

29 See Leo Ou-fan Lee, *Shanghai Modern: The Flowering of a New Urban Culture in China, 1930–1945* (Cambridge: Harvard University Press, 1999), 74. Essays by Yingjin Zhang and Carrie Waara in Jason Kuo's 2007 anthology, *Visual Culture in Shanghai 1850s–1930s*, further testify to the enthusiasm with which publishers and artists pitched images of women's bodies to China's modern audiences. Zhang analyzes China's pictorials of the 1930s to argue that the female body was manipulated in three often overlapping modes: transformed by photography or painting into a work of art; packaged as a marketing device to encourage publishing sales; or held up as a signifier of culturally significant undertakings such as China's zealous participation in the physical education movement. In Waara's view, the sexual power of nudes possessed a "destabilizing potential." She concludes that a middle-class modernization project employed images of nudes as it struggled to characterize modern femininity for Chinese women. Zhang Yingjin, "Artwork, Commodity, Event: Representations of the Female Body in Modern Chinese Pictorials," in *Visual Culture in Shanghai, 1850s–1930s*, ed. Jason C. Kuo (Washington, DC: New Academia Publishing, 2007), 123–24; Carrie Waara, "The Bare Truth: Nudes, Sex, and the Modernization Project in Shanghai Pictorials," in *Visual Culture in Shanghai, 1850s–1930s*, ed. Jason C. Kuo (Washington, DC: New Academia Publishing, 2007).

30 Lang Jingshan's numerous art photographs evidence that the predominant characteristics found in painted images of nudes also extended to fine art photography. *Arts & Life* published several of his works in 1934, a few of which may be found republished in Waara's article. Lang Jingshan's photographs take full advantage of the sexuality of his subjects yet carefully avoid what he considered to be vulgarity. For a brief discussion of Lang Jingshan, see Waara, "The Bare Truth," 192, 196.

31 Published by the China Art Publishing Society, the set of books, touted itself as a reference tool for a strong and healthy feminine physique. See the back covers of *Shidai huabao* 時代畫報 *[Modern Miscellany]* 1, no. 4 (June 1930) and *Shidai huabao* 時代畫報 *[Modern Miscellany]* 2, no. 5 (1 March 1931). Other publishing houses produced similar publications. Zhang documents a range of such contributions from the publishers of *The Young Companion* in 1933—on topics such as art photography, famous nude paintings, and the nudist movement—and from *The Chin-Chin Screen*, a popular Shanghai film magazine, the following year. Zhang Yingjin, "Artwork, Commodity, Event," 135 and n. 29.

32 So far as popular publications are concerned, the mid 1930s witnessed a rise in *jianmei* imagery concurrent with nationalist sentiments, while the number of images meant for the passive appreciation of the feminine form solely on aesthetic terms appears to have declined. For information on the *jianmei* movement see Yunxiang Gao, "Nationalist and Feminist Discourses on Jianmei (Robust Beauty) during China's National Crisis in the 1930s," in *Translating Feminisms in China: A Special Issue of Gender & History*, ed. Dorothy Ko and Wang Zheng (Malden, MA: Blackwell Publishing, 2007), 104–37; Denise Gimpel, "Freeing the Mind through the Body: Women's Thoughts on Physical Education in Late Qing and Early Republican China," *NAN NÜ* 8, no. 2 (2006): 316–58; Denise Gimpel, "Exercising Women's Rights: Debates on Physical Culture since the Late Nineteenth Century," in *Beyond the May Fourth Paradigm: In Search of Chinese Modernity*, ed. Kai-Wing Chow et al. (New York: Lexington Books, 2008), 95–130.

33 My examination of the nude in popular culture includes images of semiclothed women as well as depictions with no inherent artistic content, such as shots of female athletes in their swimsuits. I use the terms naked and nude interchangeably, as I feel that they were conceptually held to be in Republican-period China. While, in English, nude typically refers to an image with aesthetic value and naked implies an absence of clothes in opposition to commonly held mores, a single image could bear both conceptual readings. An artist may paint an image of a female nude, but its viewership may choose to see a naked woman, and editors with an eye to both the censors and to sales figures might happily accommodate the slippage between the two readings. In truth, the Chinese term does not differentiate: *luo* can be translated as both naked and nude; *luoti* means naked body and nude. Zhang Yingjin, "Artwork, Commodity, Event," n. 6.

34 Louise Edwards, "The Shanghai Modern Woman's American Dreams: Imagining America's Depravity to Produce China's 'Moderate Modernity,'" *Pacific Historical Review* 81, no. 4 (2012): 567–601. Most issues of this periodical are available online through the C.V. Starr East Asian Library website. An onomatopoeia, *linglong* refers to the tinkling sound of jade trinkets clinking together. For a discussion of periodical's romanized title, see C.V. Starr East Asian Library, "The Magazine," Columbia University Libraries Online Exhibitions: Ling long Women's Magazine, accessed

June 21, 2019, https://exhibitions.library.columbia.edu/exhibits/show/linglong/about_linglong/magazine.

35 The photographs are labeled with rather mundane captions such as "Ms. Liu Yunying in winter attire" and "Ms. Cao Jiahua leaning against a small railing." For the benefit of aspiring socialites, the pictorials also carried educational articles that specifically targeted women's display of their own bodies and instructed women on how to cultivate a modern image. The article in the October 1934 issue of *The Cosmopolitan*, "Careful of Your Sitting Position," serves as an illustrated manual on proper ways for women to govern their bodies in public. "Dangxin, ni zuo shi de zishi 當心,你坐時的姿勢[Careful of Your Sitting Position]," *Dazhong huabao* 大眾畫報 *[The Cosmopolitan]*, no. 12 (October 1934): 26–27. The ladies illustrating the improper forms of repose are all labeled with a caption indicating that their stance was for demonstration purposes only and not reflective of their natural posture. An earlier article in the same pictorial, "The Beautiful Form of Breasts" explains how the shape of the breasts betray the owner's level of sophistication and, providing a Western advertisement for corsets as an illustration, discusses how a new way of clothing the body could produce positive results. Huang Ping, "Rufang de xingtai mei 乳房的形態美 [The Beautiful Form of Breasts]," *Dazhong huabao* 大眾畫報 *[The Cosmopolitan]*, no. 4 (February 1934): 26–27. Thus, although the intentional display of a body within Republican-period popular culture generally relates to a modernist agenda, the body itself did not inherently symbolize modernity. Women needed to wear modern support garments and sit in modern poses in order to become modern. Youth of the modern era required healthy athletic bodies in order to compete at an international level. Ethnic minorities unconcerned or unaware with the concept of nakedness were presented as holdouts from a bygone era against which magazine readers could gauge the modernity of their own cosmopolitan lifestyle. An anthropomorphized depiction of China as a defenseless nude female served as a commentary on the country's present condition and imparted a sense of timelessness and unresponsiveness instead of dynamic modernity.

36 Edwards, "The Shanghai Modern Woman's American Dreams," 585.

37 This same sly juxtapositioning is used by the editors of *Pei-yang Pictorial News* (*Beiyang huabao* 北洋畫報). The lovely local socialite frequently gracing the center of the front page nicely balances the pin-up style nude included on the arts page. In this way, the European erotic postcards could suggest to the readership the Tianjin socialite's appearance in the boudoir or the bath.

38 The two double-page spreads ran back to back in *Shidai huabao* 時代畫報 *[Modern Miscellany]* 4, no. 12 (16 August 1933).

39 While the fine art nude may not have had much precedent in China, erotic imagery certainly did. As Francesca Dal Lago's examination of *yuefenpai* (calendar posters) illustrates, generic Modern Girl images reference traditional Chinese erotica in subtle yet numerous ways, from her own suggestive poses to voyeuristic glimpses of her boudoir. Francesca Dal Lago, "How 'Modern' Was the Modern Woman? Crossed Legs and Modernity in 1930s Shanghai Calendar Posters, Pictorial Magazines, and Cartoons," in *Visualizing Beauty: Gender and Ideology in Modern East Asia*, ed. Aida Yuen Wong (Hong Kong: Hong Kong University Press, 2012), 45–62.

40 Notably, the majority of young Chinese women featured in the magazines were not anonymous models but the named daughters of prominent families. Often such women received expensive educations for the express purpose of increasing their marriageability and the publication of their photographs and short biographical information signaled that they were "on the market," so to speak. The emancipation of women, however, presented a challenge to the potential suitor, who might have expected his wife to assume a more traditional role of domesticity following marriage. For a discussion about the "woman question" and the presentation of career women in the Republican press see, Wright, "Qiu Ti's Contributions to Juelanshe," 21–30. Jun Lei similarly notes that anxiety over changing gender roles impacted the presentation of women in contemporary print media. Jun Lei, "Producing Norms, Defining Beauty: The Role of Science in the Regulation of the Female Body and Sexuality in Liangyou and Furen Huabao," in *Liangyou: Kaleidoscopic Modernity and the Shanghai Global Metropolis, 1926–1945*, ed. Paul Pickowicz, Kuiyi Shen, and Yingjin Zhang (Boston: Brill, 2013), 129.

41 The cartoon seems to be a humorously ridiculous image, but it may have some basis in reality. Pan Yuliang is widely believed to have served as her own nude model.

42 "Pan Yuliang nüshi zhi huihua zhanlanhui 潘玉良女士之繪畫展覽會 [Pan Yuliang's Painting Exhibition]," *Shanghai manhua* 上海漫畫 *[Shanghai Sketch]* 33 (1928): 6; "Huajia Pan Yuliang nüshi jiqi zuopin 畫家潘玉良女士及其作品 [The Painter Miss Pan Yuliang and Her Artwork]," *Qingdao huabao* 青島畫報 [*Qingdao Pictorial*], no. 17 (1935); "Liuxue Fa Yi xianren Zhongda huashi Pan Yuliang nüshi jinying 留學法意現任中大畫師潘玉良女士近影 [A Recent Photograph of Pan Yuliang, Exchange Student of France and Italy and Painter of the Central University]," *Weimei* 唯美 *[Aesthetics]*, no. 4 (1935).

43 Sun argues that transculturation transformed European photographs of nudes into versions of an exotic self but

says nothing about women's role in the process. Zhang briefly raises the question of how a female viewership might receive these images and closes his essay with a call for additional scholarship on the issue. Zhang Yingjin, "Artwork, Commodity, Event," 153–54. Waara gives a bit more consideration to women's hand in the popularity of the nude but argues that the female art nude "signifies passive submission." She resolves potential discomfort on the part of the female viewers by assigning them the role of wishful spectators: a role in which women elevated their level of aesthetic appreciation, identified with the sexual objectification of the nudes, and longed for greater sexual attractiveness for themselves. Waara, "The Bare Truth," 185, 196–97. Edwards gives women a more active role when she posits nudes and semiclothed Western women as models of depravity against which Chinese women could fashion their own relative modernism, but, again, this is a case of women as passive consumers and not producers of images, as Edwards concedes that even the women's magazine *Lin Loon* may have had an all-male editorial staff. Edwards, "The Shanghai Modern Woman's American Dreams," 576–77. Though most studies acknowledge that the way in which Republican-period women received these plentiful images of nudes is problematic, scholarship so far does not account for the women's authorship of female nude images. Even Clarke, who specifically contemplates the (male) makers of these images and the iconographic importance of the female nude, does not acknowledge women artists as cocreators. Clarke, "Iconicity and Indexicality."

44 Patricia Mathews, "Returning the Gaze: Diverse Representations of the Nude in the Art of Suzanne Valadon," *Art Bulletin* 73, no. 3 (September 1991): 415.

45 It must be noted, however, that Pan Yuliang created more female nudes than any of the other women artists of her generation and her interest in the feminine form may spring from her personal history. Pan spent her adolescence in a brothel, as is widely known, where she most likely served as an indentured servant. This early and direct exposure to the commodification of women's bodies may have profoundly altered her view of women's sexuality and its uses in society. For a brief note about Pan's employment as a servant girl, see Sung, "Redefining Female Talent," n. 422.

46 For more information about the importation of Western-style painting to Japan and the nude as subject matter, see Alice Y. Tseng, "Kuroda Seiki's 'Morning Toilette' on Exhibition in Modern Kyoto," *The Art Bulletin* 90, no. 3 (September 1, 2008): 417–40, https://doi.org/10.2307/20619620; Bryson, "Westernizing Bodies."; Jaqueline Berndt, "Nationally Naked? The Female Nude in Japanese Oil Painting and Posters (1890s–1920s)," in *Performing Nation: Gender Politics in Literature, Theater, and the Visual Arts of China and Japan, 1880–1940*, edited by Doris Croissant, Catherine Vance Yeh, and Joshua S. Mostow, 307–45 (Leiden: Brill, 2008).

47 Alicia Volk writes, "Women could paint if they wished, but only as amateurs, and with the style and subjects that preserved their sanctioned role as protectors of the state's conservative values." Alicia Volk, "Katsura Yuki and the Japanese Avant-Garde," *Woman's Art Journal* 24, no. 2 (October 1, 2003): 3, https://doi.org/10.2307/1358780. See also Laura W. Allen, "Modern Girls, Working Women and Housewives: Japanese Women Artists in the Interwar Years," in *Essays on Women's Artistic and Cultural Contributions 1919–1939: Expanded Social Roles for the New Woman Following the First World War*, ed. Paula Birnbaum and Anna Novakov (Lewiston: Edwin Mellen Press, 2009).

48 Some few brave women did enroll in nude figure painting classes at private schools at a much earlier date. For example, the feminist poet and painter Takamura Chieko painted nude models during her 1907–11 study at the Pacific Ocean Painting Research Institute (Taiheiyō Yōgakai Kenkyūjo), the same art school Qiu Ti was to attend nearly two decades later when it was renamed the Pacific Ocean Art School (Taiheiyō Bijutsu Gakkō). Phyllis Birnbaum, *Modern Girls, Shining Stars, the Skies of Tokyo: Five Japanese Women* (New York: Columbia University Press, 1999), 76–77. Little is known about Qiu Ti's study in Japan, but it is possible that she took life drawing classes during her brief attendance—perhaps no longer than a semester—at the Pacific Ocean Art School. See Wright, "Qiu Ti's Contributions to Juelanshe," 17, 98.

49 Allen, "Modern Girls, Working Women and Housewives," 104–5; also 102. Volk quotes Katsura Yuki's (1913–91) parents' response when initially forbidding their daughter to pursue oil painting as: "Painting nudes and getting covered in oil paints is only for boys and is an inappropriate accomplishment for an unmarried girl." Volk, "Katsura Yuki," 3.

50 Shunted to the more docile *nihonga* sidelines, women avoided contact with risqué content. Though few dared try the nude as painting subject, some women *nihonga* artists did specialize in *bijinga* (paintings of beautiful women). During the Meiji, the art establishment had effectively severed the *bijinga's* ties to erotic art and infused the newly sanitized genre with a moralistic tone aimed at the education of women. *Bijinga* imagery of the twentieth century now represented the ideal Japanese woman and as such promoted the nation-building rhetoric of women as Good Wives and Wise Mothers as well as perpetuated a fashionable consumer culture in magazine and poster advertisements. Doris Croissant, "Icons of Femininity: Japanese National Painting and the

Paradox of Modernity," in *Gender and Power in the Japanese Visual Field*, ed. Joshua S. Mostow, Norman Bryson, and Maribeth Graybill (Honolulu: University of Hawaii Press, 2003), 137–38; Allen, "Modern Girls, Working Women and Housewives," 102.

51 Bryson, "Westernizing Bodies"; Wright, "Qiu Ti's Contributions to Juelanshe," 93–98.

52 In fact, female students matriculated into the Shanghai Academy of Art the same exact year that the school introduced female models to its classrooms. Jane Zheng, "The Shanghai Fine Arts College: Art Education and Modern Women Artists in the 1920s and 1930s," *Modern Chinese Literature and Culture* 19, no. 1 (Spring 2007): 201–2.

53 Tao Yongbai and Li Shi, *Shiluo de lishi*, 121.

54 Tao Cuiying 陶粹英, "Nuzi fayu mei yu renti huafa 女子發育美與人體畫法 [Women's Physical Development and the Techniques of Figure Painting]," *Funü zazhi* 婦女雜誌 *[Ladies' Journal]* 15, no. 7 (July 1929).

55 Like many Japanese art critics in the early twentieth century, Tao Cuiying disparages Asian women's natural features and feels them to be typically unsuited for the nude painting genre.

56 Jin Qijing, "Nüxing yu meishu."

57 Jin Qijing cites four images of nudes as the most famous examples from the First National Art Exhibition of Japanese paintings: *Harmony in Silver* (*Yin zhi xiehe*) by Okada Saburosuke (1869–1939); *Tulips* (*Tirenlitian de hua*) by Wada Eisaku (1874–1959); *Woman* (*Nü*) by Mitsutani Kunishiro (1874–1936); and *After the Bath* (*Yuhou*) by Ishikawa Toraji (1875–1964).

58 Although in comparison to twenty first-century American feminism Jin Qijing's argument seems odd, her article leaves no doubt that she was striving to equalize the status of women.

59 Jin Qijing, "Nüxing yu meishu."

60 Although these two artists are neither female nor Chinese, Jin Qijing and her coeditors considered the works especially successful entries in the exhibition and appropriate to the women's journal on the basis of subject matter. Images of nudes from the exhibition reproduced in the special issue include the works by Pan Yuliang, Terauchi Manjirō, and Ishikawa Toraji mentioned above, as well as *Axiang Che* (*Chariot of the Thunder Goddess, Axiang*) by Chen Xiaojiang, *Beautiful Countenance* (*Huarong*) by Wada Eisaku, *Male Lying under a Light* (*Deng xia wo nan*) by Pan Yuliang, and *Image of a Woman* (*Nüxiang*), a sculpture by Wang Jingyuan.

61 For more on Pan Guangdan, see Leon Antonio Rocha, "Quentin Pan 潘光旦 in The China Critic," *China Heritage Quarterly*, no. 30/31 (September 2012). For a summary of Pan's writings on Feng Xiaoqing, see Jingyuan Zhang, *Psychoanalysis in China: Literary Transformations, 1919–1949* (Ithaca, NY: East Asia Program, Cornell University, 1992), 134–36. Tani E. Balow discusses Pan Guangdan's psychoanalytical research on Feng Xiaoqing in connection with Wen Yiduo's illustration for Pan's 1927 book and the motif of a woman looking into a mirror. Tani E. Barlow, "Commercial Cartoon Genre and the Cliché Mise-En-Scene of the Gazing Girl," in *A Companion to Chinese Art* (Chichester, West Sussex: Wiley-Blackwell, 2016), 434–36.

62 Barlow's article touches on the link between images self-gazing women and masturbation, whether depicted or implied. She also notes that Pan positions Feng's tragically youthful death as her own active choice and a form of martyrdom. Barlow, "Commercial Cartoon Genre," 435–36, 446.

63 The word *guying* is half of the idiom "*guying zilian*," which the Oxford Chinese-English Dictionary defines as to "look at one's shadow and lament one's lot" or to "look at one's reflection and admire oneself," generally implying feelings of self-pity and isolation.

64 *Renjia bu aixi wo, wo ziji aixi ziji!* 人家不愛惜我，我自己愛惜自己！

65 Li Yuyi 李寓一, "Jiaoyu bu quanguo meishu zhanlanhui teji hao 教育部全國美術展覽會特輯號 [Special Issue on the National Art Exhibition of the Ministry of Education]," *Funü zazhi* 婦女雜誌 *[Ladies' Journal]* 15, no. 7 (July 1929): editor's note on Pan Yuliang's painting. Li Yuyi further observes that the beauty of Pan Yuliang's paintings rests in the factual description of the body rather than in adherence to any stylistic convention.

66 In a note, Sun briefly mentions that the nude fell out of favor as subject matter in the *Pei-yang Pictorial News* after 1933, a decline in interest that she similarly links to the New Life Movement. Sun Liying, "An Exotic Self? Tracing Cultural Flows of Western Nudes in Pei-Yang Pictorial News (1926–1933)," in *Transcultural Turbulences*, ed. C. Brosius and R. Wenzlhuemer, Transcultural Research-Heidelberg Studies on Asia and Europe in a Global Context 3 (Dordrecht: Springer, 2011), n. 13.

67 Based on the contents of the catalogue, it is safe to conclude that the exhibition included at least eleven nudes.

Chapter 4

1 Zhou Jin 周今, "Meishu jie: Zhongguo xin huajia 美術界：中國新畫家 [Art World: China's New Painters]," *Xingqi wenyi* 星期文藝 *[Weekly Literature and Art]* 9 (1931): 3. This article contains short critiques of ten artists, both men and women.

2 It is noteworthy that the author does not suggest that Guan failed to measure up as a professional artist, but rather that she—and all *nühuajia* by extension—should alter her content so as to continue her career and

improve her artistic output. Although war was on the horizon, the Shanghai art community of the early 1930s still widely accepted women artists as professionals within the field.

3 Kuiyi Shen, "Modernist Movements in Pre-War China" (April 13, 2002).

4 See Chapter 6, "Petty Urbanites and Tales of Woe" in Wen-hsin Yeh, *Shanghai Splendor: Economic Sentiments and the Making of Modern China, 1843–1949* (Berkeley: University of California Press, 2007).

5 Kuiyi Shen, "The Lure of the West: Modern Chinese Oil Painting," in *A Century in Crisis: Modernity and Tradition in the Art of Twentieth-Century China*, ed. Julia F. Andrews and Kuiyi Shen (New York: Guggenheim Museum, 1998), 178–79.

6 Shen, "Modernist Movements."

7 Multiple periodicals publicized the two groups' exhibitions with side-by-side coverage. See *Liangyou huabao* 良友畫報 *[The Young Companion]*, 111 (November 1935) and *Shidai huabao* 時代畫報 *[Modern Miscellany]* 8, no. 10 (October 1935).

8 Karl Gerth, *China Made: Consumer Culture and the Creation of the Nation* (Cambridge: Harvard University Asia Center, 2003), 286 n. 2.

9 Duara argues that women were not forced back into the home but ushered into gender-segregated jobs and he states that with the war, "the fundamental conceptions of women and strategies for directing their role in society appear not to have so much changed as intensified, extended, and expanded." However, these regimes unquestionably placed greatest emphasis on women's roles within the home as supportive wives and mothers, which led to greater gender segregation and undermined women's professional advancements. Prasenjit Duara, *Sovereignty and Authenticity: Manchukuo and the East Asian Modern* (Lanham: Rowman & Littlefield Publishers, 2004), 143.

10 "Nüxing de lunkuo 女性的輪廓 [Women's Silhouette]," *Jiating zazhi* 家庭雜誌 *[Household Magazine]*, no. 2 (1937): 24. The caption for Zhong Duqing describes her as an artist who had studied in France (*Liu Fa meishujia Zhong Duqing nüshi* 留法美術家鍾獨清女士).

11 The entire text states: "時代的輪子，把婦女從家裏叫了出來；雖然現在又有人提倡把她們趕回家裏去，可是，也正如叫她們出來一樣，這倒不是一下子就辦得到的事了。在這混亂的過渡時期中，學會上有的是各種各樣的女性影子，她們散佈在交際場中，學術界裏，她們也留戀着溫馨的家！然而，她們的地位狀況雖不同，却都不再羞人答答了。"

12 Shui Tianzhong discusses some of the problems faced by women artists at this time in his article on Republican-period artist couples. Shui Tianzhong 水天中, "Yishu yu jiehun—20 shiji qianqi de meishujia fufu 艺术与婚姻--20 世纪前期的美术家夫妇 [Art and Marriage: 20th Century Artist Couples]," in *Zhongguo nüxing zhuyi 1* 中国女性主义 1 *[Feminism in China 1]*, ed. Huang Lin 荒林 (Guilin: Guangxi Shifan Daxue Chubanshe, 2004).

13 Shortly after the family fled the bombing of Beiping, Pang Xunqin followed the Beiping Art Academy to Yuanling in 1938. After a conflict between the Beiping Art Academy and the Hangzhou Art Academy later that same year, he relocated his family to Kunming where he became an independent artist. In Kunming, Pang Xunqin worked as a research fellow in the planning department of the relocated National Central Museum (*Zhongyang bowuguan*). He then moved with the Academia Sinica to Lizhuang, Sichuan in 1940, but later that same year resigned and moved his family again so that he could teach at the Chengdu Provincial Art Academy. Xiaoqing Zhu, "Pang Xunqin (1906–1985): A Chinese Avant-Garde's Metamorphosis, 1925–1946, and Questions of 'Authenticity'" (PhD diss., University of Maryland, College Park, 2009), 128–33; Ni Jun, "Schudy: Her Art and Life," 101.

14 Ni Jun dates this period to 1940, but Zhu Xiaoqing gives the summer of 1941 as the year of the book's completion. See Ni Jun, "Schudy: Her Art and Life," 103; Zhu, "Pang Xunqin," 133.

15 Li Chao 李超, *Kuangbiao jiqing—Juelanshe ji xiandai zhuyi yishu xiansheng* 狂飆激情--决澜社及现代主义艺术先声 *[Hurricane Passion: The Storm Society and the Modernist Art Prelude]* (Shanghai: Shanghai Jinxiu Wenzhang Chubanshe, 2008), 75.

16 Ni Jun, "Schudy: Her Art and Life," 103. While in Sichuan, Pang Xunqin held five solo shows (in 1941, 1943, 1944, 1945, and 1946). Pang Tao, ed., *The Storm Society and Post-Storm Art Phenomenon* (Taibei: Chin Show Publishing, 1997), 18. In 1942 he showed two paintings in the Third National Art Exhibition. Zhu, "Pang Xunqin," 190.

17 Pang Tao, email correspondence, September 2010.

18 Wilma Fairbank compiled and edited Liang Sicheng's *A Pictorial History of Chinese Art.*

19 "每当我做些家务活儿时，我总觉得太可惜了，觉得我是在冷落了一些 素昧平生但更有意思，更为重要的人们." Xiao Qian 萧乾, "Yidai cainü—Lin Huiyin" 一代才女--林徽因 [The Talented Woman of a Generation], *Dushu* 读书 10 (1984): 115. Translation from Shu-mei Shih, *The Lure of the Modern: Writing Modernism in Semicolonial China, 1917-1937* (Berkeley: University of California, 2001): 209.

20 Wilma Fairbank, *Liang and Lin: Partners in Exploring China's Architectural Past* (Philadelphia: University of Pennsylvania, 1994): 111.

21 While in Kunming Liang Sicheng and Pang Xunqin were professional colleagues and Liang Sicheng's younger brother, the renowned archeologist Liang

Siyong, gave Pang Xunqin access to the excavation findings of the National Central Museum's Department of Archaeology. Zhu, "Pang Xunqin," 129–30. It is quite probable that, more than simple acquaintances, Lin Huiyin and Qiu Ti became familiar friends.

22 Fairbank, *Liang and Lin*, 129.

23 Ibid., 131.

24 Shu-mei Shih observes that Liang's "contribution to her husband's work as a professional architectural historian has so far been systematically ignored, although, according to several close friends who knew her professional relationship with her husband, it was she who was the major inspiration behind what passed as Liang Sicheng's work." Shih, *Lure of the Modern*, 209.

25 The catalogue for the 2002 exhibition of Fang Junbi's and Zeng's art collection alongside Fang's paintings notes that the couple collected literati artworks only. Frank Dunand, ed., *The Pavilion of Marital Harmony: Chinese Painting and Calligraphy Between Tradition and Modernity* (Genève: Collections Baur, 2002), 6.

26 Fang Junbi's son Chunglu Tsen wrote her biography for the 2002 exhibition catalogue. Frank Dunand, ed., *The Pavilion of Marital Harmony*, 25.

27 Information about Fang Junbi's life comes primarily from two retrospective exhibitions: Dunand, *The Pavilion of Marital Harmony* and *A Retrospective Exhibition of the Works of Fan Tchun-pi* (Hong Kong: Department of Fine Arts of the University of Hong Kong, 1978). The Hood Museum of Art held another retrospective of her work in 2013. See Michael R. Taylor and Xinyue Guo, *Between Tradition and Modernity: The Art of Fan Tchunpi* (Dartmouth, NH: Hood Museum of Art, 2013), https://hoodmuseum.dartmouth.edu/explore/exhibitions/between-tradition-and-modernity. Another source of information on Fang Junbi is the pro-Wang Jingwei website: "Fang Junbi (1898–1986)," 汪精衛 | Wang Jingwei, accessed June 20, 2018, http://wangjingwei.org/en/associates-en/fang-junbi/.

28 The charismatic Wang Jingwei continued to gain political power and the Guomindang split into two factions: one led by Wang in Hankou and the other headed by Generalissimo Chiang Kai-shek in Nanjing. After an assassination attempt in 1935, Wang resigned, and between 1936 and 1938—while tensions with Chiang Kai-shek's government grew and the Second Sino-Japanese War began—Wang and Zeng traveled extensively through Europe, China, and French Indochina (Vietnam). Following Wang Jingwei's announcement at the end of 1938 of his intention to negotiate with the Japanese, Chiang Kai-shek sent assassins to kill his troublesome adversary. In March 1939, the assassins tracked Wang to a residence in Hanoi and riddled with bullets the bedroom in which they believed he was staying, but which actually contained Zeng and Fang, who had just arrived on a visit to her husband that day.

29 The exhibition was held October 11–15, 1941, in the Tokyo Ginza Kōjunsha, which was the residence of a modern social club founded in 1880. "Dongjing tongxun: Fang Junbi Dongjing huazhan canguan ji 東京通訊:方君璧東京畫展參觀記 [Tokyo News Dispatch: Notes from a Visit to Fang Junbi's Tokyo Exhibition]," *Guomin xinwen zhoukan* 國民新聞周刊 *Citizens News Weekly*, no. 1 (1941): 8.

30 *The Pavilion of Marital Harmony* states that Wang Jingwei had requested Fang Junbi recreate a lost painting titled, *A Morning Lesson in an Autumn Courtyard*, that had depicted his mother teaching him as a boy. Dunand, *The Pavilion of Marital Harmony*, 26. The painting cited as number seventeen in this exhibition review is a picture commissioned by Wang depicting him receiving a lesson as a youth, and it would seem to be the same painting. However, the review article precisely describes the instructor as an old man stroking his beard and identifies him as Wang's father.

31 As the text relates, "*mei yi ge binke dou qinpei zhe Fang nüshi de duoneng* 每一個賓客都欽佩着方女士的多能."

32 Wang Jingwei referred to his alliance with the Japanese as the Peace Movement. Taylor has written about Wang's cultivation of his image as willing martyr for this Peace Movement and notes that regime propagandists endlessly circulated in the press an image of his hospitalization following the first assassination attempt on his life. Taylor states that there was no image associated with the second attempt to be similarly deployed by propagandists, but in fact this painting served that very purpose. Jeremy E. Taylor, "From Traitor to Martyr: Drawing Lessons from the Death and Burial of Wang Jingwei, 1944," *Journal of Chinese History*, March 2018, 6, https://doi.org/10.1017/jch.2017.43.

33 The Shanghai exhibition took place in April 1942 and is mentioned in Yun Duan 雲端, "Fang Junbi nüshi fangwen ji 方君璧女士訪問記 [Notes on an Interview with Madam Fang Junbi]," *Funü shijie* 婦女世界 *[Women's World]*, Mingren fangwen ji 名人訪問記 [Notes on Interviews with Famous People], 3, no. 6 (1942): 3.

34 Yu Zhong 羽中, "Fang Junbi nüshi huazhan yipie 方君璧女士畫展一瞥 [A Glimpse at Fang Junbi's Painting Exhibition]," *Guomin xinwen zhoukan* 國民新聞周刊 *Citizens News Weekly*, no. 8 (1941): 8.

35 Based on the series title, this article belongs to a larger collection of celebrity interviews. The source of the article, a women's magazine begun in 1940 in Guangzhou during the occupation, was another pro-Wang Jingwei publication. Yun Duan, "Fang Junbi nüshi fangwen ji."

36 Interestingly, the article also notes that Fang Junbi participated in the event at the invitation of Chairman Chen—Wang Jingwei's wife, who would later be criticized and imprisoned for taking a strong, active role in the Reorganized National Government. For information about the condemnation Chen received for her "manly" involvement in the collaborationist government, criticism that continued even years after her death, see Charles D. Musgrove, "Cheering the Traitor: The Post-War Trial of Chen Bijun, April 1946," *Twentieth-Century China* 30, no. 2 (April 2005): 25.

37 Lingnan School cofounder Gao Jianfu spearheaded the fundraising event and Fang Junbi first met him there. According to *The Young Companion*, the oil painting captioned *Shen yu meihua yiyang qing* was purchased for 1,000 yuan by the Nationalist Government for the Sun Yat-sen Memorial Hall. Fang sold other artworks as well, including a painting that Chiang Kai-Shek bought for 100 yuan. See "Shen yu meihua yiyang qing 神與梅花一樣清 [A Diety and Plum Blossoms Equally Pure]," *Liangyou huabao* 良友畫報 *[The Young Companion]*, November 30, 1927. For this information, I would like to thank Qingqi Xia, who presented an insightful conference paper on the painting and shared her copy of the pictorial's article with me.

38 The New Life Movement, a social reform campaign that the Guomindang began in 1934, preached frugality and modesty and sought to control women's dress and shopping habits through propaganda campaigns while Chiang Kai-shek's forces terrorized and murdered women perceived as insufficiently chaste and decorous. Louise Edwards, "Policing the Modern Woman in Republican China," *Modern China* 26, no. 2 (April 1, 2000): 119–20, 133, https://doi.org/10.1177/009770040002600201. Hung-Yok Ip examines how Communist rhetoric strongly discouraged self-beautification, pointing out that, "Communists viewed nonadornment pragmatically: it was construed as an attitude and a practice that women revolutionaries should adopt so that they could contribute to the political—in this case, Communist—project of strengthening the nation and reshaping society." Hung-Yok Ip, "Fashioning Appearances Feminine Beauty in Chinese Communist Revolutionary Culture," *Modern China* 29, no. 3 (July 1, 2003): 335, https://doi.org/10.1177/0097700403029003003. Of the PGROC, a Japanese-controlled puppet state in north China from 1937 to 1940, Taylor writes, "gendered archetypes employed by this regime were reminiscent of figures celebrated under the preceding Nationalist regime of Chiang Kai-shek, which the PGROC professed to loathe." Jeremy E. Taylor, "Gendered Archetypes of Wartime Occupation: 'New Women' in Occupied North China, 1937–40," *Gender & History* 28, no. 3 (November 1, 2016): 682, https://doi.org/10.1111/1468-0424.12244. Wang Jingwei, for his part, similarly embraced social reform modeled on Confucian morals and instructed women to recycle the traditional feminine virtue of self-sacrifice. Prasenjit Duara, "The Regime of Authenticity: Timelessness, Gender, and National History in Modern China," *History and Theory* 37, no. 3 (1998): 299–300. Wang Jingwei conspicuously fashioned himself as a morally righteous ruler who, besides modeling moral integrity and propriety in his own behavior, was willing to die for his convictions. Taylor, "From Traitor to Martyr." In an interesting quote from the pro-Wang Jingwei website, Fang says of Wang, "Although he was at times humorous, he was also very reserved and kept to old traditions in his code of ethics . . . I never saw any action that overstepped proper etiquette and never heard him say anything that was impolite . . . He kept himself pure, like a woman from antiquity . . . " "Fang Junbi (1898–1986)."

39 Duara, "The Regime of Authenticity," 299. Duara is borrowing this term from Partha Chatterjee. See Partha Chatterjee, *Nationalist Thought and the Colonial World: A Derivative Discourse* (London: Zed Books for the United Nations University, 1986).

40 Duara identifies this discourse as "subterranean in the communist case." Duara, "The Regime of Authenticity," 301.

41 Taylor, "Gendered Archetypes of Wartime Occupation," 682.

42 Taylor writes that the policies of the briefly lived PGROC puppet state "promoted a return" to Confucianism and family, but "[r]ather than advising educated young women to return to their homes then, the PGROC encouraged them to take to the streets, to engage in campaigns and to celebrate the birth of the 'New Order' by chasing Chiang Kai-shek from China, as her predecessors had done to warlords some years earlier." Taylor, 665, 667. Of Manchukuo, Duara writes, "After 1937, and especially after 1941, the regime's attitude toward women was by no means a mere return to the past. The ideal was not to confine women to the home, but to contain and deploy them in the public in a way that would serve state and regime interests." Duara, *Sovereignty and Authenticity*, 146–47. Speaking more broadly, he also notes, "while twentieth-century women were not necessarily discouraged from involvement in the public sphere, nationalist patriarchy in China sought to mobilize the weight of these historical representations to discipline women's bodies within the public sphere as figures of self-sacrifice." Duara, "The Regime of Authenticity," 300.

43 Huang Miaozi 黃苗子, ed., *Quanguo manhua zuojia kangzhan jiezuo xuanji* 全國漫畫作家抗戰傑作選集 *[Selection of War of Resistance Masterpieces by the National Cartoonists,* hereafter *War of Resistance Masterpieces]* (Guangzhou: Zhanwang Shushe, 1938).

44 The end of the volume contains an accidental duplication of fifteen images; as a result, pages 95–110 are identical to pages 79–94.

45 Li Hui 李辉, *Ren zai xuanwo—Huang Miaozi yu Yu Feng* 人在漩涡—黄苗子与郁风 *[People in a Whirlpool: Huang Miaozi and Yu Feng]* (Jinan: Shandong Huabao Chubanshe, 1998), 71–72.

46 Sources for biographical information on Liang Baibo include, Tao Yongbai and Li Shi, *Shiluo de lishi*, 217–22; Jaeyeon Ahn, "Gendering Cartoons, Representing Woman's Desire," *Zhongguo xiandai wenxue* 中國現代文學 *[Modern Chinese Literature and Culture]*, no. 58 (September 2011): 157–85; John A. Lent and Xu Ying, "Chinese Women Cartoonists: Historical and Contemporary Perspectives," *International Journal of Comic Art* 5, no. 2 (2003): 351–55; Martina Caschera, "Women in Cartoons: Liang Baibo and the Visual Representations of Women in Modern Sketch," *International Journal of Comic Art* 19, no. 2 (Fall/Winter 2017): 224–52.

47 Liang illustrated *Children's Pagoda* (*Haier ta*), written by Yin Fu; a short story titled "Country Scenes" by Mu Shiying; and "Hongcai moyan [Inflammation of the Iris]" by the Shanghai male writer Lin Huiyin (1899–1982), not to be confused with the female architect and poet of the same name (1904–55). Lynn Pan, *Shanghai Style: Art and Design between the Wars* (San Francisco: Long River Press, 2008), 127. The text and illustrations for "Hongcai moyan" were published in *Modern Miscellany*. Lin Huiyin 林微音, "Hongcai moyan 虹彩膜炎 [Inflammation of the Iris]," *Shidai huabao* 時代畫報 *[Modern Miscellany]* 8, no. 12 (1935): 26–27.

48 Zhi zhi 知之, "Yitan yishi: Liang Baibo zhi dadan 藝壇逸事:梁白波之大膽 [Art Circle Anecdotes: Liang Baibo's Guts]," *Meishu zazhi* 美術雜誌 *Art Magazine* 1, no. 5 (1937): 136–37.

49 Pang Tao, ed., *Schudy*, 69; Ahn, "Gendering Cartoons," 162.

50 Dorothy Wong, "Huang Miaozi and Yu Feng," *Orientations* 19, no. 8 (August 1988): 32.

51 The Luguoqiao Incident (or, Marco Polo Bridge Incident) was the July 7th, 1937, event that precipitated Japan's full-scale invasion of China and marks the official start of the Second Sino-Japanese War. Tian Han's play gives some sense of just how quickly China's eastern cities succumbed to the invasion. Tian Han began writing the play not long after the incident occurred in July and staged it while Chinese and Japanese troops fought a four-month battle over Shanghai. By the end of that year, however, both Shanghai and Nanjing had fallen to Japan and many of those involved with the play had escaped to safer areas.

52 Antonia Finnane, "Yu Feng and the 1950s Dress Reform Campaign: Global Hegemony and Local Agency in the Art of Fashion," in *Voices Amid Silence (II): Women and the Society in Modern China (1600–1950)* (Taipei: Institute of Modern History Academia Sinica, 2003), 245.

53 Wong, "Huang Miaozi and Yu Feng," 32.

54 "Activities of Writers and Artists," *Kangri huabao* 抗日畫報 *[Anti-Japanese Pictorial]*, no. 3 (1937): 11.

55 Ahn, "Gendering Cartoons," 174–75.

56 Chang-tai Hung, *War and Popular Culture: Resistance in Modern China, 1937–1945* (Berkeley: University of California Press, 1994), 124–36, http://ark.cdlib.org/ark:/13030/ft829008m5/.

57 Ahn, "Gendering Cartoons," 175–77.

58 Yu Feng studied her lines for the play with another strong-willed woman, Jiang Qing, who was then known as Lan Ping (藍蘋) and who would meet and marry Mao Zedong the following year. A prescient parallel, as a few decades later Jiang Qing would likewise be demonized as a villainous and power-hungry tyrant following the close of the Cultural Revolution. Li Hui, *Ren zai xuanwo*, 79.

59 Yu Feng 郁風, "Guanyu Wu Zetian 關於武則天 [About Wu Zentian]," *Funü shenghuo* 婦女生活 *[Women's Life]* 4, no. 12 (1937): 14.

60 Liang is billed at time as China's only female cartoonist, but the slanderous source, a tabloid-style report on her relationship with Ye Qianyu, is filled with backhanded compliments (for example, she is "praised" for being romantic and knowing a lot) that are intended to discredit and shame her for her tryst. Zhi zhi, "Liang Baibo zhi dadan." The scandalous affair became a fixation in the news, which printed at least a half-dozen tabloid-style articles on the topic. In the end, the press coverage spanned more than a decade and long outlasted the romance itself. "Yishuhua de qinglü: Liang Baibo ye Ye Qianyu dingyou shenshi xieding 藝術化的情侶:梁白波與葉淺予訂有紳士協定 [Artistic Sweethearts: Liang Baibo and Ye Qianyu Draw Up a Gentleman's Agreement]," *Shidai shenghuo* 時代生活 *[Times Life]* 5, no. 4/5 (1937): 6; "Manhua quan dongjing 漫畫圈動靜 [Cartoon Group Activity]," *Feng yue huabao* 風月畫報 *[Wind and Moon Pictorial]* 9, no. 47 (1937): 2; Ru Shi 如是, "Ye Qianyu xiatang zhi qi: Liang Baibo ye wu fei jia ji 葉淺予下堂之妻: 梁白波野鶩非家雞 [Ye Qianyu's Abandoned Wife: Wild Duck Liang Baibo Wrongs Family Chicken]," *Kuaihuo lin* 快活林 *[Merry Forest]*, no. 51 (1947): 2.

61 Jack Chen, "Towards a Modern Conception of Art," *T'ien Hsia Monthly* 7, no. 4 (November 1938): 342–49.

62 This incident was not the only time that Liang Baibo's work was credited to a man. Years earlier, Lu Xun had misattributed her illustrations to the text's author, Yin Fu. See Pan, *Shanghai Style*, 127.

63 Duara, "The Regime of Authenticity," 297.

64 Although, Edwards's analysis focuses on the propaganda corps' journals, much the same imagery—including some of the images she specifically references—is also found in *War of Resistance Masterpieces.* Louise Edwards, "Drawing Sexual Violence in Wartime China: Anti-Japanese Propaganda Cartoons," *The Journal of Asian Studies* 72, no. 3 (August 2013): 563–86.

65 Edwards, 573.

66 Edwards, 573, 577–79. Edwards notes that the implied death of the raped woman also neatly eliminated the threat of racial defilement caused by the birth of children of rape, and thus—for the male viewer, at least—would be "reassuring and inspire retaliatory action, rather than despair." Edwards, 577.

67 Edwards, 571.

68 There are a couple of notable exceptions to the typical depiction of women by male cartoonists: Yu Shaofei's contrasting of female troops against the rape and murder of women who had not militarized in "Women jointly rise up and annihilate the evil enemy (*Funü gongtong qilai jian echou*)" and Wang Zimei's portrayal of the many wartime occupations for women, including that of soldier, in "Total Mobilization of Women (*Funü zongdongyuan*)." Huang Miaozi, *Quanguo manhua zuojia*, 111, 113.

69 Taylor notes that the "rhetoric of female victimhood" held little persuasive power in occupied China, "for it makes the very notion of conflating territorial and sexual conquest problematic." Instead, he finds that, "[c]ollaborationist nationalism . . . often seems to grant symbolic agency to female archetypes while downplaying notions of female victimhood." Taylor, "Gendered Archetypes of Wartime Occupation," 664.

70 Duara, "The Regime of Authenticity," 298. Duara links his observation on women's status in wartime China to "many other early twentieth-century patriarchal nationalisms." I do not disagree that the rhetoric surrounding women's place in society was closely associated with "patriarchal nationalism" throughout the early twentieth century, but as I hope to have demonstrated here, the parameters in which women professionals operated and the agency that they enjoyed did change dramatically.

71 Liang Baibo did not meet her spouse until 1938; Yu Feng did not marry Huang Miaozi and begin a family until 1944.

72 Duara, *Sovereignty and Authenticity*, 307.

Conclusion

1 Translation from Ni Yide, "A Galaxy of the Storm Society (1 October 1935)," in *Shanghai Modern, 1919–1945*, ed. Jo-Anne Birnie Danzker Danzker, Ken Lum, and Zheng Shengtian (Ostfildern-Ruit: Hatje Cantz Verlag, 2004), 236.

2 As translated in Zheng Shengtian, "Waves Lashed the Bund from the West," 196.

3 Also translated by Zheng, see Zheng Shengtian, 196.

4 Zheng Shengtian, 196.

5 Liang Xihong 梁錫鴻, "Zhongguo de yanghua yundong 中國的洋畫運動 [China's Western Painting Movement]," *Daguang bao* 大光報 *[Great Light Newspaper]*, June 26, 1948, Guangzhou edition. The other two Chinese women artists that Liang Xihong mentions are Liang Baibo and Sheng Cijun (盛此君), *both* of whom he identifies as members of the Storm Society. Liang himself had been a founding member of the Chinese Independent Art Association in Guangzhou.

6 Yang writes, "*Qiu Ti yuanshi yanjiu zhuangshi yishu de, tade zuopin budaiyan juyou zhuangshiwei* 丘堤原是研究装饰艺术的，她的作品不待言具有装饰味." Yang Qiuren 杨秋人, "Huiyi Ni Yide he Juelanshe 回忆倪贻德和决澜社 [Remembering Ni Yide and the Storm Society]," *Meishu jia* 美术家 *[Artist]* 31 (April 1983): 20.

7 Shui's words: "*Zai Pang de huiyilu Jiushi zheyang zouguolai de (1949 nian yiqian bufen) you guan 30 nian shidai shenghuo de xushu zhong, dui ta yu Qiu Ti de guanxi jingbuzhe yi zi.* 在庞的回忆录《就是这样走过来的》(1949 年以前部分) 有关30 年代生活的叙述中, 对他与丘堤的关系竟不着一字." Shui Tianzhong 水天中, "Tanxun Qiu Ti 探寻丘堤 [Searching for Qiu Ti]," *Meishu yanjiu* 美术研究 *[Art Research]* 4 (1997): 46, n. 5.

8 Pang Tao suggests the jealous influences of Pang Xunqin's second wife may account for the omission of Qiu Ti from the memoir. Political pressures also may have colored Pang Xunqin's reminiscences—for example, his characterization of the Storm Society is fairly disenchanted in general—and this may have influenced his decision to omit earlier references to his wife.

9 Michael Sullivan, *Art and Artists of Twentieth-Century China* (Berkeley: University of California Press, 1996), 64. Sullivan's dismissal of Qiu Ti's professional career began decades earlier and may be gleaned from Chinese art historian Michael Sullivan's "Reminiscences of Pang Xunqin," which he penned shortly after the family left Chengdu in 1946. The short essay, focusing exclusively on the heroic struggles faced by Pang Xunqin during his career as artist, mentions Qiu Ti in passing within the initial paragraph: ". . . Qiu Ti, studied in Japan and paints flowers when not making clothes for the children and keeping house—a hard task in these days of inflation. Pang Xunqin keeps a benign and fatherly eye on his family and in a quiet way exerts a great influence on them." A close family friend, Sullivan surely had no intention of slighting Qiu Ti, but his comments nonetheless trivialize her professional accomplishments and reinforce ancient gender roles. He makes no mention of Qiu Ti's college degree and research

appointment at the Shanghai Academy of Art, nor later in the essay does he disclose her participation in the Storm Society when he discusses Pang Xunqin's role in the group. Sullivan does observe in passing Qiu Ti's education abroad, but then labels her a flower painter, children's clothing maker, and housekeeper. In other words, Qiu Ti provides pretty and quaint flourishes while fulfilling her proper role within the home. In the following sentence, however, her husband assumes the stereotypical role of Confucian patriarch, a "benign and fatherly" ruler of the house whom all members of the family, swayed by his effortless superiority, heed. Sullivan no doubt shared a perception of Qiu Ti common within the larger art scene at that time. Considering his personal involvement with the struggling refugee artists in Chengdu and his subsequent decades-long standing as preeminent Western authority on modern Chinese art, this essay should not be read as a simple eyewitness record of the unfolding of history but, rather, as a preliminary foray into the construction of a canon. Regrettably, this emergent canon of modern Chinese art held little room for domesticated Modern Girls like Qiu Ti. Michael Sullivan's "Reminiscences of Pang Xunqin," (1946), reprinted in Danzker, Jo-Anne Birnie et al, *Shanghai Modern, 1919-1945* (Ostfildern-Ruit: Hatje Cantz, 2004): 248.

10 Sullivan, 78.

11 Sullivan, 78.

12 Sullivan, 78–79.

13 Pang Tao, ed., *Schudy*, 141. Prior to Shui Tianzhong's paper, the last time Qiu Ti's modernist painting career received attention seems to have been in Liang Xihong's lackluster evaluation, which he illustrates with her painting of sunflowers in a vase.

14 Pang Tao interview with author, August 2011.

15 Wendy M. K. Shaw, "Where Did the Women Go? Female Artists from the Ottoman Empire to the Early Years of the Turkish Republic," *Journal of Women's History* 23, no. 1 (Spring 2011): 13–37.

16 Though raised and educated in the United States, Shaw's ethnic heritage is in part Turkish and the bulk of her research for this article was conducted during her six years of employment in Istanbul, which would seem to grant her an insider view of Turkish art and culture. See Wendy M. K. Shaw, "Why Care About Ottoman Women Artists?," *Journal of Women's History* (blog), accessed June 12, 2019, http://bingdev.binghamton.edu/jwh/?page_id=385.

17 Shaw, "Where Did the Women Go?" 13.

18 Shaw writes, "Paraphrasing Linda Nochlin, there were no great women artists in the Ottoman Empire because there were no 'great' artists in the first place. The limitations which faced women in the arts also faced non-Western artists struggling to create a career in a society where painting was a very new cultural form.... In such an environment, male artists struggled to make ends meet, and often created work less with an eye to the creation of original works than with a desire to please, and thereby educate and modernize, the public. However, limited as the opportunities for male artists were, they were still more limited for women." Shaw, 31. Though Chinese modernists also faced great difficulty in 1930s Shanghai, there is no doubt that many—in particular, Xu Beihong, Lin Fengmian, Liu Haisu, and Pang Xunqin—readily emerge as the "greats" of their generation. I would also argue that many women artists—such as Qiu Ti, Pan Yuliang, and Fang Junbi—although less studied, are similarly crucial contributors to the development of modernist art in China.

19 Shaw, 14. Comparison with China is my contribution; Shaw makes no comparative reference to East Asia in her article.

20 Shaw, 14–15.

21 Shaw, 19–27.

22 The 2010 translation of Lu Peng's ambitious survey of twentieth-century Chinese art says of Qiu Ti's style: "In her expression, she moved between Impressionism and decorative painting, and possibly because of her female temperament but more likely because of the suggestions of Japanese painters her works are characterized by simplicity and gentleness." Lü Peng, *A History of Art in 20th-Century China* (Milano: Charta, 2010), 309. Pang Tao disputes the authenticity of the painting the text reproduces as an example of Qiu Ti's work.

23 Shaw, "Where Did the Women Go?," 23.

24 Information about Guan Zilan's later life and career is found in her recent retrospective catalogue. See primarily: CANS Yishu Xinwen Bianji Tuandui, ed., *Guan Zilan (1903–1985)*, 23, 26–28, 34–35.

25 See Wen Zhaotong 溫肇桐, "Nühuajia Guan Zilan 女畫家關紫蘭 [Painteress Guan Zilan]," *Yong'an yuekan* 永安月刊 *[Wing On Monthly]*, no. 26 (June 1941): 42; "Benkan benqi fengmian zuojia—yanghuajia Guan Zilan nüshi jieshao 本刊本期封面作者—洋畫家關紫蘭女士介紹 [Our Cover Artist for This Issue: Introducing Western-Style Painter Guan Zilan]," *Huawen meiri* 華文每日 *[Chinese Daily]* 9, no. 11 (1943): 45. The 1943 article mentions Guan had a solo exhibition in Shanghai after her return in 1930, but in terms of her professional activity since then it only mentions her participation in the Shanghai Lianhe Yanghuazhan (Shanghai Joint Western Painting Exhibition) the previous year. Though her recent catalogue raisonne says that Guan refused to aid the Japanese, these two articles suggest that the occupied Shanghai propaganda machine, whether with the artist's complicity or without, appropriated her persona as a cultural figure professionally successful in Japan.

26 Ahn, "Gendering Cartoons," 178.

27 A number of Liang Baibo's depictions of ethnic minorities from China's western regions were published in *Wenchao yuekan* 文潮月刊 (*Culture Current Monthly*) and *Renshijian* 人世間 (*The World*) in 1947. For a brief discussion of the album, see Xu Wenhua 徐文华 and Li Chao 李超, "Niu Yue: Zhongjian Liang Baibo de yishu shengming 纽约:重见梁白波的艺术生命 [New York: An Important Look at the Artistic Life of Liang Baibo]," *Xinmin wanbao* 新民晚报 *[New People's Evening News]*, August 29, 2009, sec. B. See also, Zhang Qiongwen, "Minguo nühuajia Liang Baibo," 184–97.

28 For what little information that is known about Liang Baibo's late life, see Zhang Qiongwen, "Minguo nühuajia Liang Baibo," 11, 210–12; Ahn, "Gendering Cartoons," 160, n. 5; Martina Caschera, "Women in Cartoons: Liang Baibo and the Visual Representations of Women in Modern Sketch," *International Journal of Comic Art* 19, no. 2 (Fall/Winter 2017): 227.

29 In her analysis of Pan Yuliang's paintings of female nudes, Phyllis Teo observes that it "is visibly undeniable that Pan was adopting certain aspects of the Western Orientalist aesthetics." Teo goes on to state that "Pan attempted to 'speak' of her distinct identity in the West by turning her race, as well as her gender, into a site of self-expression through her multiple representations of the Oriental body." Teo thus concludes that, as many of the figures resemble the artist herself, Pan's self-Orientalizing imagery represents the displaced artist's attempt to reclaim agency. Phyllis Teo, "Modernism and Orientalism: The Ambiguous Nudes of Chinese Artist Pan Yuliang," *New Zealand Journal of Asian Studies* 12, no. 2 (December 2010): 74–78.

30 Phyllis Teo has observed that "[m]ore than half of the works Pan left behind featured the non-Western female nude as their subject." Teo, 70.

31 Francesca Dal Lago recent essay looks closely at Pan Yuliang's paintings of nudes, but she points to this poster as evidence of the artist using media, subject, and style to obtain a "perfect balance" between the two cultures. Francesca Dal Lago, "The Best of Both Worlds: Pan Yu-Lin's Paintings of the Nude," in *Song of Spring* 春之歌*: Pan Yu-Lin in Paris* 潘玉良在巴黎, ed. Eric Lefebvre (Hong Kong: Yazhou Xiehui Xianggang Zhongxin, 2018), 65, https://hkupress.hku.hk/pro/1761.php.

32 Doris Sung's dissertation provides a thorough analysis of the romanticized version of Pan's life and career, which has been perpetuated by both popular culture and scholarship alike, and which is perhaps best represented by the sensationalizing 1994 movie, *Huahun* 畫魂 [A Soul Haunted by Painting]. A vehicle for Gong Li directed by Zhang Yimou, the movie is full of widely believed fictionalizations, such as false notions Pan had been a prostitute in her youth and that she relocated overseas in response to vandalization of her artwork. See chapter 3 of Doris Ha Lin Sung, "Redefining Female Talent: Chinese Women Artists in the National and Global Art Worlds, 1900s–1970s" (PhD diss., York University, 2016).

33 For an example of the sordid rumors about Fang Junbi that circulated after the fall of Wang Jingwei's regime, see lively titled, Lao Caoming 老草命, "Chen Bijun/Fang Junbi, Wang Jingwei zuoyou fengyuan—Zeng Zhongming daile lümaozi, zai Henei you zuo tisigui: touhao hanjian guifang mishi 陳璧君 / 方君璧、汪精衛左右逢源--曾仲鳴戴了綠帽子，在河內又做替死鬼：頭號漢奸閨房秘史 [Chen Bijun/Fang Junbi—Wang Jingwei Benefited from Both Sides: Zeng Zhongming Wearing a Green Hat, Also Made a Scapegoat in Hanoi: The Secret History of the Number One Traitor's Boudoir]," *Piao* 飄 *[Flutter]*, no. 3 (1946): 1. Wearing a green hat is a euphemism for a cuckolded man.

34 In 1948 with the establishment of the Communist state imminent and the political tide having firmly turned, Fang realized China was no longer safe for her and fled first to Hong Kong and then to Paris. She relocated to Paris in the fall of 1949.

35 For more information on the practice of collective painting in early decades of the PRC, see Christine I. Ho, "The People Eat For Free and the Art of Collective Production in Maoist China," *The Art Bulletin* 98, no. 3 (2016): 64–88.

36 These paintings are now lost. Pang Tao, ed., *Schudy*, 117, 121, 139.

37 Antonia Finnane, *Changing Clothes in China: Fashion, History, Nation* (New York: Columbia University Press, 2008), 206–15.

38 Writing of the social developments in China during the 1950s, Finnane observes that, "Women's liberation ceased to be a right and became a duty, and the circumstances for identity formation became rather constraining, especially given the well-documented ambiguities and contradictions in the Communist project." Finnane, "Yu Feng," 246. Noting that the fashions that Yu Feng designed in reality experienced very little application to the garments worn by the public at large, Finnane nonetheless concludes, "As an artist drawing up designs for clothes at a time when the cultural content of a 'New China' was being negotiated, Yu Feng deserves identification as an agent in a specific historical process." Finnane, "Yu Feng," 262.

39 Email correspondence with Pang Tao. Document of official recognition published in Pang Tao, ed., *Schudy*, 119.

40 Dorothy Wong, "Huang Miaozi and Yu Feng," *Orientations* 19, no. 8 (August 1988): 32.

41 For information on this group, as well as the persecution later suffered by its members, see Geremie R.

Barmé, "The People's Republic of Wine," *China Heritage Quarterly*, no. 25 (March 2011), http://www.chinaheritagequarterly.org/editorial.php?issue=025.

42 Wong, "Huang Miaozi and Yu Feng," 32; Michael Sullivan, *Modern Chinese Artists: A Biographical Dictionary* (Berkeley: University of California Press, 2006), 205. Lü Peng, *A History of Art in 20th-Century China*, 429.

43 For a group photograph of the exhibition participants, taken in April 1946, see Lü Peng, fig. 10.66.

44 Wong, "Huang Miaozi and Yu Feng," 32; Sullivan, *Modern Chinese Artists*, 205.

45 Finnane, *Changing Clothes in China: Fashion, History, Nation*, 206–15.

46 Finnane, "Yu Feng," 262.

47 Jan Marsh, *Pre-Raphaelite Sisters* (London: National Portrait Gallery, 2019); Sarah Cascone, "This New Database Aims to Become the World's Best Resource on the History of Overlooked Women Artists," *artnet News*, November 2, 2018, https://news.artnet.com/art-world/new-database-complies-info-historys-overlooked-women-artists-1384966; "AWA's Missions and Goals," Advancing Women Artists, accessed June 7, 2019, http://advancingwomenartists.org/about/mission-and-goals. Although we a currently witnessing a renewed interest in reconstituting women's careers in the arts, initial recovery work was already underway in the 1980s when Griselda Pollock first published her books documenting the systematic expulsion of women from the canon of Western art history. See Rozsika Parker and Griselda Pollock, *Old Mistresses: Women, Art and Ideology* (London: I. B. Tauris, 2013); Griselda Pollock, *Vision and Difference: Feminism, Femininity, and the Histories of Art* (New York: Routledge, 1988).

48 Joan Marter et al., *Women of Abstract Expressionism* (Denver; New Haven, CT: Denver Art Museum; Yale University Press, 2016); Ulrike Muller, *Bauhaus Women: Art, Handicraft, Design*. (Place of publication not identified: Flammarion, 2015); T'ai Lin Smith, *Bauhaus Weaving Theory: From Feminine Craft to Mode of Design*, 2014, http://public.eblib.com/choice/publicfullrecord.aspx?p=1834016; Stella Rollig and Sabine Fellner, *City of Women: Female Artists in Vienna from 1900 to 1938*, 2019; Museum Haus Konstruktiv, *Dada Differently: Sophie Taeuber-Arp, Hannah Hoech, Elsa Von Freytag-Loringhoven* (Zürich, 2016), https://www.hauskonstruktiv.ch/enUS/exhibitions/exhibition-archive/2016/-/events/archives-2016/2016/dada-differently.htm; Paula K Kamenish, *Mamas of Dada: Women of the European Avant-Garde*, 2015; Hilma af Klint, Tracey Bashkoff, and Solomon R. Guggenheim Museum, *Hilma Af Klint: Paintings for the Future* (New York: Guggenheim Museum Publishing, 2018); Städtische Galerie im Lenbachhaus München, *World Receivers: Georgiana Houghton, Hilma Af Klint, Emma Kunz and John Whitney, James Whitney, Harry Smith*, 2018; Mika Yoshitake, ed., *Yayoi Kusama: Infinity Mirrors* (New York: DelMonico Books, Prestel, 2017).

49 M. Lluïsa Faxedas, "Women Artists of Cercle et Carré: Abstraction, Gender and Modernity," *Woman's Art Journal* 36, no. 1 (Spring/Summer 2015): 37–46.

50 Faxedas, 39.

51 Françoise Gilot, *Life with Picasso* (New York: New York Review of Books, 2019).

52 "'Life With Picasso' Stands As An Invaluable Work of Art History," NPR.org, accessed June 7, 2019, https://www.npr.org/2019/06/06/729956221/life-with-picasso-stands-as-an-invaluable-work-of-art-history.

53 Karolina Ziebinska-Lewandowska, Damarice Amao, and Amanda Maddox, *Dora Maar Exhibition Catalogue* (Paris: Cente Pompidou, 2019).

Bibliography

A Retrospective Exhibition of the Works of Fan Tchun-pi. Hong Kong: Department of Fine Arts of the University of Hong Kong, 1978.

"Activities of Writers and Artists." *Kangri huabao* 抗日畫報 *[Anti-Japanese Pictorial]*, no. 3 (1937): 11.

Ahn, Jaeyeon. "Gendering Cartoons, Representing Woman's Desire." *Zhongguo xiandai wenxue* 中國現代文學 *[Modern Chinese Literature and Culture]*, no. 58 (September 2011): 157–85.

Allen, Laura W. "Modern Girls, Working Women and Housewives: Japanese Women Artists in the Interwar Years." In *Essays on Women's Artistic and Cultural Contributions 1919–1939: Expanded Social Roles for the New Woman Following the First World War*, edited by Paula Birnbaum and Anna Novakov, 97-117. Lewiston: Edwin Mellen Press, 2009.

Andrews, Julia F. "A Shelter from the Storm: Chinese Painting in a Cataclysmic Age, 1930–1979." In *Between the Thunder and the Rain: Chinese Paintings from the Opium War Through the Cultural Revolution, 1840–1979*, edited by Kuiyi Shen and Julia F. Andrews, 169-197. San Francisco: Asian Art Museum, 2000.

———. "Art and the Cosmopolitan Culture of 1920s Shanghai: Liu Haisu and the Nude Model Controversy." *Chungguksa yon'gu*, no. 35 (April 2005): 323–72.

———. "Luotihua lunzheng ji xiandai Zhongguo meishushi de jiangou 裸体画论争及现代中国美术史的建构 [The Nude Painting Debate and the Construction of Modern Chinese Art History]." In *Haipai huihua yanjiu wenji* 海派绘画研究文集 *[Studies on Shanghai School Painting]*, 117–50. Shanghai: Shanghai Shuhua Chubanshe, 2001.

Andrews, Julia F., and Kuiyi Shen. "Traditionalism as a Modern Stance: The Chinese Women's Calligraphy and Painting Society." *Modern Chinese Literature and Culture* 11, no. 1 (Spring 1999): 1–30.

———. "The Traditionalist Response to Modernity: The Chinese Painting Society of Shanghai." In *Visual Culture in Shanghai, 1850s–1930s*, edited by Jason C. Kuo, 79-93. Washington, DC: New Academia Publishing, 2007.

Andrews, Julia F., and Kuiyi Shen, eds. *A Century in Crisis: Modernity and Tradition in the Art of Twentieth-Century China*. New York: Guggenheim Museum, 1998.

———. *Between the Thunder and the Rain: Chinese Paintings from the Opium War Through the Cultural Revolution, 1840–1979*. San Francisco: Asian Art Museum, 2000.

———. "Schudy, the Storm Society, and China's Early Modernist Movement." In *Schudy* (Qiu Ti) 丘堤, edited by Pang Tao, 62–75. Nanjing: Jiangsu Jiaoyu Chubanshe, 2006.

———. *The Art of Modern China*. Berkeley: University of California Press, 2012.

"Art Exhibition of the Storm & Stress Society." *Liangyou huabao* 良友畫報 *[The Young Companion]* 82 (November 1933): 30.

"Autumn—The Season of Arts: Exhibition of works by the faculty of S. H. Academy." *Liangyou huabao* 良友畫報 *[The Young Companion]* 71 (1932).

"Bai E de qishi 白鵝的起始 [The Beginnings of White Goose]." *Bai E yishu banyue kan* 白鵝藝術半月刊, June 15, 1930, back cover.

Bailey, Paul. "Women Behaving Badly: Crime, Transgressive Behavior and Gender in Early Twentieth-Century China." *NAN NÜ* 8, no. 1 (2006): 156–97.

Barlow, Tani E. "Buying In: Advertising and the Sexy Modern Girl Icon in Shanghai in the 1920s and 1930s." In *The Modern Girl Around the World: Consumption, Modernity, and Globalization*, edited by The Modern Girl Around the World Research Group, 288–316. Durham: Duke University Press, 2008.

———. "Commercial Cartoon Genre and the Cliché Mise-En-Scene of the Gazing Girl." In *A Companion to Chinese Art*, edited by Martin J. Powers, Katherine R. Tsiang, and Dana Arnold, 432–53. Chichester, West Sussex: Wiley-Blackwell, 2016.

———. *The Question of Women in Chinese Feminism*. Durham: Duke University Press, 2004.

Barmé, Geremie R. "The People's Republic of Wine." *China Heritage Quarterly*, no. 25 (March 2011). http://www.chinaheritagequarterly.org/editorial.php?issue=025.

"Benkan benqi fengmian zuojia—yanghuajia Guan Zilan nüshi jieshao 本刊本期封面作者—洋畫家關紫蘭女士介紹 [Our Cover Artist for This Issue: Introducing Western-Style Painter Guan Zilan]." *Huawen meiri* 華文每日 *[Chinese Daily]* 9, no. 11 (1943): 45.

Berndt, Jaqueline. "Nationally Naked? The Female Nude in Japanese Oil Painting and Posters (1890s–1920s)." In *Performing Nation: Gender Politics in Literature, Theater, and the Visual Arts of China and Japan, 1880–1940*, edited by Doris Croissant, Catherine Vance Yeh, and Joshua S. Mostow, 307–45. Leiden: Brill, 2008.

Birnbaum, Paula. *Women Artists in Interwar France: Framing Femininities*. Farnham: Ashgate, 2011.

Birnbaum, Phyllis. *Modern Girls, Shining Stars, the Skies of Tokyo: Five Japanese Women*. New York: Columbia University Press, 1999.

Bryson, Norman. "Westernizing Bodies: Women, Art, and Power in Meiji Yoga." In *Gender and Power in the Japanese Visual Field*, edited by Joshua S. Mostow,

7 (July 1929).

Judge, Joan. "Blended Wish Images: Chinese and Western Exemplary Women at the Turn of the Twentieth Century." *NAN NÜ* 6, no. 1 (2004): 102–35.

———. *Republican Lens: Gender Visuality, and Experience in the Early Chinese Periodical Press*. Oakland, CA: University of California Press, 2015.

———. "The Modern Shanghai Visual Imaginary: Magazine Cover Girls and New Cultural Possibilities in the Early Twentieth Century." University of California, Berkeley, 2010. http://www.youtube.com/user/calcommunitycontent#p/c/3B4BC26C0768B4E2/11/xGb3PaZWMAU.

"Juelan huazhan 决瀾畫展 [Storm Society Painting Exhibition]." *Xinren zhoukan* 新人周刊 *[New People's Weekly]* 2, no. 10 (November 2, 1935).

"Juelanshe de yi qun jiqi zuopin 决瀾社的一群及其作品 [The Storm Society's Group and Their Works]." *Qingnian jie* 青年界 *[Youth World]* 8, no. 3 (October 1935).

"Juelanshe di san jie huazhan 决瀾社第三屆畫展 [The Third *(sic)* Storm Society Exhibition]." *Liangyou huabao* 良友畫報 *[The Young Companion]* 111 (November 1935).

"Juelanshe di si jie zhanlanhui 决瀾社第四屆展覽會 [The Fourth Storm Society Exhibition]." *Shidai huabao* 時代畫報 *[Modern Miscellany]* 8, no. 10 (October 1935).

"Juelanshe jiang 决瀾社獎 [The Storm Society Award]." *Shidai huabao* 時代畫報 *[Modern Miscellany]* 5, no. 4 (16 December 1933): unnumbered pages.

"Juelanshe xuanyan 决澜社宣言" [The Storm Society Manifesto]." *Yishu xunkan* 藝術旬刊 *[L'Art]* 1, no. 5 (October 1932): 8.

Kao, Mayching Margaret. "China's Response to the West in Art: 1898–1937." PhD diss., Stanford University, 1972.

Karetzky, Patricia. "Four Artists from Beijing: Li Hong, Feng Jyali, Cai Jin, Xing Fei." *Woman's Art Journal* 23, no. 2 (Autumn 2002–Winter 2003): 28–32.

Ko, Dorothy. *Cinderella's Sisters: A Revisionist History of Footbinding*. Berkeley, CA: University of California Press, 2005.

Ko, Dorothy, and Wang Zheng, eds. *Translating Feminisms in China: A Special Issue of Gender & History*. Oxford: Malden Blackwell Publishing, 2007.

Kuo, Jason C., ed. *Visual Culture in Shanghai, 1850s–1930s*. Washington, DC: New Academia Publishing, 2007.

Laing, Ellen Johnston. "Women Painters in Traditional China." In *Flowering in the Shadows: Women in the History of Chinese and Japanese Painting*, edited by Marsha Weidner, 81–101. Honolulu: University of Hawaii Press, 1990.

Lao Caoming 老草命. "Chen Bijun/Fang Junbi, Wang Jingwei zuoyou fengyuan—Zeng Zhongming daile lümaozi, zai Henei you zuo tisigui: touhao hanjian guifang mishi 陳璧君 / 方君璧、汪精衛左右逢源--曾仲鳴戴了綠帽子，在河内又做替死鬼：頭號漢奸閨房祕史 [Chen Bijun/Fang Junbi—Wang Jingwei Benefited from Both Sides: Zeng Zhongming Wearing a Green Hat, Also Made a Scapegoat in Hanoi: The Secret History of the Number One Traitor's Boudoir]." *Piao* 飄 *[Flutter]*, no. 3 (1946): 1.

Lee, Leo Ou-fan. *Shanghai Modern: The Flowering of a New Urban Culture in China, 1930–1945*. Cambridge: Harvard University Press, 1999.

Lefebvre, Eric, ed. *Song of Spring* 春之歌*: Pan Yu-Lin in Paris* 潘玉良在巴黎. Hong Kong: Yazhou Xiehui Xianggang Zhongxin, 2018. https://hkupress.hku.hk/pro/1761.php.

Lei, Jun. "Producing Norms, Defining Beauty: The Role of Science in the Regulation of the Female Body and Sexuality in Liangyou and Furen Huabao." In *Liangyou: Kaleidoscopic Modernity and the Shanghai Global Metropolis, 1926–1945*, edited by Paul Pickowicz, Kuiyi Shen, and Yingjin Zhang, 111–31. Boston: Brill, 2013.

Li Chao 李超. *Kuangbiao jiqing—Juelanshe ji xiandai zhuyi yishu xiansheng* 狂飙激情—决澜社及现代主义艺术先声 *[Hurricane Passion: The Storm Society and the Modernist Art Prelude]*. Shanghai: Shanghai Jinxiu Wenzhang Chubanshe, 2008.

Li Hui 李辉. *Ren zai xuanwo—Huang Miaozi yu Yu Feng* 人在漩涡--黄苗子与郁风 *[People in a Whirlpool: Huang Miaozi and Yu Feng]*. Jinan: Shandong Huabao Chubanshe, 1998.

Li Ying. "Zuo yi wei xiandai nüzi 做一位現代女子 [Being a Modern Woman]." Translated by C.V. Starr East Asian Library. *Linglong tuhua zazhi* 玲瓏圖畫雜誌 *[Lin Loon Ladies' Magazine]* 4, no. 10 (April 4, 1934): 583–84.

Li Yuyi 李寓一. "Jiaoyu bu quanguo meishu zhanlanhui teji hao 教育部全國美術展覽會特輯號 [Special Issue on the National Art Exhibition of the Ministry of Education]." *Funü zazhi* 婦女雜誌 *[Ladies' Journal]* 15, no. 7 (July 1929): editor's note on Pan Yuliang's painting.

Li Yuyi 李禹一, Jin Qijing 金啟靜, and Jiang Zhaohe 蔣兆和, eds. "Jiaoyu bu quanguo meishu zhanlanhui teji hao 教育部全國美術展覽會特輯號 [Special Issue on the National Art Exhibition of the Ministry of Education]." *Funü zazhi* 婦女雜誌 *[Ladies' Journal]* 15, no. 7 (July 1929).

Liang Xihong 梁錫鴻. "Zhongguo de yanghua yundong 中國的洋畫運動 [China's Western Painting Movement]." *Daguang bao* 大光報 *[Great Light Newspaper]*, June 26, 1948, Guangzhou edition.

Lien, Ling-ling. "Leisure, Patriotism, and Identity: The Chinese Career Women's Club in Wartime Shanghai." In *Creating Chinese Modernity: Knowledge and Everyday Life, 1900–1940*, edited by Peter Zarrow, 213–42. New

York: Peter Lang, 2006.

———. "Searching for the 'New Womanhood': Career Women in Shanghai, 1912–1945." PhD diss., University of California, 2001.

Lin Huiyin 林微音. "Hongcai moyan 虹彩膜炎 [Inflammation of the Iris]." *Shidai huabao* 時代畫報 *[Modern Miscellany]* 8, no. 12 (1935): 26–27.

"Liuxue Fa Yi xianren Zhongda huashi Pan Yuliang nüshi jinying 留學法意現任中大畫師潘玉良女士近影 [A Recent Photograph of Pan Yuliang, Exchange Student of France and Italy and Painter of the Central University]." *Weimei* 唯美 *[Aesthetics]*, no. 4 (1935).

Lü Peng. *A History of Art in 20th-Century China*. Milano: Charta, 2010.

Lu Yin 廬隱. "Huaping shidai 花瓶時代 [The Age of Flower Vases]." *Shishi xinbao* 時事新報, Qingguang 青光 supplement, August 11, 1933. Reprinted in *Lu Yin daibiaozuo* 庐隐代表作, Beijing: Huaxia Chuban She, 1998, 373–74.

Lum, Ken. "Aesthetic Education in Republican China: A Convergence of Ideals." In *Shanghai Modern, 1919–1945*, edited by Jo-Anne Birnie Danzker Danzker, Ken Lum, and Zheng Shengtian, 216–33. Ostfildern-Ruit: Hatje Cantz Verlag, 2004.

Ma, Lesley W. "Blossoming Beyond the Pages: Female Painterly Modernities in Liangyou." In *Liangyou: Kaleidoscopic Modernity and the Shanghai Global Metropolis, 1926–1945*, edited by Paul Pickowicz, Kuiyi Shen, and Yingjin Zhang, 203–25. Boston: Brill, 2013.

Ma Yuxin. "Male Feminism and Women's Subjectivities: Zhang Xichen, Chen Xuezhao, and The New Woman." *Twentieth-Century China* 29, no. 1 (November 2003): 1–37.

"Manhua quan dongjing 漫畫圈動靜 [Cartoon Group Activity]." *Feng yue huabao* 風月畫報 *[Wind and Moon Pictorial]* 9, no. 47 (1937): 2.

Maske, Huajing Xiu. "Three Generations of Chinese Women Painters in Pang Family, Part I." In *Three Generations of Chinese Modernism: Qiu Ti, Pang Tao, Lin Yan*. Vancouver: Art Beatus Gallery, 1998.

Mathews, Patricia. "Returning the Gaze: Diverse Representations of the Nude in the Art of Suzanne Valadon." *Art Bulletin* 73, no. 3 (September 1991): 415–30.

"Miss Kuan Chi-lan, a Chinese painter, tendered a reception to Japanese painters." *Tuhua shibao* 圖畫時報 *[The Eastern Times Photo Supplement]*, no. 388 (1927): 2.

"Miss Kuan Chi-lan in Japan." *Tuhua shibao* 圖畫時報 *[The Eastern Times Photo Supplement]*, no. 383 (1927): 1.

"Miss Kwan Tsu-lan, whose works recently exhibited in Japan." *Liangyou huabao* 良友畫報 *[The Young Companion]* 30 (September 1928): 4.

Musgrove, Charles D. "Cheering the Traitor: The Post-War Trial of Chen Bijun, April 1946." *Twentieth-Century China* 30, no. 2 (April 2005): 3–27.

Nead, Lynda. *Female Nude: Art, Obscenity and Sexuality*. London: Routledge, 1992.

Ni Jun. "Schudy: Her Art and Life." In *Schudy* (Qiu Ti) 丘堤, edited by Pang Tao, 79–133. Nanjing: Jiangsu Jiaoyu Chubanshe, 2006.

"Ni Yide Zhejiang Hangzhou ren 倪貽德浙江杭州人 [Ni Yide from Hangzhou, Zhejiang]." *Meishu shenghuo* 美術生活 *[Arts & Life]*, no. 7 (October 1934): 12.

Ni Yide 倪貽德. "A Galaxy of the Storm Society (1 October 1935)." In *Shanghai Modern, 1919–1945*, edited by Jo-Anne Birnie Danzker Danzker, Ken Lum, and Zheng Shengtian, 236–41. Ostfildern-Ruit: Hatje Cantz Verlag, 2004.

———. "Lun luoti yishu 論裸體藝術 [Considering Nude Art]." *Shishi xinbao* 時事新報 *[The China Times]*. December 14, 1924, Shanghai: A Daily Supplement of China Times (312) edition, sec. Yishu [Art] no. 82.

———. "Lun luoti yishu 論裸體藝術 [Considering Nude Art]." *Chenbao fukan* 晨報副刊 *[Morning News Supplement]*, September 17, 1925.Reprinted in Lang Shaojun 郎紹君 and Shui Tianzhong 水天中, eds. *Ershi shiji Zhongguo meishu wenxuan (I)* 二十世纪中国美术文选(上卷) [20th Century Chinese Art Literary Selections]. Shanghai: Shanghai Shuhua Chubanshe, 1999, 123–29.

———. "Luoti yishu zhi zhenyi 裸體藝術之真義 [The True Meaning of Nude Art]." *Chenbao fukan* 晨報副刊 *[Morning News Supplemental]*. September 17, 1925, 1274 edition.

———. "Xin de guohua 新的國畫 [New Guohua]." In *Yishu mantan* 藝術漫談. Shanghai: Guanghua Shuju, 1928.

———. "Yiyuan jiaoyou ji: Juelanshe de yi qun 藝苑交遊記: 决瀾社的一群 [Notes on Friendly Connections in the Art Community: The Storm Society's Group]." *Qingnian jie* 青年界 *[Youth World]* 8, no. 3 (October 1935): 65–70.

Nivard, Jacqueline. "Women and Women's Press: The Case of the *Ladies' Journal* (Funü Zazhi) 1915–1931." *Republican China* 10, no. 1 (1984): 37–55.

Nochlin, Linda. "Why Have There Been No Great Women Artists?" *ARTnews* (January 1971): 22–39, 67–71.

Nochlin, Linda, and Maura Reilly. *Women Artists: The Linda Nochlin Reader*. New York, NY: Thames & Hudson, 2015.

"Nüxing de lunkuo 女性的輪廓 [Women's Silhouette]." *Jiating zazhi* 家庭雜誌 *[Household Magazine]*, no. 2 (1937): 24.

O'Brien, Elaine, ed. *Modern Art in Africa, Asia, and Latin America: An Introduction to Global Modernisms*. Malden, MA: Wiley-Blackwell, 2013.

"Pan Yuliang nüshi zhi huihua zhanlanhui 潘玉良女士之繪畫展覽會 [Pan Yuliang's Painting Exhibition]." *Shanghai*

manhua 上海漫畫 *[Shanghai Sketch]* 33 (1928): 6.
Pang Tao. “Early Works of Qiu Ti and Pang Xunqin.” *Meishu yanjiu* 美术研究 *[Art Research]* 104 (2001).
———, ed. Schudy (Qiu Ti) 丘堤. Nanjing: Jiangsu Jiaoyu Chubanshe, 2006.
———, ed. *The Storm Society and Post-Storm Art Phenomenon*. Taibei: Chin Show Publishing, 1997.
Pang Xunqin 龐薰琹. *Jiushi zheyang zou guolai de* 就是这样走过来的 *[It Happened Just Like This]*. Beijing: Shenghe, Dushu, Xinzhi Sanlian Shudian, 1988.
———. “Juelanshe xiaoshi 决澜社小史 [The Brief History of the Storm Society].” *Yishu xunkan* 藝術旬刊 *[L'Art]* 1, no. 5 (October 11, 1932): 9.
Parker, Rozsika, and Griselda Pollock. *Old Mistresses: Women, Art and Ideology*. London: I. B. Tauris, 2013.
Perry, Gillian. *Women Artists and the Parisian Avant-Garde: Modernism and “Feminine” Art, 1900 to the Late 1920s*. Manchester: Manchester University Press, 1995.
Pickowicz, Paul, Kuiyi Shen, and Yingjin Zhang, eds. *Liangyou: Kaleidoscopic Modernity and the Shanghai Global Metropolis, 1926–1945*. Boston: Brill, 2013.
Pollock, Griselda. *Vision and Difference: Feminism, Femininity, and the Histories of Art*. New York: Routledge, 1988.
“Qing zhuang jiu shi 輕妝就試 [Trying on a Bit of Makeup].” *Shidai huabao* 時代畫報 *[Modern Miscellany]* 1, no. 7 (1 August1930): 25.
Qiu Jin. “An Address to My Two Hundred Million Women Compatriots in China [Trans.].” In *The Search for Modern China: A Documentary Collection*, edited by Janet Y Chen, Pei-kai Cheng, Michael Elliot Lestz, and Jonathan D Spence, 185–87. Vancouver: Langara College, 2017.
“Qiu Ti nüshi 丘堤女士 [Miss Qiu Ti].” *Dazhong huabao* 大眾畫報 *[The Cosmopolitan]*, no. 13 (November 1934): 33.
“Renti, Fang Junbi zuo 人體, 方君璧作 [Figure, by Fang Junbi].” *Meishu shenghuo* 美術生活 *[Arts & Life]*, no. 4 (July 1934): 5.
Rocha, Leon Antonio. “Quentin Pan 潘光旦 in The China Critic.” *China Heritage Quarterly*, no. 30/31 (September 2012).
“Rowing in a lake near Kobe: Miss Kuan Tsu-lan, a famous Chinese painter, is first from right. Mr. C. T. Pao, our correspondent in Japan, is fourth from right.” *Tuhua shibao* 圖畫時報 *[The Eastern Times Photo Supplement]*, no. 393 (September 11, 1927): cover.
Ru Shi 如是. “Ye Qianyu xiatang zhi qi: Liang Baibo ye wu fei jia ji 葉淺予下堂之妻: 梁白波野鶩非家雞 [Ye Qianyu's Abandoned Wife: Wild Duck Liang Baibo Wrongs Family Chicken].” *Kuaihuo lin* 快活林 *[Merry Forest]*, no. 51 (1947): 2.
Sang, Tze-lan Deborah. “Failed Modern Girls.” In *Performing Nation: Gender Politics in Literature, Theater, and the Visual Arts of China and Japan, 1880–1940*, edited by Doris Croissant, Catherine Vance Yeh, and Joshua S. Mostow, 179–202. Leiden: Brill, 2008.
Shanghai Wenguang Xinwen Chuanmei Jituan 上海文广新闻传媒集团 [Shanghai Media Group] et al. *Minghua mingjia mi'an* 名画名家谜案 *[Mysteries of Famous Paintings and Famous Artists]*. Vol. 4, “Faxian” Guan Zilan 发现关紫兰 [‘Discovering’ Guan Zilan]. Beijing: Zhongguo Guoji Dianshi Zonggongsi, 2009.
Shaw, Wendy M. K. “Where Did the Women Go? Female Artists from the Ottoman Empire to the Early Years of the Turkish Republic.” *Journal of Women's History* 23, no. 1 (Spring 2011): 13–37.
———. “Why Care About Ottoman Women Artists?” *Journal of Women's History* (blog). Accessed June 12, 2019. http://bingdev.binghamton.edu/jwh/?page_id=385.
Shen, Kuiyi. “A Modern Showcase: *Shidai (Modern Miscellany)* in 1930s Shanghai.” *Yishuxue yanjiu* 12 (September 2013): 129–70.
———. “Modernist Movements in Pre-War China.” Paper presented at the Urban Cultural Institutions in Early Twentieth-Century China Symposium, Ohio State University, April 13, 2002.
———. “The Lure of the West: Modern Chinese Oil Painting.” In *A Century in Crisis: Modernity and Tradition in the Art of Twentieth-Century China*, edited by Julia F. Andrews and Kuiyi Shen, 172–80. New York: Guggenheim Museum, 1998.
———. “Traditional Painting in a Transnational Era, 1900–1950.” In *A Century in Crisis: Modernity and Tradition in the Art of Twentieth-Century China*, edited by Julia F. Andrews and Kuiyi Shen, 80–95. New York: Guggenheim Museum, 1998.
“Shen yu meihua yiyang qing 神與梅花一樣清 [A Diety and Plum Blossoms Equally Pure].” *Liangyou huabao* 良友畫報 *[The Young Companion]* 21 (November 30, 1927): 28.
Shih, Shu-Mei. “Shanghai Women of 1939: Visuality and the Limits of Feminine Modernity.” In *Visual Culture in Shanghai, 1850s–1930s*, edited by Jason C. Kuo, 205–40. Washington, DC: New Academia Publishing, 2007.
———. *The Lure of the Modern: Writing Modernism in Semicolonial China, 1917–1937*. Berkeley: University of California Press, 2001.
Shui Tianzhong 水天中. “Tanxun Qiu Ti 探寻丘堤 [Searching for Qiu Ti].” *Meishu yanjiu* 美术研究 *[Art Research]* 4 (1997).
———. “Yishu yu jiehun—20 shiji qianqi de meishujia fufu 艺术与婚姻--20 世纪前期的美术家夫妇 [Art and Marriage: 20th Century Artist Couples].” In *Zhongguo nüxing zhuyi 1* 中国女性主义 1 *[Feminism in China 1]*, edited by Huang Lin 荒林. Guilin: Guangxi Shifan Daxue Chubanshe, 2004.
“Some Masterworks of Miss C. L. Kuan.” *Shidai huabao* 時代畫報 *[Modern Miscellany]* 1, no. 6 (1930): 8.

Stevens, Sarah E. "Figuring Modernity: The New Woman and the Modern Girl in Republican China." *NWSA Journal* 15, no. 3 (2003): 82–103.

Sullivan, Michael. *Art and Artists of Twentieth-Century China*. Berkeley: University of California Press, 1996.

———. *Modern Chinese Artists: A Biographical Dictionary*. Berkeley: University of California Press, 2006.

———. "Reminiscences of Pang Xunqin (1946)." In *Shanghai Modern, 1919–1945*, edited by Jo-Anne Birnie Danzker Danzker, Ken Lum, and Zheng Shengtian, 248–53. Ostfildern-Ruit: Hatje Cantz Verlag, 2004.

Sun Liying. "An Exotic Self? Tracing Cultural Flows of Western Nudes in Pei-Yang Pictorial News (1926–1933)." In *Transcultural Turbulences*, edited by C. Brosius and R. Wenzlhuemer, 271–300. Transcultural Research—Heidelberg Studies on Asia and Europe in a Global Context 3. Dordrecht: Springer, 2011.

———. "Engendering a Journal: Editors and Nudes in Linloon Magazine and Its Global Context." In *Women and the Periodical Press in China's Long Twentieth Century: A Space of Their Own?*, edited by Michel Hockx, Joan Judge, and Barbara Mittler, 57–73. Cambridge, UK: Cambridge University Press, 2018.

Sung, Doris Ha Lin. "Redefining Female Talent: Chinese Women Artists in the National and Global Art Worlds, 1900s–1970s." PhD diss., York University, 2016.

Tao Cuiying 陶粹英. "Nuzi fayu mei yu renti huafa 女子發育美與人體畫法 [Women's Physical Development and the Techniques of Figure Painting]." *Funü zazhi* 婦女雜誌 *[Ladies' Journal]* 15, no. 7 (July 1929).

Tao Yongbai 陶咏白, and Li Shi 李湜. *Shiluo de lishi: Zhongguo nüxing huihua shi* 失落的历史: 中国女性绘画史 *[Lost History: The History of Chinese Women's Painting]*. Changsha: Hunan Meishu Chubanshe, 2000.

Taylor, Jeremy E. "From Traitor to Martyr: Drawing Lessons from the Death and Burial of Wang Jingwei, 1944." *Journal of Chinese History* 3, no. 1, March 2018, 1–22. https://doi.org/10.1017/jch.2017.43.

———. "Gendered Archetypes of Wartime Occupation: 'New Women' in Occupied North China, 1937–40." *Gender & History* 28, no. 3 (November 1, 2016): 660–86. https://doi.org/10.1111/1468-0424.12244.

Taylor, Michael R., and Xinyue Guo. *Between Tradition and Modernity: The Art of Fan Tchunpi*. Dartmouth, NH: Hood Museum of Art, 2013. https://hoodmuseum.dartmouth.edu/explore/exhibitions/between-tradition-and-modernity.

Teo, Phyllis Hwee Leng. "Alternative Agency in Representation by Contemporary Chinese Women Artists." *Asian Culture and History* 2, no. 1 (January 2010): 3–13.

———. "Modernism and Orientalism: The Ambiguous Nudes of Chinese Artist Pan Yuliang." *New Zealand Journal of Asian Studies* 12, no. 2 (December 2010): 65–80.

The Li-ching Cultural & Educational Foundation. PAN YU LIN 潘玉良. Accessed June 29, 2019. http://www.panyulin.org/index.php.

"Third Exhibition of The 'Torrents Society.'" *Meishu shenghuo* 美術生活 *[Arts & Life]*, no. 21 (December 1935).

Three Generations of Chinese Modernism: Qiu Ti, Pang Tao, Lin Yan. Vancouver: Art Beatus Gallery, 1998.

Tseng, Alice Y. "Kuroda Seiki's 'Morning Toilette' on Exhibition in Modern Kyoto." *The Art Bulletin* 90, no. 3 (September 1, 2008): 417–40.

Universität Heidelberg. Chinese Women's Magazines in the Late Qing and Early Republican Period, 2015. http://kjc-sv013.kjc.uni-heidelberg.de/frauenzeitschriften/index.php.

Volk, Alicia. "Katsura Yuki and the Japanese Avant-Garde." *Woman's Art Journal* 24, no. 2 (October 1, 2003): 3–9. https://doi.org/10.2307/1358780.

Waara, Carrie. "The Bare Truth: Nudes, Sex, and the Modernization Project in Shanghai Pictorials." In *Visual Culture in Shanghai, 1850s–1930s*, edited by Jason C. Kuo, 163–203. Washington, DC: New Academia Publishing, 2007.

Wang, Bo. "'Breaking the Age of Flower Vases:' Lu Yin's Feminist Rhetoric." *Rhetoric Review* 28, no. 3 (2009): 246–64.

Wang, Peggy. "Subversion, Culture Shock, and 'Women's Art': An Interview with Lin Tianmiao." *n. paradoxa* 29 (January 2012): 22–31.

Wang, Sumei. *The East Asian Modern Girl: Women, Media, and Colonial Modernity in the Interwar Years*. Leiden: Brill, 2021.

Wang Yilun 王益論. "Sheying 攝影 [Photography]." *Shidai huabao* 時代畫報 *[Modern Miscellany]* 5, no. 8 (16 February1934).

Wang Zheng. *Women in the Chinese Enlightenment: Oral and Textual Histories*. Berkeley: University of California Press, 1999.

Wangwright, Amanda. "Double Vision: The Culture China Overseas Chinese Women's Invitational Exhibition [Review]." *SECAC Review* 16, no. 5 (December 2015): 661–64.

———. "The Sick Man of Asia and the Anatomically Perfect Woman: Remodeling China's (Body) Image through the Visual Arts." In *Visualizing the Body in Art, Anatomy, and Medicine since 1800: Models and Modeling*. Science and the Arts since 1750. Routledge, 2019.

Weidner, Marsha, ed. *Flowering in the Shadows: Women in the History of Chinese and Japanese Painting*. Honolulu: University of Hawaii Press, 1990.

———. "Women in the History of Chinese Painting." In *Views from Jade Terrace: Chinese Women Artists 1300–1912*, edited by Marsha Weidner, 13–30. Indianapolis, IN: Indianapolis Museum of Art, 1988.

Wen Zhaotong 溫肇桐. “Nühuajia Guan Zilan 女畫家關紫蘭 [Painteress Guan Zilan].” *Yong'an yuekan* 永安月刊 *[Wing On Monthly]*, no. 26 (June 1941): 42.

Widmer, Ellen. “Gentility in Transition: Travels, Novels, and the New Guixiu.” In *The Quest for Gentility in China: Negotiations beyond Gender and Class*, edited by Daria Berg and Chloe Starr, 21–44. New York: Routledge, 2007.

Wong, Dorothy. “Huang Miaozi and Yu Feng.” *Orientations* 19, no. 8 (August 1988): 31–40.

Wright, Amanda S. “Qiu Ti's Contributions to Juelanshe and the Intersection of Modernist Ideology, Public Receptivity, and Personal Identity for a Woman Oil Painter in Early Twentieth-Century China.” PhD diss., University of Kansas, 2011.

Wu Fangcheng 吳方正. “Luode liyou—ershi shiji chuqi Zhongguo renti xiesheng wenti de taolun 裸的理由—二十世紀初期中國人體寫生問題的討論 [The Reason for the Nude: Questions Concerning Nude Figure Drawing in China at the Beginning of the Twentieth Century.” *Xin shixue* 新史學 *[New Studies in History]* 25, no. 2 (June 2004): 55–110.

Xiao Qian 萧乾. “Yidai cainü—Lin Huiyin 一代才女—林徽因 [The Talented Woman of a Generation: Lin Huiyin].” *Dushu* 讀書10 (1984): 113–21.

Xiu (Maske), Huajing. “Shanghai–Paris: Chinese Painters in France and China, 1919–1937.” PhD diss., University of Oxford, 2000.

Xu Hong. “Dialogue: The Awakening of Women's Consciousness.” Translated by Claire Roberts. *Art AsiaPacific* 2, no. 2 (1995): 44–51.

———. “Early 20th-Century Women Painters in Shanghai.” In *Shanghai Modern, 1919–1945*, edited by Jo-Anne Birnie Danzker, Ken Lum, and Zheng Shengtian, 200–215. Ostfildern-Ruit, Germany: Hatje Cantz Verlag, 2004.

Xu Wenhua 徐文华, and Li Chao 李超. “Niu Yue: Zhongjian Liang Baibo de yishu shengming 纽约:重见梁白波的艺术生命 [New York: An Important Look at the Artistic Life of Liang Baibo].” *Xinmin wanbao* 新民晚报 *[New People's Evening News]*, August 29, 2009, sec. B.

Xue Fen. “Guan Zilan gezhan de guangan 關紫蘭個展的觀感 [View of Guan Zilan's Solo Exhibition].” *Shenbao* 申報 *[Shun Pao]*, no. 4 (August 29, 1927).

Yang Qiuren 杨秋人. “Huiyi Ni Yide he Juelanshe 回忆倪贻德和决澜社 [Remembering Ni Yide and the Storm Society].” *Meishu jia* 美术家 *[Artist]* 31 (April 1983): 18–22.

Yang Taiyang 陽太陽. “The Storm Society (Interview).” In *Shanghai Modern, 1919–1945*, edited by Jo-Anne Birnie Danzker Danzker, Ken Lum, and Zheng Shengtian, 242–45. Ostfildern-Ruit: Hatje Cantz Verlag, 2004.

“Yanghuajia Guan Zilan nüshi 洋畫家關紫蘭女士 [Western Painter Miss Guan Zilan].” *Tuhua shibao* 圖畫時報 *[The Eastern Times Photo Supplement]*, no. 375 (1927): 3.

Yeh, Wen-hsin. *Shanghai Splendor: Economic Sentiments and the Making of Modern China, 1843–1949*. Berkeley: University of California Press, 2007.

“Yishu huabao: guben duizhao 藝術畫報: 古本對照 [Literature and Art Pictorial: Comparison with the Ancient Books].” *Xiaoshuo yuebao* 小說月報 *[Fiction Monthly]*, July 1934.

“Yishuhua de qinglü: Liang Baibo ye Ye Qianyu dingyou shenshi xieding 藝術化的情侶: 樑白波與葉淺予訂有紳士協定 [Artistic Sweethearts: Liang Baibo and Ye Qianyu Draw Up a Gentleman's Agreement].” *Shidai shenghuo* 時代生活 *[Times Life]* 5, no. 4/5 (1937): 6.

“Yishujia Pang Xunqin shi 藝術家龐薰琴氏 [Artist Mr. Pang Xunqin].” *Liangyou huabao* 良友畫報 *[The Young Companion]* 90 (July 1934): 14.

Yiu, Josh, and Seattle Asian Art Museum, eds. *Writing Modern Chinese Art: Historiographic Explorations*. Seattle, WA: Seattle Art Museum, 2009.

“You tian le ji wei nüyishujia 又添了幾位女藝術家 [A Few More Female Artists].” *Shenbao* 申報 *[Shun Pao]* 20385 (December 21, 1929): 17.

Yu Feng 郁風. “Guanyu Wu Zetian 關於武則天 [About Wu Zentian].” *Funü shenghuo* 婦女生活 *[Women's Life]* 4, no. 12 (1937): 14.

Yu Zhong 羽中. “Fang Junbi nüshi huazhan yipie 方君璧女士畫展一瞥 [A Glimpse at Fang Junbi's Painting Exhibition].” *Guomin xinwen zhoukan* 國民新聞周刊 *Citizens News Weekly*, no. 8 (1941): 8.

Yuan Yunyi 袁韵宜. *Pang Xunqin zhuan* 庞薰琹传 *[Biography of Pang Xunqin]*. Beijing: Beijing Gongyi Meishu Chubanshe, 1995.

Yun Duan 雲端. “Fang Junbi nüshi fangwen ji 方君璧女士訪問記 [Notes on an Interview with Madam Fang Junbi].” *Funü shijie* 婦女世界 *[Women's World]*, Mingren fangwen ji 名人訪問記 [Notes on Interviews with Famous People], 3, no. 6 (1942): 3.

Zhang, Jingyuan. *Psychoanalysis in China: Literary Transformations, 1919–1949*. Ithaca, NY: East Asia Program, Cornell University, 1992.

Zhang Qiongwen 張瓊文. “Minguo nühuajia Liang Baibo huihua zhong de nüxing zhanxian 民國女畫家梁白波繪畫中的女性展現 [Female Representation in the Paintings of Republican Period Woman Artist Liang Baibo].” Master's thesis, National Taiwan Normal University, 2016.

Zhang Ruogu 張若谷, ed. “Nüzuojia hao: Zhen mei shan zazhi yi zhou nian jinian haowai 女作家號: 真美善雜誌一周年紀 念號外 [Women Writers Issue: Truth, Beauty, Good Magazine's First-Year Anniversary Special Issue].” In *Zhen mei shan zazhi* 真美善雜誌 *[Truth, Beauty, Good Magazine]*. Shanghai: Zhen Mei Shan Shudian, 1929.

Zhang Yingjin. "Artwork, Commodity, Event: Representations of the Female Body in Modern Chinese Pictorials." In *Visual Culture in Shanghai, 1850s–1930s*, edited by Jason C. Kuo, 121–61. Washington, DC: New Academia Publishing, 2007.

Zhao Li 赵力, and Yu Ding 余丁, eds. *Zhongguo youhua wenxian* 中国油画文献 *[Literature on Chinese Oil Painting]*. Changsha: Hunan Meishu Chubanshe, 2002.

Zheng, Jane. "A Local Response to the National Ideal: Aesthetic Education in the Shanghai Art School (1913–1937)." *Art Criticism* 22, no. 1 (2007): 29–56.

———. *The Modernization of Chinese Art: The Shanghai Art College, 1913–1937*. Leuven: Leuven University Press, 2016.

———. "The Shanghai Art School and the Modern Mechanism of Artistic Celebrity (1913–1937)." *Art Criticism* 22, no. 1 (2007): 7–28.

———. "The Shanghai Fine Arts College: Art Education and Modern Women Artists in the 1920s and 1930s." *Modern Chinese Literature and Culture* 19, no. 1 (Spring 2007): 192–235.

Zheng Shengtian. "Waves Lashed the Bund from the West: Shanghai's Art Scene in the 1930s." In *Shanghai Modern, 1919–1945*, edited by Jo-Anne Birnie Danzker Danzker, Ken Lum, and Zheng Shengtian, 174–99. Ostfildern-Ruit: Hatje Cantz Verlag, 2004.

Zhi zhi 知之. "Yitan yishi: Liang Baibo zhi dadan 藝壇逸事: 梁白波之大膽 [Art Circle Anecdotes: Liang Baibo's Guts]." *Meishu zazhi* 美術雜誌 *Art Magazine* 1, no. 5 (1937): 136–37.

"Zhonghua Yishu Daxue meishu zhanlanhui zhi yibufen zuopin ji zuozhe 中華藝術大學美術展覽會之一部分作品及作者 [A Few Artworks and Artists from the Chinese University of the Arts' Fine Art Exhibition]." *Liangyou huabao* 良友畫報 *[The Young Companion]* 17 (August 1927): 20.

Zhongyang Dianshitai Wenhua Zhuantibu, Bi Hong, Zhang Fan, and Li Xin. *Zhaopian beihou de gushi* 照片背后的故事 *[The Story behind the Photograph]*. DVD. *Tansuo faxian* 探索发现 [Explore, Discover]. China: Zhongguo Guoji Dianshi Zonggongsi, 2005.

Zhou Jin 周今. "Meishu jie: Zhongguo xin huajia 美術界: 中國新畫家 [Art World: China's New Painters]." *Xingqi wenyi* 星期文藝 *[Weekly Literature and Art]* 9 (1931): 3.

Zhu Boxiong 朱伯雄, and Chen Ruilin 陈瑞林. *Zhongguo xihua wushinian, 1898–1949* 中国西画五十年, *1898–1949 [Fifty Years of Western Painting in China, 1898–1949]*. Beijing: People's Art Publishing House, 1989.

Zhu, Xiaoqing. "Pang Xunqin (1906–1985): A Chinese Avant-Garde's Metamorphosis, 1925–1946, and Questions of 'Authenticity.'" PhD diss., University of Maryland, College Park, 2009.